SPIRIT CARE

SPIRIT CARE

Aspire – Affirm – Transform

Richard Gordon Zyne, MDiv, DMin, BCC

SPIRIT CARE
ASPIRE – AFFIRM – TRANSFORM

iUniverse books may be ordered through booksellers or by contacting:

iUniverse
1663 Liberty Drive
Bloomington, IN 47403
www.iuniverse.com
844-349-9409

ISBN: 978-1-6632-6298-1 (sc)
ISBN: 978-1-6632-6299-8 (e)

Library of Congress Control Number: 2024909878

Print information available on the last page.

iUniverse rev. date: 05/20/2024

Dedication

To Paula

To Danny, Nick, and Jessica

To all who are called to the Sacred Work of Spirit Care.

Contents

Preface

Spirit Care is a resource designed for spiritual care providers, those dedicated souls—chaplains, ministers, nurses, healthcare workers, educators, family and friends—who provide love and support to those in crisis or trauma. It is based on the concept of dialogue, which is a vehicle for self-exploration, insight, and growth. It is a fundamental aspect of the spirit care process, allowing the patient, the person in need, to engage in a meaningful exploration of their inner world with the guidance and support of a trained professional.

Spirit Care, functioning within the concept of dialogue, is based on the foundational message of Jesus, in the Bible, where he says, "For where two or three are gathered in my name, there am I among them." (Matthew 18:20)

Throughout my career in Christian ministry, spanning many decades and in various roles including administrator, chaplain, counselor, and educator, I have experienced the profound reward of serving others in their time of need. At every step, I have been guided by the personal, incarnate God – Jesus Christ – who has illuminated my path and provided light and strength, especially in times of struggle and doubt.

As an ordained minister, and a Board Certified Chaplain (BCC) credentialed by both the Spiritual Care Association and the World Spiritual Health Organization, and with degrees from The School of Theology at Virginia Union University, including a Master of Divinity and Doctor of Ministry, my journey has been shaped by rigorous training and hands-on experience. Clinical pastoral education at Johns Hopkins Hospital and Academic Medicine has further equipped me for the spiritual care ministry in the health care environment.

Currently serving as a hospice chaplain at Gilchrist Hospice in Maryland, one of the nation's leading hospice organizations, I have also held leadership positions at CurePSP (Foundation for Progressive Supranuclear Palsy and Related Brain Diseases), Mount Olive College, Volunteers of America, and Virginia Union University. Through these experiences, I have come to understand that Christian ministry is an embodiment of "love in action," a tangible expression of the Spirit of God inherent in every individual.

For me, Spirit Care is a journey of discipleship, following in the footsteps of Jesus Christ and allowing His transformative power to flow through me to serve others. It is a source of immense joy and fulfillment, affirming the inherent dignity and worth of every person. I have witnessed firsthand the transformative impact of compassionate care on both caregivers and recipients, and it is my hope that this book will serve as a guide and inspiration for all those called to the sacred work of Spirit Care.

May this book be a testament to the enduring power of love, compassion, and faith in the service of others.

Warm regards,

Richard Gordon Zyne, MDiv, DMin, BCC

Introduction

Spirit Care

Spirit Care is an active and creative process of encouraging and healing persons to aspire, affirm, and transform into the full human beings we are meant to be. We are all made in the image of God, and Jesus Christ provides the model. His total being shows us the way, the truth, and the life. It is simple, and the only thing we need to do is to surrender to God's love, as offered by Jesus as the Christ, and walk behind him as his disciples.

By surrendering to God's love and following Jesus, individuals can experience transformation and fulfillment. This surrender involves acknowledging God's presence in our lives and allowing his love to guide our actions and decisions. Walking as disciples of Jesus means learning from his teachings, emulating his virtues, and participating in his mission to bring about the kingdom of God on earth.

Spirit Care encourages nurturing the spiritual growth of oneself and others, recognizing the inherent dignity and worth of every individual, and aligning one's life with the example and teachings of Jesus Christ.

Dialogue

Foundational to the concept of Spirit Care is the process of dialogue, the interactive exchange between the spiritual care provider and the patient. It is a dynamic process whereby both parties engage in a conversation aimed at exploring the patient's thoughts, feelings, experiences, behaviors, and especially their spiritual needs, concerns and difficult issues.

Dialogue in Spirit Care includes the following activities:

Communication: Dialogue involves open and honest communication between the spiritual care provider and the patient. It is not about the spiritual care provider giving advice or instruction but rather a mutual exchange of ideas and perspectives.

Exploration: Through dialogue, the spiritual care provider helps the patient explore their thoughts, feelings, emotions, and behaviors in a safe and non-judgmental space. This exploration can lead to deeper insights and understanding of oneself.

Collaboration: Spirit Care is a collaborative process, and dialogue reflects this collaboration. Both the spiritual care provider and the patient work together to assess needs, identify goals, develop strategies for change, navigate challenges, and enable appropriate interventions.

Reflection: Dialogue allows the patient to reflect on their experiences and gain new insights into their patterns of thinking, feeling, and behaving. The spiritual care provider may ask probing questions or offer reflections to facilitate this process.

Empowerment: Through dialogue, the spiritual care provider empowers the patient to express themselves freely and to take an active role in their own healing and growth. It fosters a sense of agency and self-awareness.

Building Trust: Dialogue is built on trust and empathy. The spiritual care provider creates a supportive environment where the patient feels safe to share their innermost thoughts and feelings without fear of judgment.

Dialogue in Spirit Care serves as a vehicle for self-exploration, insight, and growth. It is a fundamental aspect of the healing process, allowing the patient to engage in a meaningful exploration of their inner world with the guidance and support of a trained professional and a truly caring, empathic, person.

While I consider my book to be a devotional and inspirational resource, and not a research dissertation or scholarly treatise, I highly recommend to readers the following books which have enhanced my understanding of the concept and use of dialogue in spiritual care and therapy. These are: Martin Buber's, *I and Thou*, and Maurice Friedman's, *The Healing Dialogue in Psychotherapy*.

Aspire, Affirm, Transform

To *aspire, affirm, and transform* encapsulates key aspects of the Christian faith journey, with Jesus Christ serving as the ultimate guide, light, and direction in this process. Jesus always points to the Ultimate Transcendent Reality, which is God.

To aspire in the Christian faith involves setting one's sights on spiritual growth and living in alignment with the teachings and example of Jesus. Jesus provides the guidance by showing believers what it means to aspire to a life of love, compassion, humility, and service. His teachings challenge Christians to aspire to virtues that reflect the character of God and to seek first the kingdom of God and his righteousness (Matthew 6:33).

To affirm in the Christian faith entails acknowledging and embracing the core values and principles as established by Jesus, as set forth in scripture. Jesus serves as the light by illuminating the truth of God's Word and revealing the nature of God's love and grace. Through his life, teachings, death, and resurrection (the ultimate transformation), Jesus affirms the foundational truths of Christianity, such as God's love for humanity, the need for salvation (ultimate healing), and the promise of eternal life.

To transform is a central tenet and principle of the Christian life, and Jesus provides the direction for this process. He offers the light of his presence through the Holy Spirit, who empowers believers to be transformed into his likeness. By following Jesus' example, surrendering to his power, and allowing the Holy Spirit to work within them, Christians can experience personal growth, spiritual renewal, grace, and the ultimate transformation of their hearts and minds.

In summary, for a Christian, "to aspire, affirm, and transform" means striving to live according to the example and teachings of Jesus Christ, affirming the truths of the faith, and allowing God to continually transform them into his image. Jesus provides the guidance, light, and direction by showing believers the way to abundant life and by empowering them through his Spirit to live as his disciples in the world. These values and principles are essential aspects in order to offer and provide Spirit Care to all people.

Christian Universalism and Christian Humanism

Christian Universalism is a theological viewpoint that challenges the traditional notion of eternal damnation and instead emphasizes the inclusivity of God's love and mercy. According to Christian Universalism, salvation is not limited to a select few who adhere to specific beliefs or practices, but is available to all people, regardless of their faith tradition, actions, or circumstances during their earthly lives.

At its core, Christian Universalism asserts that God's love is universal and extends to every individual without exception. It suggests that God's desire for reconciliation with humanity is so profound that it encompasses all people, regardless of their past or present condition. This perspective rejects the idea of a punitive God who condemns some to eternal suffering and separation, and instead focuses on the redemptive power of God's love to bring all individuals back into a harmonious relationship with the divine.

In contrast to more traditional Christian views that emphasize the importance of accepting specific beliefs or adhering to particular religious practices in order to attain salvation, Christian Universalism posits that salvation is ultimately achieved through the transformative work of God's grace. It suggests that divine love has the power to overcome sin and separation, leading to the eventual reconciliation of all individuals with God.

Christian Universalism acknowledges the diversity of religious beliefs and practices across cultures and traditions but maintains that God's love transcends these differences and encompasses all people equally. It promotes the idea of universal reconciliation, wherein every individual, regardless of their background or beliefs, will ultimately experience the fullness of God's love and restoration to wholeness.

Overall, Christian Universalism offers a hopeful and inclusive vision of salvation and ultimate healing, emphasizing the boundless nature of God's love and the possibility of redemption for all humanity. It stands in contrast to more exclusive interpretations of Christianity, emphasizing the inherent worth and dignity of every individual and the ultimate triumph of divine love over sin and separation.

Christian humanism is a philosophical and theological perspective that seeks to harmonize humanistic values with Christian teachings and traditions. At its core, it upholds the belief that human beings possess inherent dignity, worth, and potential as they are created in the image of God. This perspective emphasizes the importance of individual agency, free will, and the capacity for moral and spiritual growth.

Central to Christian humanism is the idea that Jesus Christ serves as a model of ethical living, emphasizing principles of love, compassion, and social justice. Christian humanists draw inspiration and guidance from Jesus' teachings and seek to apply them to contemporary societal issues and challenges.

In addition to focusing on human dignity and ethical living, Christian humanism values the pursuit of knowledge and understanding. It encourages critical thinking, intellectual inquiry, and engagement with the arts and sciences as avenues for exploring the mysteries of existence and deepening one's understanding of the creative aspects of God in the world and the universe.

Historically, Christian humanism emerged during the Renaissance as a reaction to the rigid scholasticism of medieval Christianity. Figures such as Erasmus of Rotterdam and Thomas More promoted a more humane and rational approach to Christian faith and practice. They advocated for the study of classical literature, the promotion of education, and the reform of corrupt religious institutions.

In modern times, Christian humanism continues to influence various branches of Christianity. It remains a dynamic intellectual tradition that seeks to reconcile faith with reason, spirituality with intellectual inquiry, and the pursuit of individual flourishing with the pursuit of the common good.

The Stories

In each narrative contained within this volume, we encounter real characters, genuine individuals grappling with the weighty issues of life and death. While names and locations may have been altered to protect privacy, the essence of each story remains authentic and a genuine experience of the author's chaplain ministry.

These stories offer a window into the world of spirit care, revealing the compassionate responses of chaplains, healthcare workers, volunteers, friends, and family members as they navigate the challenges of supporting those in need. Through their actions, we witness the profound impact of human connection, dialogue, and the transformative power of faith. There is also the essential connection to Christian universalist/humanist values and biblical scripture.

Furthermore, these narratives illustrate how each person involved in the journey—both caregivers and recipients alike—manages their struggles and ultimately finds hope and healing through the grace of God. Through the process of aspiring to something greater, affirming their worth and purpose, and being transformed by divine love, these individuals emerge from their trials with newfound strength and resilience.

Christian Themes and Values

Christian themes and values are foundational to the beliefs and teachings of Christianity, as expressed in the words of Jesus and the Prophets found in scripture. Here are some of the key themes and values:

Love: The foundational principle of Christianity is love. Jesus Christ taught that the greatest commandments are to love God with all your heart, soul, and mind, and to love your neighbor as yourself (Matthew 22:37-39). Christians are called to love one another as Christ loved them (John 13:34-35).

Forgiveness: Christians believe in the importance of forgiveness, both receiving God's forgiveness for their sins and extending forgiveness to others. Jesus taught his followers to forgive others as God forgives them (Matthew 6:14-15).

Grace: Grace is the unmerited favor and kindness of God extended to humanity. Christians believe that salvation is a gift of God's grace, not earned through works (Ephesians 2:8-9).

Redemption: Redemption is the act of being saved or delivered from sin and its consequences. Christians believe that Jesus Christ's sacrificial death on the cross provides redemption for humanity, reconciling them with God (Romans 3:23-24).

Hope: Christians find hope in the promises of God, including the hope of eternal life through Jesus Christ. They believe that God's plans for them are good, and they trust in His faithfulness (Jeremiah 29:11, Romans 15:13).

Faith: Faith is central to Christianity. Christians believe in placing their trust and confidence in God and His promises, even when circumstances may seem uncertain (Hebrews 11:1, Romans 10:17).

Compassion: Christians are called to show compassion and mercy to those in need, following the example of Jesus Christ who ministered to the sick, the marginalized, and the oppressed (Matthew 25:35-36).

Humility: Christians are encouraged to cultivate humility, recognizing their dependence on God and acknowledging their own imperfections (Philippians 2:3-4).

Service: Christians are called to serve others, following Jesus' example of selfless service. They believe that true greatness comes from serving others rather than seeking to be served (Matthew 20:26-28).

Justice: Christians are called to seek justice and act with righteousness, standing up for the oppressed and marginalized (Micah 6:8, Isaiah 1:17).

These themes and values are woven throughout the teachings of Jesus Christ and the writings of the Bible, shaping the beliefs and practices of Christians around the world.

The Prayer

Each story in Spirit Care concludes with a heartfelt prayer, seeking Divine Guidance and ongoing strength to walk in the footsteps of Jesus, as a disciple of Christ. These prayers serve as a reflection of the deep connection between the spiritual caregivers, their patients, and their faith, acknowledging the importance of divine intervention in their endeavors to offer love and support. Through these prayers, the caregivers express their reliance on God's wisdom and grace as they navigate the complexities of their roles and seek empowerment to embody the compassionate spirit of Jesus Christ.

Spiritual Care and Redemption

On the medical-surgical floors of the downtown city hospital, where the conflicting aromas of sweaty bodies and antiseptics often seem to intertwine, there is a room where light falls softly through half-drawn blinds. The emergency department exam room is quiet except for the low hum of machinery and the occasional murmur of nurses outside the door. Melissa, the chaplain, pauses before entering, taking a moment to clear her mind and focus her heart on her next patient. She whispers a prayer, not for outcomes but for the right words, or perhaps for no words at all.

Inside, she finds a woman lying back against her pillow, her face drawn and tired but her eyes alert. There is a deep seriousness to her gaze, a weight that seems to pull at Melissa as she takes a seat beside the woman's bed.

"Good morning," Melissa says, her voice kept low and gentle, not to disturb the medical sanctity of the room.

"Morning," the woman replies, her voice rustling, like dry leaves stirred by wind.

They talk, or rather, the woman talks while Melissa listens. She listens to the rhythm beneath the woman's words, a melody of fear and bravery mixed together. The chaplain is not there to preach or to teach; she is there to hear, to listen, to acknowledge, and to affirm the woman's life and the reality of her suffering.

Sometimes, Melissa offers a word, a gentle nudge in their winding path of conversation, but often, she just listens, her presence a silent support. There are moments when the woman falters, her eyes welling up, and in those moments, Melissa offers the simple comfort of a hand outstretched, her touch light but firm.

The machines beep. The woman sighs—a sound that seems to carry the weight of her world. "It's hard," she says, "not knowing how many mornings I have left."

"It is," Melissa agrees, not shying away from the truth of her words. "It's very hard."

The woman looks at Melissa then, really looks, and in her gaze, she feels seen, understood in a way words can never fully capture. They sit together like that for a while, in communion not just with each other but with something larger, something divine that neither of them can name but both can feel.

When the time comes for Melissa to leave, she stands slowly, and they clasp hands, their grip a testament to the connection they've forged. "Thank you," the woman whispers, and Melissa nods, feeling the weight and the worth of the woman's thanks.

Walking back through the hospital corridors, Melissa feels the echo of their encounter settle around her like a cloak. She knows she will carry the woman's story, her strength and her fear, with her long after she steps out of the hospital into the light of day.

She will document the visit, note down the necessary details in her clinical records, but the essence of their meeting—the shared humanity and the touch of grace—belongs to a narrative far greater than can be captured in words on paper. It is written instead in the quiet chambers of the heart, in the sacred spaces where souls meet and recognize each other. Here, in these liminal spaces, healing happens, and the spirit is cared for, beyond the reach of medicine but within the gentle grasp of understanding and love.

Christian Themes and Values

Compassion and Presence: The story underscores the chaplain Melissa's role as a compassionate listener and a supportive presence, which aligns with the Christian call to "mourn with those who mourn" (Romans 12:15) and to embody the comfort that God provides us so that we may comfort others

(2 Corinthians 1:3-4). Her approach is not to preach or teach but to listen and affirm the woman's experiences and feelings. This reflects Jesus' own ministry, where He was often present with individuals in their suffering, offering compassion and understanding rather than immediate solutions.

Spiritual Accompaniment: Melissa's interaction with the patient showcases spiritual accompaniment, where she joins the patient in navigating the emotional and spiritual dimensions of her suffering. This practice echoes the Biblical idea of walking alongside someone in their journey—similar to how Jesus walked with the disciples on the road to Emmaus, listening to their concerns and gradually revealing His presence in the midst of their conversation (Luke 24:13-35).

Acknowledgment of Human Limitation and Divine Presence: The chaplain's prayer for the right words—or perhaps for no words at all—before entering the room acknowledges human limitations and the need for divine assistance. This humble approach is reflective of the Psalms, where the psalmists often cry out for God's guidance and wisdom in times of trouble.

The Power of Silent Solidarity: The narrative also highlights the power of simply being present with someone in their pain, which can be more impactful than any words spoken. This is a powerful testament to the ministry of presence, often considered a form of nonverbal pastoral care that underscores the belief that God is present in every moment of human suffering.

Recognition of Shared Humanity and Divine Grace: The moments of connection and the shared feeling of something larger and divine between Melissa and the patient illustrate the Christian belief in the imago Dei—the image of God in every person. This connection transcends words and is where true spiritual communion and healing can occur, as both individuals recognize and honor the divine spark within each other.

The essence of this encounter, where healing and spiritual care occur beyond the reach of medicine but within the realm of understanding and love, captures the Christian perspective on pastoral care and the redemptive, sustaining presence of God in human suffering.

Prayer

Heavenly Father, In Your boundless mercy and grace, we come before You seeking spiritual care and redemption. You are the source of all healing and restoration, and we humbly ask for Your presence to fill our hearts and souls. Grant us the wisdom to recognize the needs of those around us, both physically and spiritually. Help us to be vessels of Your love, offering comfort, guidance, and support to those who are seeking redemption and spiritual healing. May Your Holy Spirit work within us, guiding us to offer compassionate care to those who are hurting and broken. Help us to walk alongside them, offering words of hope and encouragement, and pointing them towards the ultimate redemption found in You. May we experience Your peace that surpasses all understanding and find redemption through the saving work of Jesus Christ. In His holy name, we pray, Amen.

Living Faith in the Real World

Taylor had been driving long-haul routes for two decades, his world confined mostly to the interior of his truck cab and the endless stretch of highway. Over the years, the road had become both a home and a prison. As the miles passed under his wheels, the solitude gave him ample time to think, to listen to radio preachers, and to wrestle with the bigger questions that often seemed to loom just beyond the headlights.

Tonight, the road was particularly quiet, the only sound, the hum of the engine and the occasional crackle and static of the truck's old radio. His route took him through the heart of the country, landscapes sprawling under a sky full of stars. It was on nights like these that Taylor found his thoughts drifting towards the teachings of Jesus—teachings on the radio he had encountered through sermons that filled the long, lonely hours.

The simplicity of Jesus's message—love, justice, compassion—seemed at odds with the world Taylor saw through his windscreen. A world of sharp contrasts; of glaring billboards next to dilapidated homes, of luxury cars speeding past homeless hitchhikers. The disconnect between the gospel's call and the reality of the road troubled him.

"Help the poor," Jesus had said. Taylor saw poverty from coast to coast, felt the ache of it in old industrial towns where jobs had vanished, and hope seemed outdated. He remembered a radio preacher saying that to follow Jesus was not just to feel pity but to foster a radical kind of community where everyone had enough. Taylor wondered, often, what that would really look like.

"Empower women," was another thing those radio preachers often glossed over, but which Jesus had emphasized by his actions. Taylor thought of his daughter, Jenna, back home, bright and full of opinions, and how he wanted her to grow up in a world where her voice mattered just as much as any man's.

The inclusivity Jesus preached—opening up family boundaries, creating space at the table—challenged Taylor. On the road, he met many outsiders, people who drifted from job to job, town to town. He tried, in his own way, to practice this openness, sharing a meal with a fellow trucker, offering a ride to a stranded traveler, listening to their stories.

And then there was the radical call to nonviolence—never retaliate, forgive your enemy. On the road, anger was often just a lane-change away; tempers flared easily at 70 miles an hour. But Taylor tried to keep his cool, to let go of slights, to wave a hand in forgiveness rather than clench it in anger.

"Don't be greedy, live simply," another cornerstone of Jesus's teaching, hit home for Taylor. The road tempted him with endless consumerism—every stop filled with gadgets, gizmos, and apps for phone, meant to make life easier, to make the miles pass quicker. But he resisted as much as he could, saving his money, focusing instead on what truly fed his soul.

And always, there was the call to be present, to heal wounds. Taylor knew his limitations—he was no miracle worker. But he could listen, could offer a word of encouragement, could share his own struggles and, in doing so, maybe lighten someone else's load.

As Taylor drove through the night, the stars overhead seemed to burn brighter with each mile. Jesus's teachings, a radical manifesto of love and justice, illuminated his journey. They didn't provide all the answers, but they gave him a way to steer by, a horizon to head towards. In the quiet sanctuary of his truck, with the road rolling endlessly on, Taylor felt a part of something larger, a breathing testament to a faith that was lived, mile by mile, in the real world.

Christian Themes and Values

Love, Justice, and Compassion: Taylor ponders the core teachings of Jesus, such as love, justice, and compassion, contrasting them with the harsh realities he observes on the road. This mirrors the biblical call to "love your neighbor as yourself" (Mark 12:31) and to act justly and love mercy (Micah 6:8). His reflections prompt thoughts on how these principles can be lived out authentically in a world full of contradictions.

Service to the Poor and Marginalized: Reflecting on Jesus' directive to help the poor, Taylor contemplates the pervasive poverty he witnesses across America. This aligns with numerous biblical exhortations to care for the poor and oppressed (Proverbs 14:31, Matthew 25:35-40). Taylor's thoughts on what it means to create a community where everyone has enough echoed the early Christian communities' practices of sharing resources (Acts 2:44-45).

Empowerment and Inclusivity: Considering the empowerment of women and the inclusivity preached by Jesus, Taylor thinks about his daughter and the kind of world he desires for her—a world where gender does not limit one's opportunities or silence one's voice. This reflects Jesus' radical inclusion of women in his ministry, as seen in his interactions with women throughout the Gospels (e.g., John 4:1-42, Luke 8:1-3).

Nonviolence and Forgiveness: The story also touches on the theme of nonviolence and the challenge of forgiveness, particularly in high-stress environments like driving on a busy highway. Jesus' teachings on turning the other cheek (Matthew 5:39) and forgiving others (Matthew 18:21-22) are crucial here, illustrating how these principles can be applied even in small, everyday interactions.

Simplicity and Rejection of Consumerism: Taylor's resistance to consumerism and his focus on living simply resonate with Jesus' teachings about not storing up treasures on earth (Matthew 6:19-21) and being content with what one has (Hebrews 13:5). His choice reflects a deliberate attempt to live a life not dictated by materialism but guided by more meaningful spiritual values.

Presence and Healing: Lastly, Taylor's commitment to being present for others and offering whatever healing he can—be it through listening or sharing his own experiences—captures the essence of Jesus' healing ministry, where presence and attention to individual suffering were paramount (e.g., Mark 1:40-42, Luke 7:12-15).

Overall, the story of Taylor is an exploration of how the teachings of Jesus can illuminate and guide one's life journey, even in the mundane or isolating contexts, making it a testament to living one's faith in the real world.

Prayer

Heavenly Father, help us to live out our faith in practical ways that honor and glorify You. Give us the strength and courage to show love, kindness, and compassion to those around us, reflecting Your character in all that we do. As we navigate the challenges of the real world, may our faith be a guiding light, illuminating the path before us and inspiring others to seek You. Help us to be salt and light in a world that desperately needs Your presence. Lord, may our lives be a testament to Your faithfulness and goodness, drawing others to You through our words and actions. Fill us with Your Holy Spirit, empowering us to live boldly for You, even amid challenges and trials. We surrender our lives to You, Lord, and ask that You use us as instruments of Your love and grace in this world. May our faith be evident in every aspect of our lives, bringing glory to Your name. In Jesus' name we pray, Amen.

3

Finding God in the Challenges of Daily Life

In the small, Maryland coastal town of St. Mary's, where the Chesapeake Bay spoke in whispers and the sky stretched wide and clear, there lived an old waterman named Kai. Each morning, as the sun crept over the horizon, he would push his worn boat into the shallow water, his eyes scanning the vast expanse with a mixture of reverence and yearning. He was a man of few words, his hands weathered by salt and time, his face lined with the stories of the sea, oysters, and crabs.

Kai had always felt a deep connection to the water, seeing in its depths a mirror of his own soul—vast, mysterious, and beckoning. He believed that to crab and fish was not just to seek sustenance from the sea, but to commune with a greater force, a divine presence that pulsated through all of creation.

His life, much like his boat, had seen better days. The fishing nets were frayed, the wood splintered, and the paint faded. But every morning, as he set out into the great Bay, he carried with him a simple prayer, not for bounty, but for the clarity and strength to continue his journey.

One morning, as the sky blazed with the first light of dawn, Kai felt a stirring within, a whisper that seemed to echo across the water. It was a call to aspire, to affirm, and to transform. As he cast his bait into the shimmering sea, his thoughts turned to Jesus Christ, the fisher of men, who had walked on such waters, who had calmed storms with a word, and whose teachings had spread like ripples across the globe.

Kai reflected on how Jesus had shown the way to find God not through grand deeds, but through love, humility, and the quiet surrender of one's

9

heart to the divine will. Each day on the water was an opportunity for Kai to seek this path, to aspire to something greater than himself, to affirm his faith through the rhythm of his daily toil, and to transform the simplicity of his life into a testament of his belief.

As the sun climbed higher, warming his back, Kai felt a tug on his line. Pulling it in, he found not the fish he had expected, but a startling array of sea life—bright starfish, a couple of crabs, and even a small, gleaming fish that shimmered like a sliver of the sky itself. It was a modest catch by any standard, yet it filled him with an inexplicable sense of accomplishment and gratitude.

Kai realized then that his life, much like his fishing line, was woven with threads of joy and sorrow, gain and loss. Yet, through the act of casting it daily, with Jesus as his guide, he was engaging in a deeper act of faith, affirming his place in the universe, and transforming each ordinary moment into something sacred.

As he sailed back to shore, his boat heavy with his modest catch, Kai looked towards the horizon, his heart swelling with a peace he hadn't felt in years. The sea, with its endless mysteries and its steadfast promise, had shown him the way. In the simplicity of his life, in the solitude of his boat, he had found a profound connection to the divine, a path to follow, a life transformed by the teachings of Jesus, where every wave and every whisper of the wind spoke of love and redemption.

Christian Themes and Values

Stewardship of Creation: Kai's connection to the sea and his view of fishing as a way to commune with the divine mirror the Biblical theme of stewardship, where humans are entrusted with the care and appreciation of God's creation (Genesis 1:28). Kai's reverence for the sea and the life within it reflects a deep appreciation and respect for nature, consistent with biblical teachings on stewardship.

Faith and Providence: Kai's prayer for clarity and strength rather than a bountiful catch emphasizes a Biblical understanding of faith in God's provision (Matthew 6:33-34). His trust in the divine even in the face of material scarcity reflects the scriptural call to rely on God for daily needs.

Reflection of Jesus's Teachings: The story subtly parallels Kai's life with the life of Jesus, notably in his identity as a fisher of men (Matthew 4:19). Like Jesus who called his disciples to fish for people, Kai casts his net into the sea, reflecting on the spiritual lessons inherent in his daily routine. His approach to life embodies the Christian virtues of love, humility, and the pursuit of divine will, similar to the teachings and life of Jesus.

Transformation through Simplicity: Kai's life transformation through simple, routine acts connects with the themes of finding greatness in small things and the transformative power of faith (Luke 16:10). His experience of catching diverse sea life, while modest, leads to profound spiritual fulfillment and gratitude, showcasing the theme that spiritual wealth often supersedes material gain.

Sanctity of Daily Work: The narrative portrays Kai's daily fishing routine as an act of worship and a pathway to deeper faith, aligning with the Biblical view that all forms of work can glorify God (Colossians 3:23-24). His work is not merely a means of sustenance but a form of spiritual discipline and meditation.

Peace and Redemption: Finally, Kai's peaceful and redemptive experience on the sea encapsulates the Biblical promise of peace that surpasses understanding (Philippians 4:7). His journey on the water becomes a metaphor for life's journey guided by faith, revealing the redemptive power of God's love through Christ.

Overall, Kai's story is a vivid illustration of how an individual's life and work, when intertwined with faith and reflection on Jesus's teachings, can lead to a profound understanding of one's place in the cosmos and a deeper connection to the divine. This story emphasizes that every aspect of life, even the seemingly mundane tasks, can be imbued with spiritual significance and can lead to transformative experiences.

Richard Gordon Zyne

Prayer

Heavenly Father, Amid the challenges we face each day, help us to find You. Open our eyes to see Your presence in every moment, Your guidance in every decision, and Your comfort in every trial. Give us the strength to trust in Your plan, even when we cannot see the way forward. Help us to lean on Your promises and rely on Your unfailing love to carry us through challenging times. When we feel overwhelmed, remind us that You are our refuge and strength, a very present help in trouble. Help us to surrender our worries and fears to You, trusting that You will work all things for good. May Your peace, which surpasses all understanding, guard our hearts and minds in Christ Jesus. And may Your presence be our constant companion as we navigate the challenges of daily life. In Jesus' name we pray, Amen.

4

Nurturing and Transforming Faith

In the sparse room where the light filtered through half-closed blinds, Darla sat quietly beside Earl's bed. His breathing was shallow, uneven, marked by the illness that had taken so much from him. ALS, a cruel thief, had stripped him of movement, of speech, but not of his presence, which filled the room as much as the soft hum of the medical equipment.

Darla was worn thin. Her face, once vibrant and expressive, had settled into lines of enduring fatigue. Yet, there was a steadiness in her eyes, a quiet resolve that spoke of a depth of strength not easily shaken. She administered the medication and pain killers with a practiced hand, her touch gentle on Earl's jaw, coaxing him to swallow.

Their family home had become a world unto itself, defined by the rhythms of care, of long nights and fleeting days. The others, their siblings, floated on the periphery, appearing briefly in moments of acute crisis, their voices on the phone a reminder of lives moving in different orbits.

"Here we are, brother," she whispered to Earl, brushing a lock of hair from his forehead. Her voice carried a soft certainty, fortified by faith. In the evening stillness, she often read aloud from Paul's letters, her voice threading through the verses about suffering and endurance, about grace sufficient for every moment of weakness.

It was during one of these readings that I visited, a chaplain accustomed to offering comfort, yet finding myself unexpectedly in the role of the comforted. Darla's resilience, her unwavering commitment to her brother, spoke of a profound spiritual grounding, a belief in a walking, present Jesus that sustained her even as the path grew steep.

When Earl passed, it was in the quiet hush, just before dawn, when the birds were still asleep. Darla had been by his side, her hand clasped in his, her prayer a soft murmur that seemed to guide him gently towards something beyond this tattered room, beyond the pain.

The aftermath was also quiet. The funeral was small, attended by those few who truly knew Earl, who understood the space he had occupied in the world. Darla stood by the graveside, her sorrow immense but her face serene, as if she had long ago reconciled with the inevitable passage, her faith a bridge spanning the chasm of her grief.

Now, Darla faced the task of reassembling a life that had for so long been oriented around Earl's care. It was a daunting horizon, yet she faced it as she had everything else—with a quiet, firm certainty in her step, a trust in a guidance unseen but deeply felt.

In the days that followed, as I returned to the routine of my rounds, I carried with me the image of Darla, her resilience a testament not just to human strength but to the power of faith to anchor us in the tumult of life. She had, in her quiet, determined way, taught me something vital about the nature of spiritual service—it is not always about giving, but often, simply about being present, a witness to the small, sacred dramas unfolding in the hidden corners of the world.

Christian Themes and Values

Sacrificial Love: Darla's dedication to caring for her brother Earl, despite the heavy toll it takes on her physically and emotionally, reflects the biblical notion of sacrificial love (John 15:13). This type of love is exemplified in the Christian tradition by Jesus Christ, who sacrificed His own life for the sake of humanity. Darla's actions embody this deep, selfless commitment to caring for another person, mirroring Christ's commandment to love others as oneself.

Grace and Strength in Suffering: The narrative mentions Darla reading from Paul's letters, likely referring to passages such as 2 Corinthians 12:9, where Paul discusses how God's grace is made perfect in weakness and how God's strength is manifested during times of struggle. Darla's ability to continue providing care and maintaining her faith in the face of hardship illustrates the themes that God provides spiritual strength and grace to endure and grow through suffering.

The Sanctity of Presence: Darla's constant and comforting presence by Earl's bedside, especially during his final moments, underscores the Christian value of simply being present in another's time of need. This idea resonates with the ministry of Jesus and His disciples, who often provided comfort by their mere presence. It also reflects the role of a community or a family member as a source of spiritual and emotional support, illustrating how the ministry of presence can be a profound act of faith and love.

Transformation Through Suffering: The story subtly explores how suffering and caregiving transform Darla, forging in her a serene acceptance of life's inevitable hardships and a deep, resilient faith. This transformation through suffering is a central theme in Christianity, where trials are often viewed as opportunities to grow closer to God and to deepen one's faith, much like the refining fire that purifies gold.

Faith as a Guiding Force: Darla's faith acts as a guiding force throughout her journey, providing her with the strength to face the challenges of caring for a loved one with a debilitating disease. This reflects the biblical teaching that faith is not merely a belief in God but an active trust that influences and shapes one's actions and responses to life's difficulties.

Eternal Perspective: The peace with which Darla accepts Earl's death and faces life afterwards reflects an eternal perspective, a key aspect of Christian faith. This perspective helps believers navigate grief and loss with hope, focusing on the Christian promise of eternal life and reunion after death.

In summary, the story captures themes of Christian faith, depicting how spiritual beliefs can deeply influence how individuals cope with suffering, provide care, and find meaning and strength in the most challenging circumstances. Through Darla's story, we see a portrayal of faith that is both nurturing and transformative, anchoring her through the storms of life.

Prayer

Heavenly Father, we come before You with hearts open to Your nurturing and transforming power. We long to deepen our faith and become more like Christ each day. Lord, strengthen our faith as we seek You in prayer, study Your Word, and worship You in spirit and truth. May our relationship with You grow deeper, rooted in Your love and grace. Transform us, O Lord, from the inside out. Shape us into vessels of Your love, compassion, and mercy, that we may reflect Your light to the world around us. Lord, we surrender ourselves to Your will and ask that You continue to mold us into the image of Your Son. May our lives bear witness to Your transforming power, bringing glory to Your name. In Jesus' name we pray, Amen.

5

Struggle, Endurance, and Hope

Ted stood by the window, his gaze fixed on the fading light that painted the hospital's courtyard in soft gold and grays. The chapel's silence around him was deep, thick enough to feel like a living thing. It was the hour when day slid into night, a time Ted had come to recognize as the threshold of many transformations.

Today, he had been summoned to a different kind of bedside. A young soldier, wounded, both in body and spirit, lay in one of the upstairs rooms, his family quietly torn between hope and the kind of despair that filled intensive care rooms with heavy, burdensome air.

Ted walked the bustling halls, his footsteps echoing in the quiet, his heart preparing for the courage he needed to lend and the despair he must share. As he approached the room, he heard low voices, the murmur of a family clinging together in their vigil.

The door was ajar, and he knocked softly, pushing it open at the nod of a weary mother seated closest to the entrance. The soldier, a young man with sharp features softened by pain, turned his head slightly to acknowledge Ted.

"Evening," Ted said softly, moving to stand beside the bed. His presence was a silent announcement of his role, his hospital badge reflecting a small beacon of light in the dim room.

"Chaplain," the soldier acknowledged, his voice rough with disuse.

"I'm Chaplain Ted," he introduced himself simply, pulling a chair closer. "I heard you might want some company."

The soldier nodded, his eyes holding a mixture of gratitude and something fiercer that Ted recognized as the struggle to remain strong in the face of relentless pain.

They spoke of many things—of mundane details at first, the weather, the hospital food, the noise of the night shift. But as the light outside the window faded, their conversation deepened, touching on fears, on dreams paused, on the courage it took to face each morning.

Ted listened, mostly, providing the space for the soldier to find his own strength in the telling. When he spoke, his words were deliberate, chosen for their ability to comfort but not to cajole.

"You know," Ted said as a silence fell between them, thick with the heaviness of unshed tears, "courage doesn't always roar. Sometimes, it's the quiet voice at the end of the day saying, 'I will try again tomorrow.'"

The young man's eyes, glazed with a mixture of painkillers and fatigue, focused intently on Ted. "Feels like I'm always waiting for tomorrow," he confessed.

"And yet, every morning is a little victory," Ted responded. "It's a testament to your strength, even when you feel most barren, like a garden waiting for rain. The drought's harsh, but it makes the return of rain that much sweeter."

The soldier's breathing slowed, steadied by the imagery. "I just need to keep finding that strength until the rain comes, huh?"

"Yes," Ted smiled, his voice a soft echo in the quiet room. "And remember, even the smallest light pierces through the darkness. Like right now," he gestured to the lamp by the bed, its light casting a warm glow over them, "it doesn't light up the whole room, but it makes this corner a little less daunting."

The soldier nodded, his eyes closing slowly, a tear escaping the corner of his eye. Ted reached out, a gentle touch, acknowledging the pain, the courage, the shared human frailty.

As Ted left the room later, stepping back into the solitude of the chapel, he carried with him the solemn weight of their exchange, the sacredness of shared burdens, and the flickering light of a courage that whispered of rains to come, and gardens rejuvenated. It was the essence of his calling, found not in grand gestures but in quiet presences, in the gentle tending to the spirit of those who felt most barren, guiding them through their darkest nights towards the dawn of new days.

Christian Themes and Values

Ministry of Presence: Ted's role as a chaplain emphasizes the Christian concept of the ministry of presence—being physically, emotionally, and spiritually present for others in their time of need. This mirrors the example of Jesus, who often provided comfort simply by being with people in their moments of distress, as seen in His visits with the sick and the grieving.

Endurance Through Suffering: The conversation between Ted and the soldier touches on enduring pain and finding strength in difficult times. This reflects the biblical teaching found in Romans 5:3-5, which speaks about suffering producing perseverance, character, and hope. Ted's encouragement to the soldier to find strength each day aligns with the idea that faith can provide the resilience to face ongoing challenges.

Hope and Restoration: Ted's dialogue about the "garden waiting for rain" symbolizes hope and renewal, which are central themes in Christianity. This imagery is reminiscent of biblical passages such as Isaiah 35:1, where the wilderness and dry land will rejoice and blossom. It portrays the idea that even in times of spiritual or physical drought, there is the promise of rejuvenation and growth ahead.

The Light in Darkness: Ted's mention of the small light that pierces the darkness echoes the biblical metaphor of light as a symbol of hope, guidance, and the presence of God. This is a recurring motif in the Bible, notably in Psalms 119:105 ("Your word is a lamp for my feet, a light on my path") and in John 8:12 where Jesus refers to Himself as the "light of the world." It emphasizes the belief that even a small amount of faith or hope can illuminate the darkest situations.

Shared Burdens and Compassionate Support: The story illustrates the importance of sharing burdens and providing compassionate support, reflecting Galatians 6:2, which urges believers to "carry each other's burdens, and in this way, you will fulfill the law of Christ." Ted's gentle and understanding approach helps the soldier bear his physical and emotional pain, showcasing the Christian duty to care for one another.

The themes of this story highlight the importance of faith, hope, and compassionate presence in the face of suffering. It showcases the profound impact of spiritual ministry that doesn't rely on grandiose acts but rather the quiet, steadfast accompaniment of those enduring their darkest hours. This narrative serves as a reminder of how faith can guide individuals through suffering, offering them strength and solace when they feel most vulnerable.

Prayer

Heavenly Father, In the midst of our struggles, we turn to You, knowing that You are our source of strength and hope. Grant us the endurance to persevere through difficult times, trusting in Your promises and your unfailing love. Help us to find hope in the midst of our trials, knowing that You are working all things together for our good. May we cling to the hope found in Your Word, which is a lamp to our feet and a light to our path. May Your peace, which surpasses all understanding, guard our hearts and minds in Christ Jesus. Give us the courage to face each day with hope and confidence, knowing that You are with us, guiding us every step of the way. In the name of Jesus, our Rock and Redeemer, we pray. Amen.

6

Resilience Amidst Despair

In a dimly lit room of the medical-surgical floor, I stood by the bedside of yet another terminally ill patient. It was my second week as a chaplain intern in Beckham City Hospital. The weight of suffering hung heavy in the air, suffocating me like a thick blanket. It was a feeling I knew all too well—a sense of helplessness, of being powerless in the face of overwhelming pain and suffering. I reached out, offering what little comfort I could muster, but it felt inadequate, like trying to stop a flood with a bucket. In moments like these, the work of God seemed distant, intangible, like trying to grasp at smoke.

I prayed silently, desperately seeking peace, solace, and guidance in the midst of the chaos. But the answers, if there were any, remained elusive, slipping through my fingers like grains of sand. There were times when I left a patient's room exhausted, drained by the emotional toll of bearing witness to so much suffering.

And there were times when I couldn't hold back the tears, when the weight of it all became too much to bear. But amidst the darkness, there were moments of light—a peaceful death, a sense of surrender, a quiet gratitude from the patient's family. In those moments, I glimpsed a flicker of hope, a reminder that even in the darkest of times, there is still grace to be found and received.

And so, I continued on, navigating the murky waters of life and death, clinging to the fragile thread of faith that sustained me, praying for the strength to carry on, one day at a time.

Christian Themes and Values

Compassion in Suffering: The chaplain's role in the story reflects Jesus's compassion towards those who are suffering. Jesus often ministered to those in pain, whether it was physical, emotional, or spiritual. The chaplain, through his service, embodies this compassionate approach, reaching out to offer comfort even when it feels like a small gesture against overwhelming odds.

Presence of God in Suffering: The story delves into the common struggle of feeling God's absence in moments of intense suffering. This mirrors the biblical Psalmist's lamentations, such as in Psalm 22, where David expresses feeling forsaken yet continues to seek God's presence. Similarly, the chaplain prays for solace and guidance, grappling with the elusive nature of divine intervention but persisting in faith.

Endurance and Faith: The chaplain's experience of continuing his work amid suffering, and clinging to faith, aligns with the themes of perseverance. In the New Testament, James 1:12 praises those who persevere under trial, promising the crown of life to those who have stood the test. The chaplain, by continuing to serve despite the hardship, practices this biblical principle of enduring faith.

Hope and Grace: Despite the darkness surrounding the situations of terminal illness, the story highlights moments of light—peaceful deaths and gratitude from families. This aspect of the story captures the biblical promise of peace and grace that surpasses all understanding (Philippians 4:7). It underscores that grace often manifests in subtle but profound ways during trials.

The Power of Prayer: The chaplain's reliance on prayer for strength and guidance reflects the biblical teaching on the power and necessity of prayer in times of distress. In Philippians 4:6, Paul instructs believers to present their requests to God through prayer and supplication with thanksgiving. The chaplain's silent prayers are an act of faith and submission to God's will, seeking not just personal strength but also divine presence in the midst of trials.

In sum, the story is a contemporary reflection of biblical teachings on suffering, service, and the sustaining power of faith. It illustrates how, even in the most trying circumstances, individuals can find strength and hope through their faith, prayer, and acts of compassion, embodying Jesus's love and endurance.

Prayer

Heavenly Father, in times of despair and darkness, we turn to You, our source of hope and strength. Grant us resilience to endure the trials that come our way, knowing that You are with us always. Help us to find courage in the midst of despair, trusting in Your promises of restoration and redemption. May we lean on You for support, finding solace in Your presence and Your Word. Grant us the grace to rise above despair and to shine Your light in the darkest of places. Use us as instruments of Your peace and love, bringing hope to those who are lost and hurting. In the name of Jesus, who conquered death and darkness, we pray. Amen.

7

Hopeful Anticipation

Milly sat in her worn recliner, her weathered hands gently cradling Elmo, the ancient cat with only one ear and clouded eyes. The room was filled with the memories of a life well-lived; photos of children, grandchildren, and great-grandchildren adorned the walls, their smiling faces a testament to the love that had filled Milly's days. I could see the pain etched into the lines of her face, but she waved it off with a dismissive gesture.

"Don't mind me," she said, her voice a raspy whisper. "I'm not feeling a thing."

She spoke of her family with pride, recounting their accomplishments and adventures with a twinkle in her eye. But there was a heaviness in her voice when she mentioned the grandson she had lost to drugs just the year before. Her grief was palpable, a silent shadow that lingered in the air. Milly tugged at the oxygen cannula that snaked across her face, the thin tube a lifeline tethering her to this world. She hadn't eaten solid food in days, her frail body growing weaker with each passing hour. But despite her pain, despite her declining health, there was a sense of peace that radiated from Milly—a quiet acceptance of what was to come.

"I'm ready to go," she said, her voice firm. "I'm ready to join Tom and my grandson up there."

She gestured towards the ceiling, a smile playing at the corners of her lips.

"Jesus can take me anytime now. I'm really looking forward to it. Real soon."

And as I sat with Milly in that dimly lit room, I couldn't help but feel a sense of awe at her strength, her resilience in the face of adversity. She was a beacon of hope, a reminder that even in our darkest moments, there is still light to be found.

Christian Themes and Values

Endurance and Faith through Suffering: Milly's resilience in the face of physical decline and personal loss mirrors the biblical teachings on suffering and endurance. In Romans 5:3-5, Paul writes, "Not only so, but we also glory in our sufferings, because we know that suffering produces perseverance; perseverance, character; and character, hope. And hope does not put us to shame, because God's love has been poured out into our hearts through the Holy Spirit, who has been given to us." Milly's endurance in her physical suffering and the loss of her grandson highlights her steadfast faith and the hope she maintains despite the challenges.

Comfort in Mourning: Milly's grief over her lost grandson resonates with the Beatitudes, where Jesus says in Matthew 5:4, "Blessed are those who mourn, for they will be comforted." The presence of comfort, even in her anticipation of joining her loved ones in heaven, emphasizes the belief that God provides peace and comfort to those in sorrow.

Peace and Readiness for Heaven: Milly expresses a peaceful readiness to join her departed loved ones, reflecting the Christian hope in the promise of eternal life. This is illustrated in Philippians 1:21-23, where Paul expresses a similar sentiment: "For to me, to live is Christ and to die is gain. If I am to go on living in the body, this will mean fruitful labor for me. Yet what shall I choose? I do not know! I am torn between the two: I desire to depart and be with Christ, which is better by far." Milly's acceptance and even longing for her heavenly reunion shows her deep-rooted faith in the promises of the gospel.

The Light in Darkness: The notion that Milly, despite her hardships, could still be a "beacon of hope" aligns with biblical imagery of light in darkness. Psalms 112:4 states, "Even in darkness light dawns for the upright,

25

for those who are gracious and compassionate and righteous." Her life story serves as an example of how faith can shine through even in the darkest times, providing hope and inspiration to others.

Strength from Faith: Milly's strength and serenity can be attributed to her faith, which is echoed in Isaiah 40:31, "But those who hope in the Lord will renew their strength. They will soar on wings like eagles; they will run and not grow weary, they will walk and not faint." This verse encapsulates how faith sustains and empowers individuals even as they face life's end.

Milly's story is a testament to the power of faith to provide hope, comfort, and peace, regardless of life's trials and the pain of loss. It demonstrates the Christian belief that with faith, the end of earthly life can be faced not just with acceptance but with a serene and hopeful anticipation of eternal life with loved ones and the divine.

Prayer

Heavenly Father, as we journey through life, we come before You with hopeful anticipation. We trust in Your promises and look forward to the blessings You have in store for us. Fill our hearts with hope, O Lord, as we wait for Your perfect timing in all things. Help us to keep our eyes fixed on You, knowing that You are faithful to fulfill Your plans for us. Grant us patience as we wait for answers to prayers and guidance for the future. May we surrender our desires to Your will, confident that Your timing is always perfect. Lord, as we anticipate the fulfillment of Your promises, help us to live each day with purpose and joy. May our lives reflect the hope we have in You, drawing others to Your love and grace. In Jesus' name we pray, Amen.

8

Enduring Love and Companionship

The sun dipped low on the horizon, casting long shadows across the quiet countryside. Inside the modest farmhouse, the air was heavy with the scent of autumn leaves and the soft hum of cicadas outside. An elderly couple, Jack and Mary, sat side by side in their cozy living room, bathed in the warm glow of the fading sunlight. Mary, her frail frame wrapped in a knitted shawl, gazed out the window with tired eyes, her once vibrant spirit now dimmed by the relentless march of cancer.

Jack, her steadfast companion of over six decades, sat beside her, his weathered hands clasped tightly in his lap. His heart ached at the sight of his beloved wife, her strength waning with each passing day. Before stepping into their room, the hospice chaplain, a man of quiet reverence and deep compassion, paused at the threshold, bowing his head in silent prayer. He whispered *"namaste,"* a sacred acknowledgment, between souls, of the Divine presence within Jack and Mary, before crossing the threshold into their sacred space.

Each encounter with the elderly couple was a delicate dance between life and death, a testament to the enduring bond that held them together through the trials of sickness and old age. The chaplain approached them with a gentle smile, his presence a beacon of solace in their time of need.

As the sun dipped below the horizon and darkness enveloped the farmhouse, the chaplain sat with Jack and Mary, his heart heavy with the weight of their shared sorrow. Together, they wove a tapestry of memories and shared laughter, finding comfort in the quiet moments of companionship.

In the stillness of the evening, as the stars twinkled overhead, the chaplain bowed his head once more, offering a silent prayer for Jack and Mary's journey ahead.

In that sacred communion, amidst the flickering candlelight and the hushed whispers of their hearts, the presence of God lingered like a gentle breeze, a comforting embrace in their time of need.

Christian Themes and Values

Enduring Love and Companionship in Marriage: Jack and Mary's lifelong relationship mirrors the biblical portrayal of marriage as a lifelong covenant. In Ecclesiastes 4:9-12, the benefits of companionship are described: "Two are better than one, because they have a good return for their labor: If either of them falls down, one can help the other up. But pity anyone who falls and has no one to help them up." Their enduring bond through health and sickness showcases the biblical ideal of marriage as a source of mutual support and love.

Comfort and Compassion in Suffering: The hospice chaplain's role as a beacon of solace for Jack and Mary reflects the biblical theme of God's compassion and comfort in times of suffering. This is similar to the comfort God promises in 2 Corinthians 1:3-4, where Paul refers to God as "the Father of compassion and the God of all comfort, who comforts us in all our troubles, so that we can comfort those in any trouble with the comfort we ourselves receive from God." The chaplain, through his gentle and reverent approach, acts as an instrument of God's comfort.

Sacred Presence in Everyday Life: The chaplain's use of *"namaste"* to acknowledge the divine in Jack and Mary reflects the themes that humans are created in the image of God (Genesis 1:27) and that the spirit of God dwells within us (1 Corinthians 3:16). This acknowledgment deepens the recognition of each person's dignity and worth, particularly in the vulnerability of illness and old age.

God's Presence in Times of Transition: The setting of the sun and the coming of night as Jack and Mary are surrounded by love and prayers can be seen as symbolic of the biblical theme of God's guidance and presence through life's transitions, including the final transition from life to death. Psalm 23:4 emphasizes this, stating, "Even though I walk through the darkest valley, I will fear no evil, for you are with me; your rod and your staff, they comfort me."

Hope and Eternal Perspective: The story, with its focus on enduring bonds and the comfort provided by faith, also echoes the Christian hope in eternal life and the belief that death is not an end but a transition to a continued existence with God. This is articulated in Christian doctrine and passages such as John 11:25-26, where Jesus says, "I am the resurrection and the life. The one who believes in me will live, even though they die; and whoever lives by believing in me will never die."

Overall, the story illustrates how faith, love, and hope intersect in the lives of believers, especially during the profound moments of life's end, offering a testament to the Christian beliefs about marriage, companionship, God's comforting presence, and the eternal hope that underpins the Christian faith.

Prayer

Heavenly Father, we thank You for the gift of enduring love and companionship. You have blessed us with relationships that reflect Your love for us, and we are grateful for the strength and comfort they provide. Lord, help us to cherish and nurture these relationships, knowing that they are a reflection of Your love for us. Grant us the grace to be patient, kind, and forgiving, even in times of difficulty and disagreement. Lord, be the foundation of our relationships, guiding us in Your ways of grace and mercy. May our love for You overflow into our love for one another, creating bonds that withstand the tests of time and trials. In Jesus' name we pray, Amen.

9

The Presence of God in Silence

Tony watched the door close with a gentle click, the silence settling back around him like a familiar blanket. Outside, the winds of autumn wrestled with the last stubborn leaves clinging to the trees, a rhythmic rustling that occasionally pressed against the windows. The room felt colder as the light outside dimmed, shifting from gold to gray, the sort of change that made evenings long and thoughts deep.

The cats, sensing the drop in temperature and perhaps the loneliness that seemed to thicken in the air, began to gather around Tony's bed. The youngest, a spry tabby named Elsie, jumped up and made her way to the pillow, her small motor of purrs running steadily. Tony looked at her and attempted a smile, the kind that didn't quite reach his eyes but showed effort, nonetheless.

"Guess it's just you and me now," he murmured, his voice rough like sandpaper. He offered a trembling hand to Elsie, letting her warmth seep into his fingertips. Memories came then, unbidden yet not unwelcome—the days of youth spent in the shop, the sharp smell of metal and the sparks flying like fleeting stars, each piece crafted with a fury and passion now lost.

Sal had been there in those days, her laughter a bright sound over the clamor of machinery. She'd bring lunch, sandwiches wrapped neatly in waxed paper, staying to watch him work, her eyes full of pride. Now the room where they had shared so much lay quiet, save for the soft purring of the cats and the ticking of the clock on the wall, each tick a heavy step towards an end he both feared and longed for.

As the light faded from the room, shadows crawled over the walls, playing tricks with their eyes. Sal seemed to move in those shadows, her figure just as he remembered, the sway of her dress, the curve of her smile. Tony knew it was the tricks of the light, the wanderings of a mind too long confined to stillness, yet he welcomed the illusion.

"You'd laugh, wouldn't you, Sal? Seeing me like this, talking to cats and shadows," he said quietly, his words floating up to the high ceilings, lost among the cobwebs and quiet dignity of old pain.

In the softening darkness, with Elsie's purrs a comforting constant, Tony thought about the prayers I had offered, straightforward and devoid of the pretense he despised. Perhaps there was something there after all, a sort of peace or acceptance in the acknowledgment of what was, what is, and what was yet to come. Maybe, just maybe, there was a kind of faith in that—the faith in seeing things through, in enduring, in not looking away when the light fades and the cold sets in.

Tony lay back against his pillows, letting the darkness envelop him fully now, the presence of his cats a weighty, comforting assurance. There was no grand epiphany, no sudden clarity or resolve, just the simple, profound comfort of presence—of shared silence and the unspoken understanding that sometimes, just being there is enough. As night fell, the room grew silent but for the steady breathing of a man and his cats, the world outside continuing on, indifferent yet oddly tender in its indifference.

Christian Themes and Values

Vanity of Life: The narrative resonates with the theme found in the book of Ecclesiastes, which speaks to the transient nature of life and the seeming futility of all human endeavors. Tony reflects on his past vigor and passion, now faded with age and sickness, mirroring the Biblical reflection on how time and death diminish all human achievements.

Job and Suffering: Tony's enduring of physical decline and his grappling with the loss of his wife echo the suffering of Job. Like Job, Tony faces his trials alone, conversing with the memories of his wife and his present loneliness. His dialogue and musings reflect a wrestling with meaning and presence in suffering, and a subtle, perhaps reluctant, leaning towards finding solace in the mere presence of his cats and the remnants of memories, similar to Job's eventual finding of peace in the presence of God amidst unanswered questions.

Lamentation: The emotional tone of the story is akin to a psalm of lament, where the protagonist expresses sorrow and loneliness yet also engages in a form of communion (with his cats and memories). This can be seen as parallel to the Biblical lamentations where the psalmists often express deep sorrow but also a profound sense of not being alone, as God is their witness.

Faith through Endurance: The theme of faith explored in the story isn't one of fervent religiosity but rather a quiet, enduring presence—akin to the Biblical notion of "faith as small as a mustard seed" (Matthew 17:20). Tony's reflection on the prayers and his possible internalization of their essence—enduring and witnessing rather than transformative miracles—mirrors the Biblical encouragement to endure in faith through trials.

The Presence of God in Silence: In the Bible, particularly in the story of Elijah (1 Kings 19:11-13), God is found not in the earthquake or fire, but in the gentle whisper. Similarly, in Tony's story, the divine or transcendent isn't present in dramatic gestures but rather in quiet moments—the steady purring of a cat, the tick of a clock, the enveloping darkness. These suggest a divine presence that is subtle and intimately woven into the fabric of everyday experiences.

Overall, Tony's story, with its reflective and subdued exploration of life's latter stages, captures a deeply human experience that aligns with several profound Biblical insights about the human condition, suffering, presence, and faith.

Prayer

Heavenly Father, In the silence, we find Your presence. Amidst the noise of the world, you speak to us in the quietness of our hearts. Teach us to embrace the silence, Lord, as a holy space where we can draw near to You and hear Your gentle voice. May we find solace in Your presence, knowing that You are always with us, even in the stillness. In the silence, we offer our prayers and our praise to You. Help us to listen attentively for Your guidance and direction, trusting in Your wisdom and understanding. May the silence be a sanctuary for our souls, where we can rest in Your love and find renewal for our spirits. Let Your peace, which surpasses all understanding, fill our hearts and minds as we dwell in Your presence. In the name of Jesus, who taught us the importance of quiet communion with You, we pray. Amen.

10

Selfless Love and Sacrifice

Tim sat by Marie's bedside, his weathered hands gently clasping hers. The faint flicker of candlelight danced across his face, casting shadows in the lines etched by years of toil and love.

"Tim," I said softly, stepping into the dimly lit room.

He looked up, his eyes tired but unwavering. "Chaplain," he greeted, his voice a low rumble.

"How are you holding up?" I asked, taking a seat beside him.

Tim sighed, his shoulders sagging with the weight of exhaustion. "Just taking it one day at a time," he replied, his words heavy with unspoken emotion.

I nodded, understanding the silent struggle that lay beneath his stoic exterior. "It's never easy," I offered, a simple acknowledgment of the pain that bound us together.

Tim glanced down at Marie, his expression a mixture of love and longing. "No," he agreed softly. "But she's worth every moment."

I reached out, placing a hand on his shoulder in a gesture of solidarity. "She is indeed," I murmured, the words hanging heavy in the stillness of the room.

We sat in silence for a moment, lost in our own thoughts and prayers. Outside, the wind whispered through the trees, a haunting melody of loss and longing.

"I don't know how you do it, Tim," I confessed, breaking the silence with a whispered admission.

Tim looked at me, his eyes reflecting the flickering candlelight. "You do what you have to," he said simply, his voice tinged with a quiet resolve.

I nodded, humbled by the depth of his wisdom. "I pray for both of you," I said softly, my voice barely more than a whisper.

Tim smiled, a weary but genuine expression of gratitude. "Thank you, Chaplain," he said, his words a balm to my troubled soul.

And in that moment, as we sat together in the quiet sanctuary of Marie's room, I knew that Tim was not just a caregiver—he was a beacon of hope in a world shrouded in darkness. And though the road ahead would be fraught with pain and uncertainty, I took solace in the knowledge that Tim would face it with the same quiet strength and unwavering love that had carried him this far.

Christian Themes and Values

Selfless Love and Sacrifice: Tim's care for Marie reflects the biblical command to love selflessly and sacrificially. This is akin to the love described in Ephesians 5:25, where husbands are instructed to love their wives "just as Christ loved the church and gave himself up for her." Tim's actions embody this sacrificial love, giving of himself tirelessly and without complaint.

The Virtue of Patience and Perseverance: Tim's continuous support and care for Marie during her illness demonstrates the virtues of patience and perseverance under trial. James 1:12 praises those who persevere under trial, stating, "Blessed is the one who perseveres under trial because, having stood the test, that person will receive the crown of life that the Lord has promised to those who love him." Tim's endurance showcases the strength that comes from a deep, abiding love and commitment.

Compassion and Mercy: Tim's tenderness towards Marie, even as Alzheimer's takes its toll, reflects the compassion and mercy that are central to Christian teachings. In Colossians 3:12, believers are urged to "clothe yourselves with compassion, kindness, humility, gentleness, and patience."

Tim lives out these virtues daily in his interactions with Marie, providing a living example of biblical compassion in action.

Bearing One Another's Burdens: The story also touches on the concept of bearing one another's burdens, which is highlighted in Galatians 6:2: "Carry each other's burdens, and in this way, you will fulfill the law of Christ." By caring for Marie and taking on the heavy load of her care, Tim not only shows his love for her but also embodies the Christian principle of helping those in need, easing their suffering through active support and love.

The Power of Prayer and Shared Burden: The chaplain's role, in praying for both Tim and Marie, underscores the importance of intercessory prayer and communal support in Christianity. This shared spiritual support is vital, as articulated in 1 Thessalonians 5:11, "Therefore encourage one another and build each other up, just as in fact you are doing." It highlights the community's role in uplifting and supporting its members through trials and hardships.

Tim's story is a profound illustration of the strength and beauty of love, patience, and faithfulness in the face of life's most challenging circumstances. It challenges and inspires believers to live out their faith through actions that reflect God's love and compassion, even under the most trying conditions.

Prayer

Heavenly Father, we come before You with hearts full of gratitude for the selfless love and sacrifice You have shown us through Your Son, Jesus Christ. He laid down His life for us, demonstrating the depth of Your love and the extent of Your mercy. Grant us the courage to lay down our desires, ambitions, and comforts for the sake of serving others. May our actions be a reflection of Your love, bringing light and hope into the lives of those around us. Fill us with Your Holy Spirit, empowering us to love unconditionally and to serve wholeheartedly. May Your love flow through us, touching the lives of those in need and bringing glory to

Your name. We surrender ourselves to Your will, Lord, asking that You use us as instruments of Your love and grace in this world. May we be willing vessels, ready to sacrifice for the sake of others, just as Christ sacrificed Himself for us. In Jesus' name, we pray, Amen.

11

Family Love at the End of a Journey

Elise lay silent on the bed, her frail form barely stirring as I sat beside her. The weight of impending death hung heavy in the room, a palpable presence that suffused the very air we breathed. Her daughters moved about the house, their actions a mixture of resignation and sorrow.

"Dana, how's she doing?" I asked, my voice a whisper in the quiet room.

Dana glanced over her shoulder from the kitchen, her eyes weary but determined. "Not good," she replied, her voice tinged with sadness. "But she's comfortable, at least."

Betty, her eyes red-rimmed from tears, emerged from Elise's room, her hands trembling as she clutched a tissue. "It won't be long now," she said softly, her voice breaking.

In the living room, Rod, Elise's husband, a man whose memory had been reduced by dementia, sat in silence, his eyes fixed on the television screen but his mind undoubtedly elsewhere, waiting for the hospice nurse to arrive and offer some semblance of comfort in the face of the inevitable.

I couldn't bring myself to eat, even when Dana offered me a bite of whatever she was cooking. My focus was solely on Elise, her spiritual needs, and on the woman whose journey was nearing its end. As the hours passed, the sense of finality grew stronger, each moment tinged with the knowledge that soon Elise would be gone. I read to her words of prayer and devotion, offering a small measure of solace in the face of the unknown.

When the nurse arrived and confirmed what we all knew in our hearts, we gathered around Elise one last time. We prayed, our voices choked with emotion, tears mingling with whispered words of love and farewell.

"Goodbye, Mom," Dana whispered, her voice trembling with grief as she leaned in to kiss Elise's forehead.

Betty reached out, clasping Elise's hand in her own, her tears flowing freely now. "We love you," she whispered, her voice breaking. Rod, now standing by the bed, simply looked at his wife.

In those last moments, as Elise slipped away from us, I couldn't help but feel the weight of the void her absence would leave behind for her family. But I also knew that she was at peace, her journey at an end, her pain finally eased in the arms of eternity. And as we stood there, united in grief but also in the knowledge that Elise was finally free from suffering, I felt a glimmer of hope amidst the sorrow.

Christian Themes and Values

Community in Suffering: The family's collective mourning and shared presence around Elise reflects the biblical notion of community in times of sorrow. Romans 12:15 instructs believers to "rejoice with those who rejoice; mourn with those who mourn." The presence of Elise's family and their collective engagement in caring for her during her final moments is a manifestation of this principle, showcasing the strength and comfort found in shared grief.

Peace Beyond Understanding: As Elise nears the end of her life, there is a sense of peace that settles over her, a peace that transcends human understanding. This peace is reminiscent of the promise found in Philippians 4:7, "And the peace of God, which transcends all understanding, will guard your hearts and your minds in Christ Jesus." Elise's peace suggests a trust in a transcendent care that soothes the fear typically associated with death.

Comfort in Mourning: The arrival of the hospice nurse and the comfort she brings to the family align with the biblical assurances of God's comfort to His people during times of distress. Psalm 34:18 says, "The LORD is close to the brokenhearted and saves those who are crushed in spirit." The nurse's role is emblematic of God's promise to be near those who are suffering and to provide solace through the hands and presence of others.

Eternal Rest: The story captures the Christian hope of eternal rest after the trials of earthly life, as described in Revelation 21:4, "He will wipe every tear from their eyes. There will be no more death or mourning or crying or pain, for the old order of things has passed away." Elise's peaceful passing into eternity is a profound reflection of this promise, offering comfort to believers that death is not an end but a transition to a place free from pain and sorrow.

Prayer and Communion: The family's gathering in prayer around Elise's bedside is a powerful testament to the role of prayer in seeking comfort and expressing love and farewell. This act of communal prayer not only fortifies their bond but also connects them spiritually as they navigate the painful reality of saying goodbye. It resonates with Matthew 18:20, "For where two or three gather in my name, there am I with them," highlighting the presence of the divine in the midst of communal prayer.

The narrative of Elise's passing weaves together these biblical themes to depict a scene of familial love, communal support, and spiritual peace at the end of life, reinforcing the Christian understanding of death as a doorway to eternal peace and a time for communal reflection and support.

Prayer

Heavenly Father, as we come to the end of our journey together, we lift our hearts in gratitude for the love and bond that has held us close through every step of the way. You have been our constant companion, guiding us with Your grace and filling our lives with Your love. We thank You for the gift of family, for the precious moments we have shared, and for the strength we have found in each other during times of joy and sorrow. Lord, help us to cherish the memories we have created together, knowing that they are a testament to Your faithfulness and goodness. May the love that binds us as family be a reflection of Your perfect love for us. We commit our family into Your hands, trusting that Your love will always be the anchor that holds us together. May Your blessings rest upon us now and forevermore. In Jesus' name, we pray, Amen.

12

Love that Transcends Death

Carla lay in her bed, the pallor of illness casting a shadow over her once vibrant features. As we spoke, she shared with me the deepest wounds of her heart—the loss of her two sons, each tragedy leaving an indelible mark on her soul. The first, taken by Covid, a cruel thief in the night, snatching away a life filled with promise and potential. The second, a motorcycle accident on the unforgiving asphalt of I-95, a sudden and senseless end to a life cut short. But amidst the grief and the pain, Carla's spirit remained unbroken.

With a quiet resolve, she spoke of her sons with a mother's love, her faith unwavering in the face of unimaginable loss. She knew, she said, that they were in a better place, waiting for her beyond the veil of mortality. Her bedroom walls bore witness to her enduring love, photographs of her sons hanging alongside the symbol of her faith, the crucifix. In their faces, I saw the echoes of Carla's strength and resilience, a testament to the bonds that transcended even death itself.

As I offered her communion, a simple ritual of faith and remembrance, Carla spoke of the Book of Job, finding a bit of comfort in the story of a man who endured suffering with unwavering faith. In her words, I heard the echoes of a soul at peace, a woman who had faced the depths of despair and emerged stronger for it. In that moment, I couldn't help but feel humbled by Carla's courage, by her unwavering trust in the face of life's greatest trials. And as I left her bedside, I carried with me the knowledge that even in the darkest of times, there is light to be found in the steadfastness of faith and the enduring power of love.

Christian Themes and Values

Faith Through Suffering: Carla's story resonates deeply with the story of Job from the Bible. Like Job, Carla has endured immense personal loss and suffering but remains steadfast in her faith. Job's story, particularly in the Book of Job, is a prime example of enduring faith under trial and the sovereignty of God, even when that sovereignty is beyond human understanding. Job 1:21 reflects this when Job says, "The Lord gave, and the Lord has taken away; may the name of the Lord be praised."

Eternal Hope: Carla's belief that her sons are "in a better place" aligns with the Christian doctrine of eternal life, where death is not an end but a transition to a new existence in the presence of God. This belief offers comfort and hope amidst grief, as outlined in 2 Corinthians 5:1, "For we know that if the earthly tent we live in is destroyed, we have a building from God, an eternal house in heaven, not built by human hands."

The Power of Communion and Remembrance: The act of taking communion at Carla's bedside is a significant one. It symbolizes the unity of believers in Christ's suffering and resurrection and serves as a reminder of Jesus' promise of eternal life. This sacrament is especially in the context of remembering her lost sons, reflecting on the sacrifice of Christ, and finding solace in the hope of reunion. As stated in 1 Corinthians 11:26, "For whenever you eat this bread and drink this cup, you proclaim the Lord's death until he comes."

Strength and Resilience in Faith: Carla's ability to speak of her trials with peace and even find solace in them showcases a remarkable spiritual resilience, similar to that praised in James 1:2-4, "Consider it pure joy, my brothers and sisters, whenever you face trials of many kinds, because you know that the testing of your faith produces perseverance. Let perseverance finish its work so that you may be mature and complete, not lacking anything."

Love That Transcends Death: The photographs of her sons beside a crucifix, a symbol of sacrificial love and victory over death, illustrate the themes that love is stronger than death. As Romans 8:38-39 asserts, "For I am convinced that neither death nor life, neither angels nor demons, neither the present nor the future, nor any powers, neither height nor depth, nor anything else in all creation, will be able to separate us from the love of God that is in Christ Jesus our Lord."

Carla's story, while marked by profound loss, is also a testament to the power of faith to provide comfort, the strength to endure unimaginable pain, and the capacity to hold onto the hope of eternal life. It highlights how, even in the darkest of times, faith can shine a light that guides one through the pain, guided by the enduring power of love and the promise of reunion beyond the veil of mortality.

Prayer

Heavenly Father, we come before You with hearts filled with gratitude for the love that transcends death, the love that You have shown us through Your Son, Jesus Christ. In His resurrection, You conquered death and gave us the hope of eternal life. Grant us the strength to face the challenges of life and death with faith and courage, knowing that Your love never fails and that You are with us always. Comfort those who are grieving the loss of loved ones, reminding them of the hope we have in Christ's resurrection. Lord, may Your love shine brightly in our lives, illuminating the darkness of death and bringing hope and healing to those who mourn. May we be a reflection of Your love, sharing Your light with others and pointing them to the eternal life found in You. We entrust our loved ones who have passed away into Your loving arms, knowing that they are safe and secure in Your presence. May we find comfort in the promise of reunion with them in Your heavenly kingdom. In Jesus' name, we pray, Amen.

13

Hope Beyond Death

Amanda lay in her hospital bed, each breath more laborious than the last, her face etched with the lines of prolonged pain. The room was quiet, save for the low hum of medical machinery—the constant beeps a somber reminder of the delicate thread between life and death. I had been assigned as her chaplain two months ago, and during that time, I'd come to know not just the clinical details of her condition, but the stories that made up her life.

Amanda was a painter, a lover of the ocean, a marine biologist, and a fiercely independent soul. She'd often speak wistfully of the mornings she'd spent by the shore, her easel anchored against the sand, capturing the sunrise. But as cancer took its toll, those mornings had become memories, framed within the confines of her mind, as tangible yet distant as the paintings that hung on the walls of her room.

"It's strange," Amanda whispered one evening, her voice hoarse yet clear, "to think of how much I took it all for granted—the ability to hold a brush, to mix paint, to see color. Now, I dream in shades of gray."

Amanda looked uncomfortable, so I asked if I could adjust her pillows, trying to ease her discomfort, a task that felt as futile as it was necessary. "Maybe," I ventured, "you're seeing in a different kind of light now. Not brighter or better, but not less beautiful either."

She smiled faintly, and it was like a brief break in the clouds on a stormy day. "I like that," she said. "Seeing in a different light. Makes it sound like there's something worthwhile to this whole ordeal."

As days turned into weeks, Amanda's body weakened, but her eyes retained a spark of defiance—a refusal to be defined by her illness. We'd talk about everything from art to marine creatures and to life's odd, unpredictable journey. In those conversations, I saw her not just as a patient suffering from a terminal disease, but as a woman who had lived passionately, loved deeply, and now, faced her reality with unimaginable courage.

But as her chaplain, I felt the weight of a different reality—the clinical assessments, the medication schedules, the gentle, yet stark discussions with caregivers, nurses, and doctors about timelines and expectations. These were the cold facts of terminal care, yet they seemed so detached from the woman who lay before me, whose presence was still vibrant with life.

One particularly difficult night, as a storm raged outside, mirroring the turmoil within the hospice unit walls, Amanda seemed restless, her breaths ragged, her brow furrowed in discomfort. I held her hand, a small gesture, yet one of the few comforts I could offer.

"Amanda," I said softly, not sure if she could hear me over the roar of the wind, "you're not alone in this."

Her grip tightened slightly, a small acknowledgment that she heard me, understood me. "I'm scared," she confessed, a vulnerability in her voice that broke my heart.

"I know," I replied, squeezing her hand. "It's okay to be scared. But I'm here with you. You have so much love around you—your family, your friends. We're all here with you."

As the night wore on, the storm subsided, and a calm settled over the room. Amanda's breathing became less labored, her face relaxed. In the dim light of early dawn, as I watched over her, I realized that my role was not just to administer the sacraments or to update charts. It was to accompany her on this last part of her journey, to be a witness to her life and to her facing of death.

When her time finally came, it was peaceful—an easing of breath, a final gentle sigh. Her family was by her side, holding her hands, a circle of love and farewell. After they had left, I stayed behind, sitting within my own silent space, a ritual that felt both sacred and heartbreakingly ordinary.

In that moment of solitude, I understood something profound about my work—not every day would bring miracles, but every day I could make a difference in small, meaningful ways. For Amanda, for all my patients, I could offer my presence, my care, and my respect for their journey.

And as I walked out of her room, I felt a flicker of peace, knowing that Amanda had found her release, perhaps on some distant shore, in a place where the sea met the sky, where the sunrise was not gray, but full of colors only she could paint.

Christian Themes and Values

Suffering and Comfort: Amanda's struggle with cancer mirrors the biblical understanding of human suffering. In Christianity, suffering is often seen as a part of the human condition that can lead to spiritual growth and deeper reliance on God. The Book of Psalms is filled with cries for help in times of distress, reflecting the natural human reaction to pain and suffering (Psalm 22). The comfort provided by the nurse, through both physical presence and emotional support, aligns with the biblical calls to comfort those in distress (2 Corinthians 1:3-4, "Blessed be the God and Father of our Lord Jesus Christ, the Father of mercies and God of all comfort, who comforts us in all our affliction...").

Presence and Companionship: The nurse's steadfast companionship with Amanda during her last days reflects the biblical theme of loving one's neighbor as oneself (Mark 12:31). The nurse's role goes beyond clinical duties, embodying the Christian act of being present in another's time of need, reminiscent of Christ's promise to be with believers always, to the very end of the age (Matthew 28:20).

Facing Mortality and Finding Peace: Amanda's vulnerability and eventual peace with her situation echo the biblical narratives where individuals face their mortality and find peace through faith. This is seen in the peaceful acceptance of death by biblical figures who trust in God's promises, such as

Simeon in the New Testament, who is content to die after seeing the infant Jesus, declaring that God's promise to him has been fulfilled (Luke 2:29-32).

Transformation and Redemption: The story hints at a transformation within Amanda, from fear to acceptance and peace. This can be likened to biblical themes of redemption and salvation where, through faith, individuals are transformed and renewed (Romans 12:2). Amanda's journey suggests a metaphorical redemption, as she comes to terms with her life and imminent death, finding peace in the knowledge that there will be a release from her suffering.

Hope Beyond Death: Amanda's final moments, where there is a suggestion of her experiencing colors in a celestial sunrise, align with Christian beliefs in an afterlife—a place where there is no more pain or suffering (Revelation 21:4). This hope beyond death is central to Christian theology, providing comfort to those facing the end of their earthly lives.

Legacy of Love and Impact: Lastly, the legacy Amanda leaves behind—a legacy of strength, love, and resilience—reflects the biblical emphasis on how individuals can impact others through their life and faith. This is the way biblical characters like the apostles left enduring legacies that continued to influence others long after their deaths.

Amanda's story is rich with elements that resonate deeply with Christian values and beliefs, portraying the redemptive power of faith, the profound impact of compassionate care, and the eternal hope that transcends even the darkest moments of human existence.

Prayer

Heavenly Father, In the face of death, we cling to the hope that You have given us through Jesus Christ. He conquered death and opened the way to eternal life for all who believe in Him. Lord, we thank You for the promise of hope beyond death, for the assurance that those who have placed their trust in You will live with You forever. Help us to hold fast to this hope, even in the midst of grief and sorrow. Grant us the strength to face the reality of death with faith and confidence, knowing that You are with us every step of the way. May Your presence bring comfort and peace to those who mourn, reminding them that death is not the end, but a gateway to a new and glorious life with You. Lord, as we walk through the valley of the shadow of death, may Your light shine brightly, guiding us and giving us courage. Help us to find strength in Your promises and to trust in Your unfailing love. May we live each day with the hope of eternity in our hearts, knowing that You have prepared a place for us in Your heavenly kingdom. And may Your grace sustain us until that day when we are reunited with our loved ones in Your presence forever. In Jesus' name, we pray, Amen.

14

Compassion for All Living Things

Kelly, a little girl stood in the sterile white room, her eyes red and swollen from tears, clutching her beloved cat, Tula, tightly to her chest. Beside her stood Aaron, the veterinarian, a kind-hearted man with gentle hands and a sympathetic gaze. The cat, once full of life and vigor, now lay still on the metal examination table, its breathing labored, and its eyes clouded with pain.

Aaron had explained to Kelly and her family that the cat's illness was terminal, and that the most humane course of action was to euthanize it to end its suffering. As Kelly struggled to come to terms with the impending loss of her beloved cat, a veterinary chaplain entered the room, her presence a silent beacon of solace amidst the somber atmosphere. With a soft smile and a reassuring touch, she approached Kelly and her family, offering words of comfort and prayers for peace.

Together, they formed a circle around Tula, their heads bowed in solemn reverence as the chaplain offered a heartfelt prayer for the animal's soul and for the family's strength in the face of loss. And as Aaron administered the final dose of medication, easing the cat's pain and granting it a peaceful passing, the chaplain stood by, offering silent support and a comforting presence to the grieving family.

In that moment of shared sorrow and shared humanity, the chaplain reminded them that even in the darkest of times, they were not alone, and that love, and compassion could transcend even the deepest pain. And as they said their final goodbyes to Tula, the chaplain's words echoed in their hearts, offering them a glimmer of hope amidst the darkness of grief.

Christian Themes and Values

Compassion and Empathy: Aaron, the veterinarian and the chaplain's approach to Kelly's situation reflects the biblical mandate to show compassion and empathy towards all of God's creations. This is seen in Proverbs 12:10, which states, "A righteous man cares for the needs of his animal." The decision to euthanize the cat to alleviate its suffering is made with a heavy heart, underscoring the deep care and compassion for the animal, as well as for the girl who loves it.

Comfort in Mourning: The role of the chaplain in providing comfort and solace to the grieving family aligns with the biblical promise found in 2 Corinthians 1:3-4, where Paul describes God as "the Father of compassion and the God of all comfort, who comforts us in all our troubles." The chaplain's presence and his comforting words help the family feel supported and less alone in their grief, embodying the spirit of divine consolation.

Prayer and Spiritual Support: The chaplain's prayer for the animal's soul and for the family's strength during loss highlights the power of prayer as a source of strength and solace. This is reflected in Philippians 4:6-7, which encourages believers to present their requests to God through prayer and supplication with thanksgiving, promising that the peace of God, which surpasses all understanding, will guard their hearts and minds.

Shared Humanity and Community: The chaplain's reminder that they are not alone in their sorrow and that love and compassion can transcend pain resonates with the biblical teaching on community and bearing one another's burdens, as instructed in Galatians 6:2, "Carry each other's burdens, and in this way you will fulfill the law of Christ." This teaches that communal support is crucial during times of loss and grief.

Hope Amidst Grief: Finally, the chaplain's message offers a glimmer of hope, echoing the biblical perspective that even in the darkest times, God's love and the community of faith can bring light. Romans 15:13 may be seen as a parallel, as it prays that "the God of hope fill you with all joy and peace as you trust in Him, so that you may overflow with hope by the power of the Holy Spirit."

This story is an illustration of how biblical principles of compassion, prayer, community support, and hope are crucial in navigating the challenges of life and death, providing a framework for understanding and processing grief and loss in a way that honors the dignity of all God's creatures.

Prayer

Heavenly Father, we come before You with hearts filled with compassion for all living things, knowing that You have created each one with love and care. Help us to see the beauty and value in every creature, and to treat them with kindness and respect. Lord, You have entrusted us with stewardship over Your creation, and we acknowledge our responsibility to care for it with compassion and reverence. Give us the wisdom to be good stewards of the earth, protecting and preserving the environment for future generations. May we be agents of healing and restoration, working to alleviate the suffering of all living things. Lord, may Your compassion flow through us, touching the hearts of others and inspiring them to join us in caring for Your creation. May Your kingdom come, and Your will be done on earth as it is in heaven, where all creatures live in harmony and peace. In Jesus' name, we pray, Amen.

15

The Ministry of Presence

The intensive care hospital room was immersed in a soft glow, shadows dancing across the walls like fleeting ghosts. The chaplain sat in the corner, his figure a silent sentinel amidst the symphony of beeping machines and whispered voices. Across from him, Cara, an oncology nurse, sat with shoulders hunched, her face etched with lines of worry. She clutched a crumpled tissue in her hand, a lifeline in the sea of uncertainty.

Her mother lay in the bed, a frail figure amidst the sterile white sheets, her breaths shallow and ragged. The machines surrounding her blinked with urgency, their red lights flashing in time with each labored exhale. Death lingered in the air, a palpable presence that weighed heavy on Cara's heart.

And at home, Cara's disabled son, Freddy, waited, innocent and unaware of the storm raging within their family. Cara carried the weight of the world on her shoulders, a delicate balance of duty as a registered nurse and responsibility as a mother. Now, faced with the imminent loss of her mother, she teetered on the edge of collapse.

The chaplain understood this burden well. He had seen it in the eyes of countless others, felt it in the heavy silence that hung in hospital rooms like a shroud. But he was not one for empty platitudes or false reassurances. He knew that sometimes, the greatest comfort one could offer was simply to be there, a silent witness to another's pain.

As Cara poured out her heart, her words rushing forth like a flood, the chaplain listened with a quiet empathy that spoke volumes. He watched as her tears fell freely, the tissue in her hand growing damp with each passing moment. There was a rawness to her grief, a primal ache that echoed through the sterile walls of the hospital room.

"My mother... she's all the original old family I have left," Cara choked out between sobs, her voice cracking with emotion. "I can't bear to lose her."

The chaplain said nothing, but reached out a hand, offering silent solidarity. Sometimes, he knew, words were inadequate in the face of such profound sorrow. Sometimes, all one could do was be present, a steady anchor in the storm.

Cara wiped her tears away with trembling hands, taking a deep, shuddering breath. The chaplain watched as she composed herself, the weight of her grief still heavy on her shoulders.

"I don't know how I'll go on without her," Cara whispered, her voice barely audible above the hum of the machines. "How will I tell Freddy? How will I face each day knowing she's not here?"

The chaplain listened, his heart heavy with the weight of Cara's pain. He knew there were no easy answers, no words of comfort that could erase the ache of loss. But he also knew that together they would find the strength to face whatever lay ahead.

"You and Freddy will take it one day at a time," the chaplain said softly, his voice a soothing balm in the darkness. "And you'll lean on each other for support. You're not alone in this, Cara. And I'm here for you, too. You can always find me walking the halls."

Cara nodded; her gratitude evident in the tearful smile she offered. In that moment, amidst the beeping machines and the fading light, she found a small amount of comfort in the chaplain's presence. She knew that together, they would navigate the storm, finding moments of peace amidst the chaos of grief.

As the night wore on, the intensive care unit grew quiet, the only sound the steady rhythm of her mother's breaths. The chaplain remained by Cara's side, a silent guardian in the darkness. And as the first light of dawn crept through the window, casting long shadows across the floor, Cara knew that she would find the strength to face another day, buoyed by the unwavering support of those who cared for her.

In the days that followed, Cara leaned on the chaplain for guidance and support, finding comfort in his quiet wisdom and steadfast presence. Together, they would navigate the difficult conversations with Freddy, gently breaking the news of his grandmother's impending passing.

And when the time finally came, when Cara's mother slipped away peacefully in her sleep, the chaplain was there to offer a shoulder to lean on, a hand to hold. Together, they mourned the loss of a loved one, finding solace in the shared understanding that life, with all its joys and sorrows, was a journey best traveled together.

Christian Themes and Values

Ministry of Presence: The chaplain's approach of simply being present with Cara as she faces the dual burdens of her mother's critical illness and caring for her disabled child underscores the themes of the ministry of presence. This idea is mirrored in the life of Jesus, who often provided comfort just by being with people in their time of need, exemplified in stories such as the raising of Lazarus (John 11), where Jesus wept alongside Mary and Martha before performing the miracle.

Bearing One Another's Burdens: The chaplain's silent support for Cara reflects the biblical injunction found in Galatians 6:2, "Carry each other's burdens, and in this way, you will fulfill the law of Christ." This scripture emphasizes the importance of empathy and shared strength in times of hardship, encouraging believers to support one another in practical and emotional ways.

Strength in Weakness: The scenario also highlights the concept that strength can be found in moments of vulnerability. This is a key message in 2 Corinthians 12:9, where Paul discusses how he has learned to rely on the grace of God, saying, "My grace is sufficient for you, for my power is made perfect in weakness." As Cara opens up about her struggles, it's suggested that her acknowledgment of vulnerability and acceptance of support can be the first steps toward finding strength in her difficult circumstances.

The Peace of God: The chaplain's role as a source of comfort and calm in the midst of chaos can also be seen as an embodiment of Philippians 4:6-7, which encourages believers to not be anxious but to present their requests to God through prayer and supplication with thanksgiving, so that the peace of God, which transcends all understanding, will guard their hearts and minds in Christ Jesus. While the chaplain does not offer overt prayer in this scenario, his empathetic listening serves a similar purpose in helping Cara find peace amidst her turmoil.

Comfort in Mourning: Finally, the interaction reflects the scriptural promise that God comforts us in our sorrows. As stated in Matthew 5:4, "Blessed are those who mourn, for they will be comforted." The chaplain's empathetic presence signifies this divine comfort, helping Cara feel less isolated in her grief and more supported in her role as both a daughter and a mother.

This story powerfully illustrates the Christian call to compassion, empathy, and the sustaining presence that we are all called to offer each other, particularly in times of deep distress and sorrow.

Prayer

Heavenly Father, We come before You with grateful hearts, recognizing the importance of the ministry of presence in our lives. You are always with us, offering Your comforting and reassuring presence in every moment. Lord, help us to be present for others as You are present for us. Teach us to listen with compassion, to offer our support without judgment, and to be a source of comfort and encouragement to those in need. Help us to be mindful of the power of our presence, recognizing that even the smallest act of kindness can make a profound difference in someone's life. May we be instruments of Your peace, spreading Your love wherever we go. Fill us with Your compassion and grace, so that we may reflect Your love to all whom we encounter. In Jesus' name, we pray, Amen.

16

Hope and Renewal

The walls of the hospital room seemed to close in on them, suffocating in their sterile white. Kathy lay in the bed, her once vibrant spirit now subdued by the relentless grip of cancer. Her husband, Vick, sat by her side, his hand clasped in hers, a silent vow of unwavering support. Across the room, their daughter Nia stood with shoulders hunched, the weight of her mother's illness pressing down upon her young heart.

For years, Kathy's battle with a rare form of blood cancer had become the defining thread in the fabric of their lives. Each passing day brought new challenges, new sacrifices, as they navigated the treacherous waters of illness and uncertainty.

Nia, barely out of her teenage years, found herself thrust into a role far beyond her years. While her classmates worried about prom and college applications, she juggled the demands of her senior year with the responsibilities of caregiving. It was a heavy burden to bear, but she did so with a quiet strength that belied her youth.

Meanwhile, Vick, a talented graphic artist by trade, found himself balancing the demands of work with the needs of his family. He became the rock upon which they all leaned, his steady presence a source of comfort in their darkest hours. Despite the mounting pressures, he never wavered, his love for Kathy shining through in every act of tenderness and sacrifice.

Their home became a sanctuary amidst the storm of illness, a place where love and support flowed freely. Despite the looming shadow of hospice care, there were moments of respite, moments when laughter echoed through the halls and the pain seemed to fade into the background.

But as the days turned into weeks and the weeks into months, Kathy's condition continued to deteriorate. Each decline brought with it a new wave of grief, a reminder of the fragility of life and the inevitability of loss.

Through it all, Vick remained by Kathy's side, a steadfast presence in the face of adversity. He tended to her needs with a quiet determination, his love for her driving him to do whatever it took to ease her suffering.

When the end finally came, it was both a relief and a devastating blow. The room was filled with a profound sense of loss as Kathy slipped away, leaving behind a void that could never be filled.

For the chaplain who had walked alongside them through their darkest hours, the pain of separation was palpable. He had witnessed their struggles, their triumphs, and their profound love for one another. And now, as he stood at the threshold of their grief, he found himself at a loss for words.

Yet, in the aftermath of Kathy's passing, life continued to unfold, albeit in a different rhythm. Nia embarked on a new chapter of her life, finding solace and strength in the love of her family and the memories of her mother.

And though the chaplain's journey with the family had reached its conclusion, the bonds forged in the crucible of suffering remained unbroken. In the quiet moments that followed, Vick's voice on the other end of the line served as a reminder of the enduring power of love and the resilience of the human spirit.

For in the face of tragedy, they had found a love that transcended all boundaries, a love that would carry them through even the darkest of nights. And as they leaned on each other for support, they knew that Kathy's spirit would live on in the love they shared, forever guiding them through life's inevitable storms.

Christian Themes and Values

Suffering and Resilience: The Bible often addresses the reality of human suffering and the resilience it can foster in individuals and communities. Romans 5:3-5 encapsulates this, explaining that suffering produces perseverance; perseverance, character; and character, hope. In Kathy's family, the trials they endure together not only test their strength but also develop a deeper sense of unity and hope among them.

Role of the Caregiver as a Servant: Vick's role as Kathy's primary caregiver exemplifies the biblical call to serve one another in love, as stated in Galatians 5:13, "You, my brothers and sisters, were called to be free. But do not use your freedom to indulge the flesh; rather, serve one another humbly in love." His devotion and the sacrifices he makes reflect Christ's command to love one another profoundly and selflessly.

Endurance Through Faith: Throughout Kathy's illness, the family's ability to cope and maintain hope reflects the biblical principle of enduring through faith. Hebrews 12:1 encourages believers to "run with perseverance the race marked out for us, fixing our eyes on Jesus, the pioneer and perfecter of faith." This endurance is crucial in helping them navigate the emotional landscape of Kathy's hospice care and eventual passing.

Comfort in Mourning: The chaplain's role in providing spiritual support and comfort aligns with 2 Corinthians 1:3-4, where God is described as the "Father of compassion and the God of all comfort, who comforts us in all our troubles." The chaplain's presence helps the family find solace and strength to continue life despite the immense loss.

Hope and Renewal Beyond Grief: After Kathy's death, Nia's continuation into a new chapter of her life symbolizes the Christian hope of renewal and continued life beyond death. Ecclesiastes 3:1-4 acknowledges there is a time for everything, including a time to mourn and a time to dance. The story reflects this cycle, showing that life's seasons of grief are followed by new beginnings.

Legacy and Love: The enduring power of love, as witnessed in Vick's ongoing strength and the family's resilience, illustrates the biblical assertion found in 1 Corinthians 13:7-8, stating that love "always protects, always trusts, always hopes, always perseveres. Love never fails." The love Kathy's family shows for each other, fortified through their shared ordeal, underpins their journey toward healing and reflects a fundamental Christian value.

In this narrative, biblical principles of enduring love, servanthood, and the redemptive quality of suffering are vividly depicted, offering a moving testament to the spiritual dimensions that underlie the human experiences of suffering, caregiving, and bereavement.

Prayer

Heavenly Father, We come before You with hearts filled with hope and gratitude for the promise of renewal that You offer us through Jesus Christ. In Him, we find the hope of new beginnings and the assurance of Your steadfast love. Lord, we thank You for the gift of hope that springs eternal in our hearts, even in the midst of trials and challenges. Help us to hold fast to this hope, knowing that You are always at work, bringing beauty from ashes and joy from mourning. May Your Spirit renew our minds and hearts, transforming us into vessels of Your grace and instruments of Your peace. Father, we pray for renewal in every area of our lives – in our relationships, our health, our work, and our spiritual journey. May Your healing touch bring wholeness and restoration, filling us with joy and gratitude for Your unfailing love. In Jesus' name, we pray, Amen.

17

Power in Testimony

Maryanne's presence filled the room like a force of nature. Despite her battle with arthritis, COPD, and the relentless pain that plagued her, her voice remained a constant, weaving tales of family, feline companions, and her unwavering faith in God.

Visiting Maryanne was always an adventure. Her home, a modest house in a trailer park, echoed with the sound of her voice, punctuated by fits of laughter that bubbled up from deep within her. All I had to do was lend an ear, nod along, and occasionally interject a word of empathy or understanding.

With two devoted sons who frequented her bedside and a daughter who had taken up residence to care for her, Maryanne was never lacking in companionship. For a chaplain, forming attachments to patients could be a slippery slope, but Maryanne made it easy. Her spirit was infectious, her resilience inspiring.

Over the span of six months, I bore witness to Maryanne's gradual decline. Her body weakened, but her spirit remained indomitable. Each visit brought with it a new revelation, a new insight into the depths of her character.

Then, one evening, as the sun dipped below the horizon, Maryanne slipped away quietly, leaving behind a void that seemed impossible to fill. Her son's voice trembled as he called for me to be by their side, to offer prayers for her final journey.

It was a struggle to maintain composure as tears welled in my eyes. Maryanne's children wept openly, their grief a tangible presence in the room. Like so many of my patients before her, I found myself silently pleading, "Please, don't leave us just yet. There's still so much left unsaid, so much left to learn."

But as the tears flowed, I found some comfort in the knowledge that Maryanne's spirit would live on, a testament to the resilience of the human soul and the enduring power of faith. And though she may have departed this world, her laughter and her stories would echo in my heart forevermore.

In the days that followed, Maryanne's absence was keenly felt. The cats still crowded around her open door, but now the food bowls were empty. The trailer park seemed quieter somehow, the air heavy with the weight of loss. But amidst the grief, there was also a sense of peace, a recognition that Maryanne's suffering had come to an end.

Her children, though heartbroken, found comfort in each other's company, drawing strength from their shared memories of their beloved mother. And for me, Maryanne's passing served as a reminder of the fragility of life and the importance of cherishing every moment.

As I sat in my home office, surrounded by the quiet purr of my own cats, I found myself reflecting on the lessons Maryanne had taught me. She had faced unimaginable pain with grace and dignity, her unwavering faith serving as a guiding light in the darkest of times.

And though she was gone, her spirit lived on in the hearts of those who had known her. Her laughter echoed in the corridors of memory, a reminder of the joy she had brought into the world.

As I closed my eyes and offered a silent prayer for Maryanne's soul, I knew that she was at peace, surrounded by the love of those who had gone before her. And though her journey had ended, her legacy would endure, a testament to the power of the human spirit to overcome even the greatest of obstacles.

Christian Themes and Values

The Power of Testimony: Maryanne's continuous storytelling and sharing of her faith even in the face of severe illness reflects the themes of testimony. In the Bible, believers are often encouraged to speak of their faith and God's work in their lives, similar to the Psalmist who declares, "I will tell of your name to my brothers; in the midst of the congregation, I will praise you" (Psalm 22:22). Maryanne uses her voice as a powerful tool to witness and uplift those around her, embodying the Christian duty to share the gospel and personal faith experiences.

Presence of God in Suffering: Throughout her battle with cancer, Maryanne's unwavering faith illustrates the biblical assurance of God's presence in suffering. Scriptures such as Psalm 23:4, which says, "Even though I walk through the valley of the shadow of death, I will fear no evil, for you are with me; your rod and your staff, they comfort me," resonate deeply with her experience. Her continual faith and joyful demeanor in spite of pain reflect a deep-rooted belief in God's steadfast presence and comfort.

Community and Support in Times of Need: The presence of Maryanne's family and the chaplain during her final days mirrors the biblical principle of community support as highlighted in Romans 12:15, "Rejoice with those who rejoice; mourn with those who mourn." The community that surrounds her, including her attentive children and the chaplain, exemplifies the Christian call to bear one another's burdens and provide support in both joyful and challenging times.

Resilience and Hope in Faith: Maryanne's indomitable spirit despite her physical decline showcases the resilience that faith can foster. 2 Corinthians 4:16-18 speaks to this, noting, "Though outwardly we are wasting away, yet inwardly we are being renewed day by day. For our light and momentary troubles are achieving for us an eternal glory that far outweighs them all." Her ability to maintain joy and hope exemplifies the transformative power of faith that looks beyond current suffering to eternal promises.

Legacy of Faith: Finally, the chaplain's reflection on Maryanne's enduring impact, with her laughter and stories echoing in their hearts, ties into the biblical idea of a spiritual legacy. Hebrews 12:1 encourages believers, surrounded by "so great a cloud of witnesses," to run the race set before them.

Maryanne leaves behind a legacy that continues to inspire and influence, much like the faithful witnesses of scripture.

Maryanne's journey is an illustration of how faith deeply interweaves with daily life and the end-of-life experience, offering strength, comfort, and a lasting testimony that impacts others profoundly. Through her story, we see the themes of witnessing, communal support, and the enduring nature of spiritual legacy brought to life.

Prayer

Heavenly Father, We come before You with hearts full of gratitude for the power of testimony in our lives. You have given us the gift of salvation through Jesus Christ, and You have called us to share the story of Your redeeming love with others. Lord, help us to recognize the significance of our testimonies and the impact they can have on those around us. Give us the boldness to proclaim Your goodness and faithfulness in our lives, so that others may come to know You and experience Your life-changing grace. We pray that our testimonies would inspire and encourage others, leading them to seek You and find hope and salvation through Jesus Christ. Use our stories to bring light into the darkness, to break chains of bondage, and to set captives free. May our testimonies be a beacon of hope in a world that desperately needs Your saving grace. In Jesus' name, we pray, Amen.

18

Strength Found in Faith

Hank's age belied the seriousness of his condition. At just thirty-eight, he was already battling a rare neurological affliction that ravaged his body and defied conventional medical treatment. When I first met his father and sister, their words hinted at a specter of discomfort that lurked behind Hank's bedroom door, a disquieting truth that I was unprepared to confront. Yet, as I stepped into his room, I found myself face to face with a man whose resilience transcended the confines of his failing flesh.

Despite the visible toll that his illness had exacted, Hank's spirit burned bright, undimmed by the shadows that loomed around him. His handshake was firm, his voice steady as he shared his story with me, a testament to his unwavering resolve in the face of adversity.

In Hank's eyes, I glimpsed a wisdom far beyond his years, a profound understanding of the transient nature of earthly existence and the enduring promise of spiritual renewal. He spoke of his imminent journey with a calm assurance, his faith unshaken by the specter of mortality that hung heavy in the air.

"Chaplain," Hank began, his voice steady but tinged with fatigue, "I've come to accept what lies ahead. It's not easy, but I know that there's a greater purpose to it all."

I nodded, listening intently as Hank shared his thoughts on life, death, and everything in between. Despite his young age, he spoke with the wisdom of someone who had lived a hundred lifetimes, his words resonating deep within my soul.

"As I face my final days," Hank continued, "I find comfort in knowing that I've lived a life of purpose. I've loved deeply, I've laughed often, and I've made a difference in the lives of those around me."

As we bowed our heads in prayer, Hank's words echoed with a resonance that transcended the confines of his frail form. In that sacred moment, I felt a profound sense of connection, a shared communion with a soul poised on the threshold of eternity.

In the days that followed, Hank's presence lingered like a gentle breeze, a reminder of the enduring power of faith and the indomitable spirit of the human soul. Though his earthly journey had come to an end soon after my visit, his light continued to shine, illuminating the path for all who crossed his path.

Christian Themes and Values

Endurance in Suffering: Hank's resilience despite his debilitating condition embodies the biblical principle of enduring suffering with faith. This is vividly illustrated in the life of Apostle Paul, particularly in 2 Corinthians 12:9, where Paul discusses how God's grace is sufficient for him, for God's power is made perfect in weakness. Like Paul, Hank's steadfastness in his affliction serves as a testament to the strength that faith in God provides.

Transcendence of the Spirit: The contrast between Hank's physical limitations and his vibrant spirit parallels the biblical view of the body and spirit as separate entities, where the spirit can remain strong even when the body is weak. This idea is echoed in Matthew 10:28, which advises not to fear those who kill the body but cannot kill the soul. Despite the decline of his physical body, Hank's spirit and faith remain robust and undiminished.

Hope in Eternal Life: Hank's calm assurance about his imminent journey into eternity reflects the Christian belief in the hope of resurrection and eternal life, which is central to Christian eschatology. John 11:25-26, where Jesus states, "I am the resurrection and the life. The one who believes in me will live, even though they die," captures the essence of this hope. Hank's acceptance of his physical mortality coupled with a firm belief in spiritual continuation offers a profound reflection on this promise.

Communion and Fellowship in Prayer: The shared prayer moment between Hank and the narrator highlights the themes of fellowship and communal prayer as sources of spiritual strength and connection. Acts 2:42 praises the early Christians who devoted themselves to the apostles' teaching and to fellowship, to the breaking of bread and to prayer. This communal aspect of faith is a powerful support system for believers, particularly in times of trial.

Legacy of Faith: Finally, Hank's story emphasizes the lasting impact of a faithful life on others. The light of Hank's spirit continues to illuminate paths for others, reminiscent of Matthew 5:16, where Jesus encourages believers to let their light shine before others, that they may see their good deeds and glorify their Father in heaven. Hank's legacy is a beacon that guides and inspires even after his passing.

Hank's life and his serene approach to death provide a powerful illustration of how deep faith can profoundly influence not only how one faces their own mortality but also how they can impact and uplift those around them. His story encapsulates the biblical teachings on the strength found in faith, the hope of eternal life, and the indelible impact of a spiritual legacy.

Prayer

Heavenly Father, We come before You, acknowledging the strength found in faith that You offer to us, Your children. In times of trial and uncertainty, You are our refuge and our strength, a present help in times of trouble. Lord, we thank You for the gift of faith that sustains us through the storms of life. Help us to trust in You completely, knowing that You are always working for our good and Your glory, even when we cannot see it. Father, we pray for strength to face the challenges that lie ahead, knowing that with You, all things are possible.

Richard Gordon Zyne

May our faith inspire others to draw near to You, Lord, and to experience the strength and comfort that only You can provide. Use us as vessels of Your grace and instruments of Your peace in a world that is desperately in need of Your love. In Jesus' name, we pray, Amen.

19

Faith and the Harsh Realities of Life

In the hospice in-patient unit, where the air hangs heavy with unspoken fears and whispered hopes, the journey towards acceptance begins. For some, like Clair, the road ahead is fraught with uncertainty, a delicate balance between faith and reality.

Her family's pleas for discretion echoed through the corridors, a desperate plea to shield Clair from the harsh truths that lurked beyond the walls of her room. They clung to the belief in a Divine intervention, praying fervently for a miracle to stem the tide of her illness.

But within the confines of her fragile existence, the specter of mortality loomed large, casting a shadow over their hopes and dreams. Despite their unwavering faith, the harsh reality of Clair's diagnosis remained a bitter pill to swallow.

As a hospice chaplain, it fell upon me to navigate the delicate terrain of belief and acceptance, offering comfort in the face of uncertainty and hope in the midst of despair. With each visit, I bore witness to the struggle that raged within Clair's heart, torn between the longing for healing and the acceptance of her mortality.

In those moments of shared vulnerability, I offered words of reassurance and prayers for strength, hoping to ease the burden that weighed heavy upon her soul. Though the path ahead was fraught with challenges, I remained steadfast in my commitment to walk alongside her, offering support and guidance as she embarked on this journey of faith and acceptance.

In the end, whether the miracle they prayed for came to pass or not,

Clair's journey was one of profound courage and resilience. For in the crucible of suffering, she found a strength that transcended the limits of mortal frailty, a testament to the enduring power of the human spirit in the face of adversity.

Christian Themes and Values

The Reality of Human Mortality and Suffering: The Bible doesn't shy away from the realities of human suffering and mortality. Clair's confrontation with her impending death echoes the existential struggles faced by biblical figures such as Job. The Book of Job particularly deals with these themes—challenging the fairness of suffering and confronting mortality, yet ultimately finding solace in God's sovereignty.

Faith Amidst Suffering: Clair's family's fervent prayers for a miracle reflect the themes of persistent prayer in the face of dire circumstances. This is similar to the persistence taught in Luke 18:1-8, where Jesus tells the parable of the persistent widow to teach His disciples to always pray and not give up, showing that faith can coexist with the challenges of grim realities.

The Role of the Chaplain as a Comforter: The chaplain's role mirrors that of the Holy Spirit, often referred to as the Comforter in scripture (John 14:16, 26). The chaplain helps navigate the emotional and spiritual turmoil of Clair and her family, offering comfort and fostering an environment where hope can persist amidst despair. This is crucial in helping them maintain their faith and find peace in their trials.

Acceptance of God's Will: Clair's eventual movement towards acceptance of her mortality can be seen in light of Jesus' prayer in the Garden of Gethsemane, where He submits to God's will despite His impending suffering (Matthew 26:39). This profound submission to the divine will, even in the face of suffering, reflects a mature faith that acknowledges God's sovereignty and the mysterious nature of His plans.

Resilience and Courage in Faith: Clair's journey and the spiritual growth that occurs through her suffering reflect James 1:2-4, which encourages believers to consider it pure joy when facing trials because these trials test faith, produce perseverance, and lead to spiritual maturity. Clair's resilience and the strength she discovers within herself demonstrate the transformative power of enduring faith through trials.

Eternal Perspective: The biblical view of eternity helps believers to cope with the pain and loss of the present life. 2 Corinthians 4:17-18 speaks of momentary troubles preparing us for an eternal glory that far outweighs them all, focusing on what is unseen rather than what is seen. Clair's situation, and the spiritual care provided, helps to shift focus from immediate suffering to the hope of eternal peace and healing.

Clair's story in the hospice illustrates these themes, showing how faith, while challenged by the harsh realities of life, also provides a framework for understanding, enduring, and ultimately accepting human suffering and mortality with grace and courage.

Prayer

Heavenly Father, As we face the harsh realities of life, we come before You with hearts filled with faith, knowing that You are our rock and our fortress, our refuge in times of trouble. Help us to trust in Your goodness and Your sovereignty, even when life feels overwhelming. Lord, we acknowledge that faith is not always easy, especially when we are confronted with pain, suffering, and uncertainty. Yet, we know that You are with us in the midst of our struggles, and that You have promised to never leave us nor forsake us. Father, we pray for those who are facing difficult circumstances, that You would surround them with Your love and peace. Give them the courage to trust in You, even when the storms of life rage around them. May our faith be a light in the darkness, a beacon of hope to those who are struggling. Use us, Lord, to demonstrate Your love and faithfulness to a world in need. In Jesus' name, we pray, Amen.

20

Earthy Realism and Eclectic Spirituality

Joe leaned back in his chair, a wisp of smoke curling lazily from the cigarette between his fingers. His eyes, weathered by years of hard living and introspection, held a glint of mischief as he spoke, his words a testament to a lifetime of searching.

"I'm not sure I believe in a higher power," he mused, his voice tinged with uncertainty. "But if there is one, I know she's more of a gentle presence, like a warm breeze on a summer day. Not some Almighty old bastard wagging his finger at me from up above, sitting on a cloud."

With a chuckle, Joe continued, his words meandering like a lazy river through the landscape of his thoughts. "My God is low wattage, you know? Not fully plugged in. Just holding me in her hands like a baby and feeding me some soft cereal."

Born of Jewish immigrants, raised on the gritty streets of the Brownsville section of Brooklyn, Joe was a product of his environment—a melting pot of cultures and beliefs that had shaped his worldview. But beneath his rough exterior lay a soul steeped in wisdom, forged in the crucible of life's trials and tribulations.

As he shared his eclectic spiritual journey, Joe's words painted a vivid portrait of a man at peace with his beliefs, unbound by the constraints of organized religion. From the earthy teachings of Jesus to the natural wisdom of Native American spirituality, Joe's faith was a soupy concoction of theological vegetables and philosophical pasta cooked in his kitchen of human experiences.

And as the smoke of an incense stick danced around him, Joe embraced his impending mortality with a quiet acceptance, finding comfort in the knowledge that, whatever lay beyond this life, he would face it with the same irreverent charm that had defined his life on earth.

Christian Themes and Values

God as a Gentle Presence: Joe's conception of a higher power as a "gentle presence" rather than an "Almighty old bastard" aligns with the biblical depiction of God as compassionate, loving, and nurturing. This can be related to scriptures like Psalm 23, where God is portrayed as a shepherd who leads, provides, and comforts. It contrasts with, yet complements, traditional images of God's might and judgment, emphasizing His closeness and tenderness—a God who is more about quiet support than overwhelming power.

Personal and Direct Relationship with the Divine: Joe's notion of God "holding me in her hands, feeding me some soft cereal" speaks to a personal and intimate relationship with the divine, which is a central theme in many parts of the Bible. In Jeremiah 1:5, God speaks of knowing us before He formed us in the womb, suggesting a deeply personal connection with each individual, much like Joe's informal and nurturing divine presence.

Eclectic Spirituality: Joe's mix of spiritual influences, from Jesus to Native American spirituality, mirrors the biblical theme of wisdom being found in various forms and places. The Bible itself contains multiple perspectives and voices, from the wisdom literature of Proverbs to the diverse views of the New Testament writers. Joe's blending of these elements reflects a modern approach to spirituality that values a broad, inclusive understanding of truth, much like the wisdom collected in the biblical canon.

Irreverent Charm and Earthy Realism: Joe's irreverent approach to his spirituality and his acceptance of mortality without fear reflect the teachings of Ecclesiastes, where the Preacher acknowledges the fleeting nature of life and the importance of enjoying the simple, earthly moments ("Eat, drink, and be merry, for tomorrow we die"). Joe's acceptance of life's impermanence and his insistence on living authentically resonate with this existential but grounded biblical wisdom.

Facing Mortality with Peace: Finally, Joe's quiet acceptance of his impending death echoes the peace and assurance that the Bible often speaks about in the face of mortality. Philippians 1:21 says, "For to me, to live is Christ and to die is gain," which shows a profound peace about the transition from life to death. Joe seems to approach his own end with a similar peace, suggesting a deep-seated faith in whatever lies beyond.

Joe's narrative, therefore, while uniquely personal and framed in non-traditional language, engages with timeless biblical themes of divine intimacy, wisdom, acceptance of human limits, and the blend of spiritual insights. His story is a modern reflection on finding and forming one's understanding of the divine through a life fully lived and deeply felt.

Prayer

Heavenly Father, As we navigate the complexities of life with its diverse spiritual paths, we come before You seeking wisdom. Help us to find our footing amidst the diverse voices and ideologies that surround us, and to discern Your truth in the midst of it all. Lord, we acknowledge that Your ways are higher than our ways, and Your thoughts are higher than our thoughts. Grant us the humility to recognize our limitations and Your guidance in all things. In Jesus' name, we pray, Amen.

21

Stewardship and Care for Creation

Ashley pulled her jacket closer as the early morning chill crept through the gaps in the old clinic's walls. It was early, yet the sun barely peeking over the horizon, painted the sky a soft pink and orange. Around her, the day was waking up; birds chirped tentatively in the budding light, and a distant dog barked as though heralding the new day.

As a veterinary assistant in a rural town, Ashley had grown accustomed to the unpredictable rhythm of her work. Each day brought new challenges—wounded strays, anxious pets, and sometimes, the quiet sorrow of saying goodbye. Her work was witness not only to her love for animals but to her deep sense of duty towards them.

This morning, she was particularly anxious about her first appointment. A week-old kitten, found abandoned in a nearby alley, was coming in, barely clinging to life. The tiny creature was fighting a severe respiratory infection, and Ashley had spent the previous night researching additional treatments, hopeful for any new insight that could save it.

The clinic door creaked open, and Dr. Hayes, the veterinarian, stepped in with the kitten wrapped delicately in a warm towel. Its frail mews were weak but determined. Ashley's heart tightened at the sight, her resolve hardening.

"Morning, Ashley," Dr. Hayes greeted her, a tired smile on his face. "Ready to work some magic?"

"Always am," Ashley replied, her voice a mix of nerves and determination.

She gently took the kitten and set to work. The examination room was her canvas, the medical tools her brushes, and each motion she made was guided by a deep, silent prayer for the tiny life in her hands. With methodical precision, she administered oxygen, hydrated the kitten with IV fluids, and prepared the antibiotics that Dr. Hayes had prescribed.

Hours passed, the clinic bustling around her, but Ashley's focus never wavered from the fragile creature fighting for its life under her care. Each small improvement—a stronger mew, a curious glance from brightening eyes—was a victory, a splash of vibrant color restoring life to a fading canvas.

By late afternoon, the kitten was stable enough to sleep peacefully, its breathing easier now. Ashley watched it, her heart swelling with relief and love. In the quiet of the examination room, with the sun casting long shadows through the window, she felt a profound connection to the small creature. It was a reminder of why she had chosen this path: not for the easy victories, but for the hard-fought battles waged in the name of care and compassion.

As she prepared to end her shift, Dr. Hayes approached her, placing a gentle hand on her shoulder. "You did good today, Ashley. Really good."

"It's all in a day's work," she replied, though her eyes reflected the deep emotion she felt.

Ashley left the clinic as the sun was setting, the sky now a canvas of deep purples and blues. She walked home, her steps light with the knowledge that the kitten was safe, for now. Her day had been a blend of art and prayer, a testament to her love for animals and the sacred trust they placed in her hands each day. And tomorrow, she would do it all over again, because for Ashley, each day was another opportunity to paint miracles, stroke by tender stroke.

Christian Themes and Values

Stewardship and Care for Creation: Ashley's work reflects the biblical theme of stewardship over God's creatures. Genesis 1:28 grants humanity dominion over animals, which is often interpreted as a call to responsible stewardship and kindness, not exploitation. Ashley's compassionate care for the animals, especially the vulnerable kitten, highlights her embodiment of this principle.

Compassion and Mercy: The compassion Ashley shows for the suffering animal resonates with biblical injunctions to show mercy. Proverbs 12:10 states, "A righteous man cares for the needs of his animal," emphasizing that kindness to animals is a mark of a virtuous character. Ashley's efforts to heal and nurture the kitten illustrate this call to mercy and compassion.

Diligence and Faithfulness in Work: Ashley's dedication to her job and her meticulous attention to the needs of the animals she cares for align with the biblical values of diligence and faithfulness in one's work. Colossians 3:23 advises, "Whatever you do, work at it with all your heart, as working for the Lord, not for human masters," suggesting that all vocations can be acts of worship when performed with dedication and a heart for service.

Hope and Perseverance: The narrative also reflects the themes of hope and perseverance in the face of adversity. Romans 5:3-5 speaks about suffering producing perseverance, character, and hope. Ashley's determination to save the kitten despite the odds, and her joy in each small improvement, mirrors this progression from struggle to hope.

Prayer and Dependence on God: Though not overtly religious, Ashley's actions are described as being guided by a "deep, silent prayer," suggesting her work is also a spiritual practice. This can be linked to the idea that in all actions, one can communicate with and depend on God, akin to 1 Thessalonians 5:17, which simply states, "pray continually."

Creation as a Reflection of the Creator: The care Ashley shows to the animals highlights a broader theme that all of creation is valuable and reflects the Creator's work. Job 12:7-10 suggests that animals have lessons to teach us about God and His creation, reinforcing the idea that by engaging compassionately with animals, humans connect with God's broader purposes for the world.

Ashley's daily work, marked by these acts of small miracles, emphasizes the impact of living one's faith through action, embodying the principles of stewardship, compassion, and diligence. Her story serves as a reminder of the sacredness in the ordinary and the potential to serve divine purposes in everyday roles.

Richard Gordon Zyne

Prayer

Heavenly Father, We lift our hearts to You in gratitude for the gift of creation, the beauty of the earth, and the wonders of nature that surround us. You have entrusted us as stewards of Your creation, and we humbly come before You seeking Your guidance and wisdom in caring for it. Lord, help us to be faithful stewards of the earth, recognizing that all we have is a gift from Your hand. Give us the wisdom to use our resources wisely, to protect the environment, and to preserve the beauty of Your creation for future generations. Give us hearts of compassion for all living creatures and help us to be responsible caretakers of the world You have entrusted to us. Lord may our stewardship of the earth be a reflection of our love for You and our desire to honor Your creation. Guide us in living in harmony with the environment and in caring for Your world with reverence and respect. In Jesus' name, we pray, Amen.

22

Divine Forgiveness

Linda sat across from me, her eyes clouded with regret as she recounted the shadows of her past. "I did a lot of rotten things," she confessed, her words heavy with the weight of years gone by. "Things that made my mother cry, things I can't forget."

Her voice trailed off, lost in the echoes of memories long buried but never truly forgotten. I listened, my presence a silent witness to the pain etched into the lines of her face.

"Have you asked God to forgive you?" I ventured, my words a tentative probe into the depths of her soul.

Linda nodded; her gaze fixed on some distant horizon. "Many times," she murmured, her voice barely a whisper.

I offered her a reassuring smile, a gesture of understanding in the face of her turmoil. "Then that's enough," I said, my tone gentle yet firm. "God's forgiveness is boundless, Linda. Sometimes we just need to forgive ourselves and let go of the past."

There was a moment of quiet reflection between us, the weight of Linda's burdens slowly lifting with each passing second. And as she laid her head back on the pillow, a flicker of hope danced in her eyes—a glimmer of light cutting through the darkness of her regrets. She then turned her head away from me and looked at the wall as if that blank space had more wisdom than the guy with the chaplain badge.

In that moment, I knew that my role as chaplain was not just about unearthing the buried relics of the past, but about guiding souls towards the healing embrace of forgiveness and redemption. It's all in her hands now.

Christian Themes and Values

Repentance and Confession: Linda's admission of her past wrongs and the regret she expresses align with the biblical principle of confession. 1 John 1:9 states, "If we confess our sins, He is faithful and just and will forgive us our sins and purify us from all unrighteousness." Her willingness to acknowledge her sins is the first step toward redemption.

Divine Forgiveness: The chaplain reassures Linda that having asked for God's forgiveness, she should trust in His boundless mercy. This echoes scriptures like Psalm 103:12, which says, "As far as the east is from the west, so far has He removed our transgressions from us." This theme underscores the complete and unconditional forgiveness that God offers, a central tenet of Christian theology.

Self-Forgiveness and Emotional Healing: The conversation hints at the often overlooked aspect of self-forgiveness. While divine forgiveness is assured, many struggle with self-condemnation. The chaplain's encouragement reflects the biblical call for peace and healing within oneself, aligning with Philippians 4:7, "And the peace of God, which transcends all understanding, will guard your hearts and your minds in Christ Jesus."

Role of Spiritual Guidance: The chaplain's role in the story is indicative of the biblical theme of pastoral care and guidance. Galatians 6:2, "Carry each other's burdens, and in this way, you will fulfill the law of Christ," highlights the responsibility of believers to support one another emotionally and spiritually, helping each other towards healing and growth.

New Beginnings and Hope: The flicker of hope in Linda's eyes at the end of their conversation symbolizes the new beginning that comes with forgiveness and the laying down of past burdens. This is reminiscent of 2 Corinthians 5:17, which declares, "Therefore, if anyone is in Christ, the new creation has come: The old has gone, the new is here!" It speaks to the transformational power of faith and forgiveness that allows one to move beyond their past.

Personal Responsibility and Agency in Redemption: Finally, the chaplain's reflection that "It's all in her hands now," underscores the biblical theme of personal responsibility in the process of redemption. While divine help is always available, the individual's choices and actions play a crucial role in their spiritual journey and healing process.

Linda's story illustrates the profound impact of spiritual counsel in helping individuals confront their past, seek forgiveness, and find peace through faith, highlighting the transformative power of grace and redemption offered through the Christian faith.

Prayer

Heavenly Father, We come before You with hearts heavy with the burden of our sins yet filled with hope in Your infinite mercy and grace. You are the God of forgiveness, who offers redemption to all who come to You with contrite hearts. We ask for Your forgiveness for the ways we have fallen short, for the times we have turned away from Your will and followed our own desires. We thank You for Your sacrificial love and the forgiveness You offer to all who come to You. Help us to forgive others as You have forgiven us, releasing the burden of bitterness and resentment from our hearts. Teach us to extend Your grace and mercy to those who have wronged us, just as You have extended it to us. Lord, may Your forgiveness transform us, renewing our hearts and minds, and empowering us to live lives of holiness and righteousness. May we walk in the freedom of Your forgiveness, experiencing the fullness of Your love and grace. In Jesus' name, we pray, Amen.

23

Spiritual Renewal and Hopeful Anticipation

Claudia arrived at hospice like a forgotten seed, scattered and trampled underfoot by the harsh winds of illness and despair. She was angry, bitter—a tiny soul lost in a vast sea of suffering and self-doubt. In her eyes, I saw the remnants of a once vibrant spirit, now eclipsed by the shadows of pain and resentment. Yet, despite her hardened exterior, there lingered a glimmer of hope—a flicker of possibility waiting to be nurtured.

With gentle hands and tender words, I sought to plant Claudia in the fertile soil of compassion and understanding. Not sure if I had a green thumb for this kind of thing, however. I listened as she poured out her grievances, her anger a torrential rain beating against the barren landscape of her parched spirit. "Those damned doctors at Saint So-and-So Hospital. I told them I was through with this dam chemo-crap!"

Together, as was her wish, we explored the realm of the afterlife—a distant horizon shrouded in mystery and uncertainty. It was a journey fraught with doubt and trepidation, tinged with a fragile sense of longing. I told her, honestly, that I really knew nothing about the afterlife. Nobody really does, although she wanted me to find some scripture and some of Jesus's words.

As the days passed, I watched Claudia's spirit begin to unfurl, her roots delving deeper into the rich soil of acceptance and peace. And though our conversations often danced around on the edge of the unknown, I found some hope in the belief that perhaps, in this moment, we were already walking the hallowed grounds of heaven or perhaps the "streets that were paved in gold," as she often joked.

With a final prayer and a gentle touch, I bid Claudia farewell, knowing that her final journey would continue long after she left our hospice care. And as I experienced her passing and watched her depart this life, a seedling no more, I couldn't help but wonder what new blooms awaited her in the gardens of eternity.

Christian Themes and Values

Suffering and Spiritual Growth: Claudia's experience reflects the biblical understanding that suffering can be a catalyst for spiritual growth and deepened faith. Scriptures such as Romans 5:3-5 highlight this process: "Not only so, but we also glory in our sufferings, because we know that suffering produces perseverance; perseverance, character; and character, hope." Claudia's transformation from bitterness to a tentative acceptance echoes this progression from suffering to hope.

Redemption and Renewal: Claudia's metaphorical description as a "forgotten seed" and her eventual growth into acceptance mirrors the biblical theme of redemption and renewal. 2 Corinthians 5:17 says, "Therefore, if anyone is in Christ, the new creation has come: The old has gone, the new is here!" This verse encapsulates the idea of spiritual rebirth through faith, akin to Claudia's gradual reawakening to hope and peace.

The Mystery of the Afterlife: The discussions about the afterlife reflect the biblical theme of heaven as a mysterious but ultimately hopeful place for believers. While the Bible offers images of heaven, such as Revelation 21:21's description of the "street of the city was pure gold, like transparent glass," it also leaves much about the afterlife shrouded in mystery. This theme aligns with the uncertain and exploratory nature of Claudia and the chaplain's conversations.

Compassionate Ministry: The chaplain's role in nurturing Claudia's spirit through listening and providing compassionate care resonates with the biblical call for believers to serve one another in love. Galatians 6:2

instructs, "Carry each other's burdens, and in this way, you will fulfill the law of Christ." The chaplain's gentle and patient ministry to Claudia exemplifies this directive.

Eternal Perspective: The notion that Claudia's journey might continue into the "gardens of eternity" after leaving hospice care is a reflection of the biblical theme of eternal life for those who believe. John 11:25-26, where Jesus says, "I am the resurrection and the life. The one who believes in me will live, even though they die," offers a profound hope that death is not the end but a transition to a new existence in God's presence.

Hope and Assurance in Faith: The underlying current of hope that permeates the chaplain's interactions with Claudia, despite the challenges and the unknowns, aligns with the biblical assurances found throughout Scripture. Psalms 23, for instance, offers comfort in the midst of the darkest valleys, emphasizing that God's presence and guidance are constants that believers can depend on.

Claudia's narrative illustrates how faith, ministered compassionately and understood within the larger context of biblical teachings, can transform suffering into an avenue for spiritual renewal and hopeful anticipation of eternal life.

Prayer

Heavenly Father, We come before You with hearts open to receive Your spiritual renewal and hopeful anticipation. In the midst of life's challenges and uncertainties, we look to You as our source of strength and our beacon of hope. Lord, we thank You for the promise of renewal that You offer us. As we seek Your face, may Your Holy Spirit breathe new life into our souls, refreshing us and revitalizing our faith. Father, we eagerly anticipate the work You are doing in our lives and in the world around us. Give us eyes to see Your hand at work, even in the midst of trials and tribulations. Help us to walk in faith, knowing that You are always with us, guiding us and leading us into Your perfect will.

May Your renewal bring healing to our brokenness, peace to our troubled hearts, and joy to our souls. Fill us with hope that transcends our circumstances and anchors us in Your promises. Lord, as we journey through life, may Your Spirit empower us to live with purpose and passion. May our lives be a reflection of Your goodness and mercy, drawing others into relationship with You. In Jesus' name, we pray, Amen.

24

The Burden of Worldly Cares

Chloe's bedroom was cluttered with the remnants of a life interrupted by illness and uncertainty. Bills lay scattered atop her bedside table, a stark reminder of the mundane tasks that loomed over her like dark clouds on the horizon.

With a weary sigh, she cast her gaze upon the daunting pile, her thin fingers tracing the edges of each envelope. The weight of responsibility pressed heavily upon her, amplified by the knowledge that time was no longer a luxury she could afford. She knew that her son, Greg was not a responsible person when it came to these details, and she felt compelled to complete these tasks before she died.

As she voiced her concerns to me, her words carried the weight of a lifetime's worth of worries. In her eyes, I saw the fear of leaving behind a tangled web of unfinished business, the burden of which threatened to overwhelm her fragile spirit.

Yet within the cloud of chaos, there lingered a glimmer of hope—a flicker of resilience that refused to be extinguished. With each passing moment, Chloe faced her tribulations with a courage born of necessity, determined to navigate the labyrinth of bureaucracy that lay before her.

In moments like these, the role of the chaplain extended beyond the realm of the spiritual, delving into the practicalities of daily life. Collaborating with the social workers, we sought to alleviate Chloe's burden, offering guidance and support as she confronted the challenges that lay ahead.

And though solutions remained elusive, and the road ahead uncertain, we stood by Chloe's side, a beacon of compassion amidst the storm. For in the midst of life's trials and tribulations, it is often the simple acts of kindness and understanding that offer solace to the weary soul.

Christian Themes and Values

The Burden of Worldly Cares: Chloe's experience reflects the biblical understanding of how earthly concerns can weigh heavily on individuals, especially when faced with mortality. This is akin to the parable of the sower in Matthew 13:22, where Jesus describes the seed that falls among thorns as someone who hears the word, but the worries of this life and the deceitfulness of wealth choke the word, making it unfruitful. Chloe's struggle with her responsibilities and the anxiety over her unfinished business echoes this parable, showcasing how worldly cares can overshadow more profound, spiritual needs.

The Role of Community and Support: The involvement of the chaplain and social workers in trying to ease Chloe's burdens mirrors the biblical exhortation to bear one another's burdens (Galatians 6:2). This principle highlights the importance of community and mutual support within the Christian faith. The chaplain's role extends beyond mere spiritual guidance to practical help, embodying the Christian call to love one's neighbor and to act as the hands and feet of Jesus in the world.

Faith Amidst Suffering: Chloe's resilience and the flicker of hope despite her circumstances can be viewed through the lens of biblical teachings on perseverance and faith through suffering. James 1:12 praises those who persevere under trial, promising the crown of life to those who love the Lord. Chloe's determination to handle her affairs responsibly, despite her declining health, reflects this call to steadfastness in faith even in dire situations.

Compassion and Kindness: The narrative also highlights the Christian virtue of compassion, as demonstrated by the chaplain and social workers. Compassion is a significant theme throughout the Gospels, where Jesus often shows compassion to the sick, the poor, and the marginalized. The practical support provided to Chloe exemplifies living out one's faith through actions of kindness and understanding, akin to the Good Samaritan's actions in Luke 10:33-34.

Hope and Redemption: Lastly, the story subtly alludes to the Christian hope in redemption and an eternal perspective. While it is not overtly mentioned, the undercurrent of hope despite uncertainty reflects the Christian belief in a transcendent purpose and assurance beyond earthly life. This aligns with verses like Romans 8:18, where Paul speaks about the sufferings of this present time not comparing to the glory that will be revealed.

In essence, Chloe's story is an illustration of several themes, particularly the intersection of faith with everyday struggles, the communal aspect of Christianity in supporting each other, and the enduring hope found in the midst of suffering.

Prayer

Heavenly Father, We come before You, burdened by cares and weighed down by the demands of life. We confess that at times we allow the worries of this world to consume us. Lord, You have called us to cast all our anxieties upon You because You care for us. You have promised to provide for our needs and to carry our burdens if only we would trust in You. Help us to trust in Your unfailing love and to find rest for our souls in Your presence. Give us the grace to live each day with hearts full of gratitude, minds filled with Your truth, and spirits surrendered to Your will. May Your light shine through us in this world, illuminating the darkness and drawing others to Your love and grace. In Jesus' name, we pray. Amen.

25

Feeling the Weight of the World

Today felt heavier than usual for Rick, a weight pressing down on his shoulders, squeezing the air from his lungs. It wasn't the chaos of the hospice schedule or the incessant demands of patients that left him feeling drained; rather, it was a suffocating sense of emptiness that lingered in the air like a fog.

The day unfolded without incident, devoid of the usual crises and conflicts that often colored Rick's interactions. Even the animals, the dogs and cats Rick often encountered on his rounds to people's homes, with their gentle presence and wagging tails, failed to lift the veil of despondency that hung over him like a shroud.

Perhaps it was the ceaseless drone of bad news, the relentless barrage of negativity that permeated the airwaves and poisoned the atmosphere. Or maybe it was the weight of the world, bearing down upon Rick's weary spirit, leaving him adrift in a sea of uncertainty and doubt.

As he sat in the quiet of his home, the emptiness seemed to stretch on endlessly, a vast expanse of nothingness yawning before him. It was as if God himself had stepped out for a moment, leaving behind only the echo of his absence.

But within the darkness, a flicker of hope remained—a glimmer of light beckoning from the horizon. Perhaps all Rick needed was to shake off the lethargy, to rise from his slumber and embrace the day with renewed vigor.

And so, with a heavy sigh and a determined resolve, Rick rose from his chair and made his way out into the world. For even in the darkest of moments, there is always the promise of a new dawn, a chance to start anew and find hope in the simple act of moving forward.

Christian Themes and Values

Lament and Despondency: The protagonist's feelings of weight, emptiness, and the sense that "God himself had stepped out for a moment," resonate with the Biblical Psalms of lament. These Psalms often express sorrow, loneliness, and a feeling of abandonment by God, yet they also maintain a thread of trust in God's ultimate goodness and deliverance. Psalm 22, for instance, starts with "My God, my God, why have you forsaken me?" yet it concludes on a note of trust and praise to God.

Renewal of Hope and Action: The turn towards action, despite feelings of emptiness and desolation, reflects the biblical theme of hope and renewal found in Lamentations 3:22-23: "The steadfast love of the LORD never ceases; his mercies never come to an end; they are new every morning; great is your faithfulness." The story's ending, where the protagonist decides to embrace the day with renewed vigor despite the darkness, embodies this scripture, emphasizing that each day brings a new opportunity for experiencing God's faithfulness and mercy.

Perseverance Through Trials: The narrative also mirrors the New Testament teachings on perseverance through suffering and trials. Romans 5:3-5 notes that "suffering produces perseverance; perseverance, character; and character, hope. And hope does not put us to shame, because God's love has been poured out into our hearts through the Holy Spirit, who has been given to us." The protagonist's decision to rise and face the world despite feeling the weight of despair aligns with this teaching, illustrating that it is through enduring difficult times that one's character is built, and hope is refined.

Presence of God in Trials: The sensation of God's absence yet the eventual stirring of hope also parallels the theme that God is present even when He feels distant. This concept is explored in many biblical narratives where God may seem absent in times of trial, yet His presence is constant and unyielding, as exemplified in the story of Job or the reassurances given in Hebrews 13:5, "I will never leave you nor forsake you."

This story, in essence, is a modern reflection of ancient biblical truths—lamenting in the midst of struggle, yet choosing to cling to hope and continue forward, trusting in God's new mercies and faithfulness each day.

Prayer

Heavenly Father, We come before You, feeling the weight of the world upon our shoulders. The burdens of injustice, pain, and brokenness surround us, and at times, they overwhelm us. Lord, You are the Rock of our salvation, our refuge in times of trouble. You understand the depths of our hearts and the struggles we face. Grant us Your strength, O Lord, to persevere in the face of adversity. Help us to cling to Your promises, knowing that You are our ever-present help in times of trouble. May Your Spirit within us bring comfort, guidance, and peace as we navigate through the storms of life. Fill us with Your compassion for those who are suffering, Your wisdom to discern Your will, and Your courage to act with love and justice. May we be Your hands and feet in a world that longs for Your healing touch. In Jesus' name, we pray. Amen.

26

Frailty and Suffering

Rachel was a force to be reckoned with a tempest in the midst of her family's calm. Despite her sharp tongue and demanding nature, there was a certain resilience about her, a strength born of a lifetime of facing life's challenges head-on.

Dementia, however, proved to be a foe unlike any other, stripping away the layers of control and leaving Rachel adrift in a sea of confusion. Her once sharp mind now dulled by the fog of forgetfulness, she found herself at the mercy of a condition she could neither understand nor control.

For months, her children bore the brunt of her frustration, their patience tested by her unpredictable behavior and irrational demands. Yet amidst the chaos, there were moments of clarity, fleeting glimpses of the woman Rachel once was—a smile, a kind word, a glimmer of recognition in her eyes.

As her condition worsened, her family made the difficult decision to place her in a nursing home, where she could receive the care and attention she so desperately needed. It was a move fraught with emotion, tinged with guilt and sorrow, but ultimately necessary for Rachel's well-being.

In those final days, as I sat by her bedside, administering communion and offering prayers of comfort, I couldn't help but feel a sense of admiration for Rachel. Despite the ravages of dementia, she remained resilient, her spirit unbroken by the trials she faced.

And when she finally slipped away, leaving behind a legacy of Love and resilience, I couldn't help but feel a sense of gratitude for having known her, if only for a fleeting moment in time.

Christian Themes and Values

Human Frailty and Suffering: Rachel's decline due to dementia underscores the biblical theme of human frailty and the inevitability of suffering in the human condition. Scriptures such as Psalm 103:15-16 remind us, "The life of mortals is like grass, they flourish like a flower of the field; the wind blows over it and it is gone, and its place remembers it no more." This theme emphasizes the transient nature of human strength and the challenges that come with aging and illness.

The Role of Caregivers: Rachel's children, and later the nursing home staff, exemplify the biblical call to care for those who are weak and vulnerable. 1 Timothy 5:8 urges individuals to take care of their relatives, especially those in their own household, asserting that failing to do so denies the faith. The care provided to Rachel, despite its emotional difficulty, aligns with these teachings, highlighting the responsibility to support and nurture the helpless.

Resilience and the Human Spirit: Despite the debilitating effects of her illness, Rachel's resilience reflects the indomitable human spirit, which can be seen as a reflection of the divine image within each person. 2 Corinthians 4:16 echoes this sentiment: "Therefore we do not lose heart. Though outwardly we are wasting away, yet inwardly we are being renewed day by day." Rachel's enduring spirit, even in diminished capacity, speaks to this mysterious renewal.

Community and Communion: The chaplain's presence and the administration of communion in Rachel's final days point to the importance of spiritual sustenance and community support in times of personal crisis. The sacrament of communion is deeply symbolic, representing not only a connection to the divine but also the fellowship of believers, as described in 1 Corinthians 10:17, "Because there is one bread, we who are many are one body, for we all partake of the one bread."

Love and Legacy: The story concludes with a reflection on the legacy of love and resilience that Rachel leaves behind, which resonates with the biblical theme of a good name being better than fine perfume (Ecclesiastes

7:1). Her life's impact, as felt by the chaplain and her family, underscores the lasting influence one's actions and character can have on others, echoing through generations.

Peace and Eternal Rest: Rachel's peaceful passing into what can be seen as eternal rest evokes the Christian hope of life after death, where there is no more suffering, pain, or tears, as promised in Revelation 21:4. This hope provides comfort to those grieving, affirming that death is not the end but a transition to a place free from the struggles of earthly life.

Rachel's story powerfully illustrates how faith, love, and communal support interplay in the human experience of aging, illness, and dying, offering a reflection on the themes of caregiving, dignity, and the enduring human spirit.

Prayer

Heavenly Father, We come before You, acknowledging our need for Your mercy and grace. We confess that in our weakness, we often feel overwhelmed by the challenges and trials of life. Lord, You are our strength in times of weakness, our healer in times of sickness. We lift up to You all who are experiencing physical, emotional, or spiritual suffering, asking for Your healing touch and Your sustaining presence. May our experiences of frailty and suffering draw us closer to You, deepening our dependence on Your grace and our compassion for others. Use our struggles to transform us into vessels of Your love and instruments of Your healing in the world. In Jesus' name, we pray. Amen.

27

Longing for Eternity

In the quiet moments of reflection, Marcie found comfort in the stories of her elderly patients, their words a testament to lives well lived and battles bravely fought. Their smiles, weathered by time and etched with the lines of experience, spoke volumes of the joys and sorrows they had known.

Barbara, one of her most spirited patients, often shared tales of her adventures with her late husband, Harold. "You should've seen him, Marcie," she would say with a twinkle in her eye. "He was a real charmer, swept me off my feet the moment we met."

As Barbara reminisced about decades spent in the embrace of loved ones, Marcie was reminded of the fleeting nature of existence, the preciousness of each passing moment. Yet beneath her tales of love and laughter, she sensed a deeper truth, a longing for something beyond the confines of mortal existence.

"It's not just about the memories," Barbara confessed one day, her voice soft with emotion. "It's about what comes next. I like to think Harold's waiting for me on the other side, but sometimes... sometimes I wonder."

Marcie nodded understandingly, knowing that beneath the surface of Barbara's cheerful demeanor lay a wellspring of emotions—a tangle of hopes and fears, desires and regrets.

"Do you truly long for the embrace of heaven, Barbara?" Marcie asked gently one afternoon as they sat together in the hospice day room.

Barbara sighed, her gaze drifting to the horizon. "I do, Marcie. But sometimes, the unknown can be scary, you know? It's hard to let go of what you've known all your life."

Marcie nodded again, offering her a reassuring smile. "It's okay to feel that way. Just know that whatever lies ahead, you won't be alone."

As a chaplain, Marcie understood that her role was not to unravel the mysteries of the human heart or dispel the shadows of doubt. It was to bear witness to their truth, to offer solace in the face of uncertainty, and to remind them that they were already whole, already complete.

"In the end," Marcie said, placing a comforting hand on Barbara's shoulder, "it's not my words that bring healing, but the quiet assurance that you are loved beyond measure. And in that simple truth, there lies the greatest comfort of all."

Barbara smiled through her tears, grateful for Marcie's presence and the reassurance she brought. In that moment, the weight on Marcie's shoulders lifted, replaced by a sense of peace that transcended words.

Christian Themes and Values

Transience of Life and Mortality: The reflections on the fleeting nature of existence draw directly from Biblical wisdom, particularly from books like Ecclesiastes, which speaks to the brevity and vanity of life (Ecclesiastes 1:2, "Vanity of vanities, says the Preacher, vanity of vanities! All is vanity."). The elderly patients' reminiscences and the chaplain's observations underscore the biblical understanding that life is temporary and should be cherished.

Longing for Eternity: The patients' mixed feelings of readiness for the next chapter and their underlying uncertainty echo the Biblical theme of eternity placed in the hearts of humans (Ecclesiastes 3:11, "He has made everything beautiful in its time. Also, he has put eternity into man's heart, yet so that he cannot find out what God has done from the beginning to the end."). This desire for something beyond mortal existence reflects a deep-seated biblical belief in an afterlife—a hope for heaven and a continued existence beyond physical death.

Presence of God and Comfort: The chaplain's role in providing solace and assurance to the patients aligns with the Biblical promise of God's presence and comfort in times of need. Psalms 23 is particularly, emphasizing God as a shepherd who comforts and guides through the valley of the shadow of death. The chaplain's ministry reflects this divine comfort, offering a presence that reassures the patients they are not alone.

Faith Amidst Uncertainty: The subtle doubts and fears that linger among the patients speak to the Biblical theme of faith amidst uncertainty. The Bible frequently addresses the fears and doubts of believers, offering reassurances of God's plan and presence (John 14:1, "Let not your hearts be troubled. Believe in God; believe also in me."). The chaplain's acknowledgment of these doubts and his role in reinforcing faith and comfort reflects this Biblical narrative.

Love and Community: The reassurance that patients are loved beyond measure taps into the Biblical commandment to love one another as a reflection of divine love (John 13:34-35, "A new commandment I give to you, that you love one another: just as I have loved you, you also are to love one another. By this all people will know that you are my disciples, if you have love for one another."). The chaplain's empathetic listening and comforting presence embody this commandment, providing a tangible sense of community and belonging.

Wholeness and Completeness in God: Finally, the chaplain's message that the patients are "already whole, already complete" aligns with the Biblical view that in God, believers find wholeness (Colossians 2:10, "and you have been filled in him, who is the head of all rule and authority"). This speaks to the spiritual fulfillment and completeness that faith provides, reassuring the elderly that in their faith, they find their completion.

These themes combine to provide a rich tapestry of Biblical reflection, offering deep comfort and profound insights into the spiritual dimensions of aging, mortality, and the enduring human quest for meaning and reassurance in the face of life's final chapter.

Richard Gordon Zyne

Prayer

Heavenly Father, We feel a longing for eternity, a yearning for something more than what this world can offer. We come before You, acknowledging that our hearts are restless until they find rest in You. Lord, You have placed eternity in our hearts, and we long to be united with You in perfect communion forever. We thank You for the hope of eternal life that You have given us through Jesus Christ. Help us to fix our eyes on the eternal truths of Your kingdom, rather than on the fleeting pleasures of this world. Holy Spirit, guide us as we navigate the challenges of this world, keeping our hearts steadfast in faith and our minds focused on the realities of Your kingdom, both now and forever more. In Jesus' name, we pray. Amen.

28

A Question of Faith

Martin's question hung in the air like a weight, heavy with expectation and curiosity. He was not one for simple answers, not when it came to matters of faith and belief. His academic Ph.D. mind, sharp as the edge of a blade, sought depth and nuance in every conversation, every exchange.

As a chaplain, I had grown accustomed to fielding such inquiries, offering reassurance and comfort in the face of uncertainty. But Martin was different, his intellect a force to be reckoned with, his thirst for understanding unquenchable.

"Do you believe in God?" he asked, his gaze piercing, his tone expectant.

I paused, considering my response carefully. The easy answer, the one I had given countless times before, hovered on the tip of my tongue. But Martin deserved more than platitudes and clichés. He deserved honesty, even if it meant delving into the depths of my own beliefs.

"No, Martin," I replied, my voice steady. "I don't believe in God."

His eyebrows arched in surprise, but he remained silent, waiting for me to continue.

"Believing in God is just a 'head thing'," I explained, my words measured. "You can believe in a lot of things because they exist in space and time. But God... God is beyond space and time. God is transcendent. Over the edge. The epitome of Holy."

I saw an understanding dawn in Martin's eyes, a flicker of recognition that mirrored my own. He knew, as I did, that faith was not bound by the constraints of logic or reason. It was a relationship, intimate and personal, a dialogue, forged in the crucible of experience.

"I have a relationship with God," I confessed, my voice softening. "A relationship that is personal because God comes to me through a person. You know, Jesus."

Martin nodded, a small smile playing at the corners of his lips. He had found what he was searching for, not in my words, but in the shared understanding that transcended language and belief.

And as we sat in silence, the weight of our conversation hanging between us, I knew that Martin had found peace in the simplicity of our exchange. For in the end, faith was not about answers, but about the journey towards Love and understanding.

Christian Themes and Values

The Nature of God: The chaplain's distinction between "believing in God" as a mere intellectual exercise and having a "relationship with God" touches on biblical descriptions of God's nature. Throughout the Bible, God is depicted not only as transcendent, beyond space and time (Isaiah 57:15), but also immanent and personally involved with His creation (Psalm 139:1-18). The chaplain's explanation echoes the biblical paradox of God's transcendence and immanence.

Faith as Relationship: The assertion that "faith is not bound by the constraints of logic or reason" aligns with biblical themes where faith is portrayed as a deep, personal relationship with God, particularly through Jesus Christ. In John 15:15, Jesus speaks about this relationship, saying, "No longer do I call you servants...but I have called you friends." This highlights the personal nature of faith as a relationship rather than merely an acknowledgement of God's existence.

Jesus as the Mediator: The chaplain mentions that God "comes to me through a person. You know, Jesus." This is a direct reference to the biblical theme of Jesus as the mediator between God and humanity (1 Timothy 2:5). The incarnation, life, death, and resurrection of Jesus are central to Christian theology and are the means through which believers can have a personal relationship with God.

Faith Beyond Understanding: The dialogue reflects the biblical notion that faith often transcends human understanding. As expressed in Hebrews 11:1, "Now faith is the assurance of things hoped for, the conviction of things not seen." The chaplain's discussion with Martin suggests that true faith involves trust and confidence that go beyond simple empirical evidence or intellectual assent.

Role of the Clergy: The chaplain's role in the story resonates with the biblical theme of spiritual guidance provided by religious leaders. In the Bible, figures such as Paul serve as guides, teachers, and comforters to those exploring their faith (1 Corinthians 11:1). The chaplain's thoughtful and respectful engagement with Martin's deep questions underscores the pastoral role of helping individuals navigate their spiritual journeys.

Shared Understanding and Community: Finally, the story closes on a note of mutual understanding and the formation of a community, however temporary, based on shared spiritual exploration. This reflects the biblical ideal of fellowship among believers, where faith is often strengthened and expressed within community settings (Acts 2:42-47).

These themes collectively depict a rich, biblically infused dialogue that emphasizes the complexity and depth of faith, the nature of God as both beyond and intimately involved with the world, and the personal journey towards understanding and embracing this dynamic.

Prayer

Heavenly Father, In times of doubt and uncertainty, we come before You with questions that weigh heavy on our hearts. We confess that there are moments when our faith wavers, when we struggle to understand Your ways and Your purposes. Lord, You are the God of all wisdom and knowledge, and You invite us to bring our questions to You. Help us to trust that You are not intimidated by our doubts but rather, You embrace us with Your love and understanding. Grant us the courage to seek answers, knowing that You are the source of all truth. Strengthen our faith, O Lord, and deepen our trust in Your goodness, even when we cannot see the full picture. Holy Spirit, guide us into all truth, illuminating Your Word and speaking to our hearts in times of uncertainty. Help us to discern Your voice amidst the noise of this world and to walk in the light of Your truth. Help us to surrender our questions into Your hands and to trust that You are working all things together for our good. In Jesus' name, we pray. Amen.

29

Grace in Weakness

Annie, a frail figure weathered by time, found grace and fulfillment in the simple refrain of faith. Her hands, gnarled with age, reached out eagerly, grasping for reassurance in a world that had grown increasingly unfamiliar. Senile degeneration of the brain had stolen much from her—her independence, her autonomy—but it could not diminish the fervent belief that burned bright within her heart.

As her hospice chaplain, Melanie often found herself drawn to Annie's room, where her presence seemed to radiate a sense of peace despite her struggles. She watched as she grappled with the trappings of modernity, her once nimble fingers now clumsy and uncoordinated. The remote control slipped from her grasp, its buttons a mystery she could no longer decipher. And yet, amidst the chaos of her failing mind, one truth remained steadfast: "Jesus Loves me, Jesus Loves me, Jesus Loves me."

"It's a beautiful song, Annie," Melanie said, offering her a gentle smile as she entered her room. "Would you like me to sing it with you?"

Annie's eyes lit up, a spark of recognition shining through the fog of confusion. "Oh, yes, please," she replied, her voice filled with childlike eagerness.

So, Melanie sat with Annie, their voices joining in harmony as they sang the familiar hymn together. In those moments, the barriers of age and infirmity seemed to fade away, leaving only the pure essence of faith and love.

"It's amazing how music can bring us comfort, isn't it?" Melanie said, as they finished the song. "Even when everything else feels uncertain, we can always find solace in the timeless truths of our faith."

Annie nodded, a contented smile gracing her lips. "That's right, dear. Jesus is always with us, no matter what."

For Annie, the best medicine was not found in pills or treatments, but in the simple act of being heard. And as she spoke, her words infused with the warmth of her faith, Melanie knew that she was witnessing something sacred—a testament to the enduring power of the human spirit, even in the face of adversity.

As Melanie left Annie's room that day, she carried with her a renewed sense of purpose, inspired by her unwavering faith and resilience. In her presence, she found a reminder of the importance of compassion and connection in her role as a chaplain, and she vowed to continue being a source of comfort and support for all those under his care.

Christian Themes and Values

Enduring Faith: Annie's unshakeable affirmation, "Jesus Loves me," despite her senility and physical frailty, highlights the biblical theme of enduring faith. This is reminiscent of Paul's declaration in 2 Corinthians 4:16, where despite outward decay, the inner self is renewed day by day. Annie's faith remains strong and is a source of comfort and assurance, mirroring the biblical promise that God's love is constant and unwavering.

Grace in Weakness: The biblical principle that God's grace is made perfect in weakness (2 Corinthians 12:9) is vividly illustrated in Annie's life. Although dementia has stripped away many of her cognitive abilities and physical independence, her spiritual vitality and connection to her faith remain intact and powerful. This suggests that spiritual strength can transcend physical and mental limitations.

Simplicity of Faith: The simplicity of Annie's faith, encapsulated in the repeated phrase "Jesus loves me," echoes Jesus' teachings on childlike faith in the Gospels (Matthew 18:3-4). Jesus emphasizes the value of receiving the kingdom of God like a child. Annie's straightforward and profound belief exemplifies how faith does not necessarily require complexity but can be deeply rooted in simple, heartfelt truths.

The Power of Presence: Melanie's role in sitting with Annie and listening to her stories reflects the biblical theme of 'bearing one another's burdens' (Galatians 6:2). The act of listening and being present with someone in their suffering is a powerful testament to the Christian call to love and support each other, showing that compassion and companionship can have healing effects.

Joy and Hope in Suffering: Despite her conditions, Annie's exuberant voice and the joy she expresses about her family indicate that her spiritual life provides her with a sense of joy and hope that transcends her physical suffering. This aligns with the biblical perspective found in Romans 5:3-5, which speaks of rejoicing in our sufferings because suffering produces perseverance, character, and hope.

Sacredness of Human Spirit: Annie's story is a testament to the sacredness of the human spirit, as mentioned in 1 Corinthians 6:19-20, which speaks of the body as a temple of the Holy Spirit. Even as her body declines, the spirit within her is portrayed as alive and vibrant, suggesting the divine image within her remains untarnished.

Annie's narrative illustrates how faith can serve as a sustaining force through the trials of life, providing not only comfort and reassurance but also a profound sense of joy and purpose, regardless of external circumstances. This story serves as a reminder of the profound impact of spiritual resilience and the enduring nature of divine love.

Prayer

Heavenly Father, In our moments of weakness, we come before You, recognizing our need for Your grace and strength. We confess that we often feel inadequate and overwhelmed by the challenges of life. Lord, Your Word tells us that Your grace is sufficient for us, that Your power is made perfect in our weakness. Help us to embrace this truth and to find comfort in knowing that Your strength is made perfect in our weakness. Grant us the humility to acknowledge our limitations and the wisdom to rely on Your grace to sustain us. May Your grace be our constant companion, lifting us up when we stumble and carrying us through the trials we face. Lord Jesus, You know what it means to endure weakness and suffering. You willingly took on human form, experiencing our frailty and pain. Help us to follow Your example, trusting in Your strength to carry us through every trial. May we boast in our weaknesses, knowing that Your grace is sufficient to see us through. May Your grace transform our weaknesses into opportunities for Your glory to be revealed. In Jesus' name, we pray. Amen.

30

Loss and Transformation

Liam sat alone at the bar, the dim light casting long shadows across the room. The glasses clinked softly in the background, a soothing, almost hypnotic sound against the low murmur of scattered conversations. The bartender, a middle-aged man with a quiet demeanor, wiped down the counter with a practiced hand, casting occasional, sympathetic glances towards Liam.

It had been a long day—a long month, actually. The firm had let him go that morning, not with a bang but a whisper, a brief meeting in a room that felt too cold, too sterile. "Restructuring," they had called it, but Liam knew the truth. His last project had failed, spectacularly, publicly. And though no one said it directly, he felt the weight of blame resting solely on his shoulders.

Now, with a tumbler of whiskey in hand, Liam wrestled with the sting of disgrace. It was more than losing a job; it was as if he had lost a part of himself, a part entwined with his career, his identity. Around him, life continued unabated, as indifferent to his suffering as it was to his successes.

A couple at the end of the bar laughed over some shared joke, their happiness a stark contrast to his inner turmoil. He sipped his drink, the whiskey sharp and burning, much like the thoughts racing through his mind.

"Rough day?" the bartender finally asked, breaking the long silence.

Liam nodded, setting his glass down a little too hard. "Feels like I've lost everything," he admitted, not looking up.

"You haven't lost everything," the bartender said softly, almost too soft for Liam to catch. "Just feels that way now."

Liam considered the words, a small part of him wanting to dismiss them as platitudes, yet another part, perhaps the part still fighting, recognized the truth in them. Acceptance seemed a distant, almost foreign concept, but as the night grew longer, the seed of it began to take root.

He thought about his old man, how he'd handled his own setbacks with a kind of stoic acceptance that Liam had always admired yet never fully understood. There was dignity in it, a quiet strength that didn't rail against the inevitable ebbs of life but instead, embraced them.

"Maybe it's time for something new," Liam finally said, more to himself than to the bartender. "Maybe it's time to accept that this isn't the end but a chance to start again."

The bartender smiled, refilling his glass. "That's the spirit," he said. "Every end is just a new beginning, if you're brave enough to see it."

Liam lifted the glass, the whiskey glowing amber in the low light. The room was still dim, the shadows still long, and the future uncertain. But as he took a drink, the warmth of the alcohol seemed to spread further than before, fueling a newfound resolve.

Tomorrow, he would begin again. Not because he was unscarred, but because he had accepted the scars as part of his story—a story that was far from over. And with this acceptance, the disgrace felt a little less sharp, a little more like a steppingstone than a stumbling block.

Christian Themes and Values

Liam's story at the bar, dealing with job loss and personal crisis, taps into several biblical themes, particularly those revolving around loss, redemption, and personal transformation.

Trials and Suffering: Liam's experience of losing his job and the subsequent feelings of disgrace mirror the biblical notion that life involves trials and suffering. This theme is prominent in books like Job, where the titular character faces immense loss and hardship, testing his faith and integrity. Liam's internal struggle and his processing of the failure reflect the existential challenges that many biblical characters face, prompting a deep personal examination and spiritual resilience.

Restoration and Redemption: As the bartender suggests that not everything is lost, he hints at the biblical promise of restoration and redemption. Scriptures such as Joel 2:25 ("I will restore to you the years that the swarming locust has eaten...") offer hope that what has been lost can be restored. This notion that Liam has not lost everything and that there is potential for a new beginning echoes the redemptive narratives found throughout the Bible.

Resilience and Hope: The conversation with the bartender and Liam's reflection on his father's stoic acceptance tie into the biblical themes of resilience and hope amidst adversity. Paul's letters in the New Testament, especially passages like Romans 5:3-5 ("...we also glory in our sufferings, because we know that suffering produces perseverance; perseverance, character; and character, hope."), highlight how trials can develop perseverance and character, leading to a hope that does not disappoint.

New Beginnings: Liam's decision to see his job loss not as an end but as an opportunity for a new beginning resonates with the biblical theme of rebirth and new life. Verses like 2 Corinthians 5:17 ("Therefore, if anyone is in Christ, the new creation has come: The old has gone, the new is here!") reflect this theme of transformation and newness, suggesting that with faith, new beginnings are always possible.

Acceptance and Moving Forward: Liam's gradual movement toward accepting his situation and considering it as a steppingstone rather than a stumbling block aligns with biblical teachings on acceptance and the pursuit of wisdom through trials. The Book of James talks about letting perseverance finish its work so that one may be mature and complete, lacking nothing (James 1:4).

The Power of Community and Counsel: The bartender's role as a listener and adviser highlights the importance of community and wise counsel found in Proverbs (Proverbs 12:15: "The way of fools seems right to them, but the wise listen to advice."). His gentle guidance helps Liam to frame his experience in a new light, showcasing the value of supportive relationships in overcoming personal crises.

Liam's story, woven with themes of despair, recovery, and hope, illustrates a journey of personal and possibly spiritual awakening, reflecting the depth and complexity of the human experience as echoed in the biblical narrative.

Prayer

Heavenly Father, In the midst of loss and change, we turn to You, our Rock and Redeemer. We bring before You the pain of our losses, the grief that weighs heavy on our hearts, and the uncertainty of transformation. Lord, You are the God who brings beauty from ashes, who turns mourning into dancing. We trust in Your promise that You are always at work, even in the midst of our losses, bringing about transformation and renewal. Help us to surrender our pain and our sorrow into Your loving hands, knowing that You are close to the brokenhearted and that You understand our every tear. Comfort us with Your presence and grant us the strength to journey through this season of loss with faith and hope. Breathe new life into our weary souls and guide us through the process of transformation. Help us to trust in Your power to bring about healing, restoration, and new beginnings. In Jesus' name, we pray. Amen.

31

Comforting Visions

Laura, a young woman with a mystical aura about her, found comfort and meaning in the ethereal whispers that danced at the edges of her consciousness. Illness had woven its tendrils around her, but within the confines of her frail body, she encountered a world that transcended the bounds of the material realm.

"I saw Uncle Ted," she would say, her voice soft and distant, as if recalling a distant dream. "He looked tired, walking the path to the workshop where he used to work alongside my dad."

Her words carried the weight of truth, her visions a testament to the unseen forces that guided her path. To some, her tales may have seemed fanciful, the ramblings of a mind touched by mental illness. But to Laura, they were tangible reminders of the spiritual realm that enveloped her.

Guardian angels, nameless and faceless, flitted through her thoughts like fleeting shadows, their presence a comforting embrace in the darkness of her illness. "Angels have been around forever," she would say, her words infused with a quiet reverence, drawing upon scripture to lend weight to her experiences and beliefs.

For most, the notion of angels and visitations from the deceased remained a distant fantasy, relegated to the realm of myth and legend. But for Laura, they were companions on her journey, guiding her through the labyrinth of joy and pain, offering glimpses of the heavenly realm that awaited her.

In my own encounters with the Divine Presence, I had felt the gentle touch of angelic guidance, a whisper in the depths of my soul. And so, I understood the significance of Laura's experiences, how they served as beacons of light in the darkness, illuminating the path towards meaning and purpose in her hospice journey.

In the end, it mattered not whether others believed in her visions. What mattered was the comfort they brought to Laura, the comfort they offered in the face of uncertainty. In the depths of her illness, angels were not just figments of imagination—they were guardians of her soul, guiding her towards a realm where pain and suffering held no sway.

Christian Themes and Values

Laura's story, rich with spiritual encounters and celestial guidance, highlights several prominent biblical themes. These include the reality of the spiritual realm, the presence and role of angels, the comfort found in spiritual experiences, and the transformative power of faith in the face of suffering.

The Reality of the Spiritual Realm: Laura's visions of her deceased Uncle Ted and her encounters with guardian angels speak to the biblical theme of a reality beyond the physical, a spiritual realm where deceased loved ones and celestial beings reside. The Bible contains numerous references to the spiritual realm as a true and active dimension of existence (Ephesians 6:12, "For our struggle is not against flesh and blood, but against the rulers, against the authorities, against the powers of this dark world and against the spiritual forces of evil in the heavenly realms.")

Angelic Presence and Intervention: The Bible depicts angels as messengers and protectors sent by God to guide and assist humans (Psalm 91:11-12, "For he will command his angels concerning you to guard you in all your ways; they will lift you up in their hands, so that you will not strike your foot against a stone."). Laura's experiences with guardian angels echo this biblical assurance of angelic guidance and protection, providing her with comfort and reassurance during her illness.

Visions as a Source of Comfort: Laura's visions and spiritual experiences bring her comfort and peace, aligning with biblical narratives where visions serve as divine communications that provide guidance, reassurance, and prophecy (Acts 2:17, "In the last days, God says, I will pour out my Spirit on all people. Your sons and daughters will prophesy, your young men will see visions, your old men will dream dreams."). These experiences help Laura cope with her illness, offering her glimpses of a heavenly realm and affirming her faith.

Endurance Through Faith: Laura's unwavering belief in the spiritual significance of her experiences, despite others' skepticism, illustrates the biblical theme of enduring faith. This theme is akin to the perseverance of biblical figures like Job, who remained faithful amidst profound suffering and loss (James 5:11, "As you know, we count as blessed those who have persevered. You have heard of Job's perseverance and have seen what the Lord finally brought about. The Lord is full of compassion and mercy.").

Heavenly Hope: Laura's anticipation of a heavenly realm where pain and suffering are absent reflects the biblical promise of heaven as a place of eternal peace and joy, free from earthly troubles (Revelation 21:4, "He will wipe every tear from their eyes. There will be no more death or mourning or crying or pain, for the old order of things has passed away."). Her spiritual journey and the comfort she derives from her angelic encounters point toward this hope, providing her with strength and peace as she navigates her final days.

These themes collectively highlight the profound impact of spiritual beliefs on individuals facing significant trials, providing them with strength, comfort, and a hopeful perspective on the challenges they encounter. Laura's story is an illustration of how deeply held faith can transform the experience of suffering, offering solace and a sense of divine presence even in the darkest moments.

Prayer

Heavenly Father, In times of darkness and despair, we seek Your comforting presence. We come before You with open hearts, longing for the light of Your love to shine upon us and bring us peace. Lord, You are the source of all comfort, the one who wipes away every tear and brings hope to the weary soul. We thank You for the comforting visions You give us in times of trouble, the glimpses of Your glory that remind us of Your eternal presence. Lord Jesus, You are the light of the world, the beacon of hope that guides us through the darkest of nights. May Your presence be a comforting vision to us, illuminating the path ahead and filling our hearts with peace. In times of trouble, may we find solace in Your comforting embrace, knowing that You are with us always, even to the end of the age. May Your love be our guiding light, leading us through every trial and into the joy of Your eternal kingdom. In Jesus' name, we pray. Amen.

32

Humility and Learning

Life after death, a topic shrouded in mystery and steeped in centuries of human contemplation. It's not a conversation one brings up lightly, especially in the somber rooms of hospice. But when Elaine broached the subject with Rick, a bereavement coordinator, her eyes aglow with curiosity, he found himself drawn into the depths of her inquiry.

"Have you ever read the Tibetan Book of the Dead?" she asked, her voice a whisper in the stillness of the room.

Rick shook his head. "I haven't delved deeply into its teachings, though I've heard whispers of its significance in the realm of spirituality and death."

Elaine nodded, her gaze fixed on a point somewhere beyond the walls of her hospice room, lost in contemplation.

As Rick began to research, he found himself overwhelmed by the wealth of spiritual concepts and content surrounding the dying process. It was a labyrinth of beliefs and rituals, each offering a unique perspective on the journey from this world to the next.

In his grief counseling sessions, Rick encountered a young woman who had found solace in the words of the Tibetan Book of the Dead, actually called the *Bardo Thodol*, reading passages aloud to her mother as she made her final journey. She spoke of the process with reverence, finding comfort in the ancient wisdom contained within its pages.

Yet, for Rick, the book remained a distant enigma, too confounding and disturbing to fully grasp. He pushed it aside, clinging to the familiarity of his own theological framework.

But as he reflected on Elaine's question, Rick realized the importance of acknowledging the unknown, of stepping outside of his comfort zone to embrace the deep spirituality found in other cultures and religions. There was wisdom to be gleaned from those who walked the threshold between life and death, a wisdom that transcended the boundaries of his own understanding.

"I still have much to learn," Rick mused to himself, "especially from those who are facing their final moments with courage and grace."

And so, he resolved to approach the subject with humility, to open himself to the teachings of the Tibetan Book of the Dead and other spiritual traditions, knowing that in doing so, he might find a deeper understanding of the mysteries that lay beyond the veil of death.

Christian Themes and Values

The story, although initially rooted in the exploration of the Tibetan Book of the Dead, touches on several Biblical themes related to life after death, the acceptance of diverse spiritual understandings, and the eternal quest for knowledge about the hereafter. These themes resonate with broader Christian theological concepts and offer a bridge between different faith perspectives:

Life After Death: The core of the narrative revolves around the contemplation of life after death, a fundamental concern in many religions including Christianity. The Bible speaks extensively about the afterlife, offering visions of heaven, hell, and the promise of eternal life through belief in Jesus Christ (John 3:16, Revelation 21:4). While the Tibetan Book of the Dead offers a different cultural and religious perspective, the shared focus on what happens after we die underscores a universal human question addressed by many theological traditions.

Exploration of Diverse Spiritual Beliefs: The chaplain's openness to exploring the Tibetan Book of the Dead despite its divergence from his own Christian beliefs reflects the Biblical theme of wisdom through understanding. Proverbs 4:6-7 emphasizes seeking wisdom and understanding: "Do not forsake wisdom, and she will protect you; love her, and she will watch over you. The beginning of wisdom is this: Get wisdom. Though it cost all you have, get understanding." This theme highlights the value of exploring and respecting diverse spiritual insights as a way to enrich one's own understanding of profound life questions.

Humility and Learning: The chaplain's acknowledgment of his limited understanding and his resolution to approach the subject with humility align with the Biblical principle of humility before God and others. James 4:6 tells us, "God opposes the proud but shows favor to the humble." This attitude fosters a greater openness to learning and spiritual growth, which is essential in the theological exploration of complex subjects such as death and the afterlife.

Comfort in Mourning: The daughter finding solace in reading passages from the Tibetan Book of the Dead to her dying mother mirrors the Biblical use of scripture to provide comfort in times of mourning. 2 Corinthians 1:3-4 discusses God as the "Father of compassion and the God of all comfort, who comforts us in all our troubles." This reflects the universal search for comfort in words and rituals during the most challenging times.

The Mystery of Death: Finally, the story taps into the Biblical theme of the mystery surrounding death and the afterlife. 1 Corinthians 13:12 mentions, "Now we see but a poor reflection as in a mirror; then we shall see face to face. Now I know in part; then I shall know fully, even as I am fully known." This verse encapsulates the idea that full understanding of life beyond death remains beyond human grasp and is known fully only in the divine presence.

These Biblical themes are woven through a narrative that, while centered on non-Christian texts, reflects a deep and respectful engagement with the universal questions of mortality, the afterlife, and the spiritual journey that transcends cultural and religious boundaries.

Prayer

Heavenly Father, In humility, we come before You, acknowledging that You alone are the source of all wisdom and knowledge. We recognize our need for Your guidance and understanding as we seek to learn and grow in faith. Lord, You have called us to be lifelong learners, to continually seek Your truth and to grow in wisdom and understanding. Help us to approach Your Word with humility, knowing that Your ways are higher than our ways and Your thoughts higher than our thoughts. Grant us teachable hearts, O Lord, that we may receive Your word with gladness and apply it to our lives. Help us to be open to correction and instruction, knowing that it is through humility that we gain wisdom. May our pursuit of knowledge be rooted in love, seeking to grow not for our own glory, but for the glory of Your name. May our learning lead us closer to You and deepen our relationship with You. In Jesus' name, we pray. Amen.

33

Faith and Doubt

Tonya lay on the sterile hospital bed, her frail frame barely stirring under the weight of her words. The soft hum of medical equipment filled the room, a constant reminder of the battles fought within its confines.

"Chemo is hell," she whispered, her voice barely more than a breath. "Damn hell."

I sat beside her, my gaze fixed on her face, searching for the shadows of pain that danced in the depths of her eyes.

"I can't take it anymore," she continued, her voice strained with exhaustion. "That's why I decided to stop and go into hospice."

I nodded, understanding the weight of her decision, the gravity of surrendering to the inevitable. But it was her next words that caught me off guard, pulling me into the labyrinth of her thoughts.

"Why do we assume that the heaven we have after death is better than the heaven we have when we are alive?" she asked, her words hanging heavy in the air. "Or the hell in the afterlife is worse than the hell of cancer?"

Her questions lingered in the silence, daring me to confront the uncertainties that lurked in the shadows of existence. I searched for answers in the depths of my own convictions but found only the echoes of her words reverberating within me.

"I don't have any pat answers to your questions," I finally admitted, my voice soft against the backdrop of the hospital's sterile walls. "But I'm more interested in knowing what you think, or better yet how you feel."

Tonya's gaze met mine, her eyes reflecting the flicker of uncertainty that danced within her soul. And in that moment, I realized that perhaps the truest answers lie not in the realm of certainty, but in the depths of our shared humanity, in the rawness of our emotions, and in the courage to confront the unknown with open hearts and unyielding grace.

Christian Themes and Values

Tonya's reflection on her suffering and existential questions about heaven, hell, and the nature of life and death introduces several profound Biblical themes.

Suffering and Endurance: Tonya's struggle with cancer and her description of chemotherapy as "hell" resonates with the Biblical understanding of suffering. Scriptures often discuss suffering not just as a consequence of sin but as a part of the human experience that can lead to spiritual growth and character development. Paul's words in Romans 5:3-5 come to mind: "...we also glory in our sufferings, because we know that suffering produces perseverance; perseverance, character; and character, hope."

Heaven and Hell: Tonya's contemplation of heaven and hell before and after death touches on the themes of eternal life and eternal separation from God. Her query about the nature of heavenly peace versus earthly suffering reflects the descriptions found in Revelation 21:4, where God will wipe away every tear, and there will be no more death, mourning, crying, or pain. Her question challenges the conventional perceptions of heaven and hell, encouraging a deeper theological exploration of what these terms mean in both the physical and metaphysical contexts.

The Value of Life: Tonya's decision to enter hospice and cease aggressive treatment for her cancer brings up the Biblical theme of the sanctity and brevity of life as described in James 4:14 ("What is your life? You are a mist that appears for a little while and then vanishes."). It poses deep questions about the quality of life versus the quantity of life, a topic deeply rooted in Biblical discussions about the meaning and purpose of human existence.

Faith and Doubt: Tonya's existential questions reflect the Biblical theme of wrestling with faith and doubt—a struggle epitomized by figures like Job and Thomas. This wrestling leads not necessarily to answers but to a deeper faith and trust in God's sovereignty, as seen in Job's life (Job 42:1-6) and Thomas' encounter with the risen Christ (John 20:24-29).

Compassion and Presence: The narrator's role as a listener and supporter for Tonya highlights the Christian duty of compassion and bearing one another's burdens (Galatians 6:2). The narrator's admission of not having "pat answers" but rather focusing on empathetic presence aligns with Jesus' model of ministry, which often emphasized being with people in their suffering rather than offering quick solutions.

Eternal Perspective: Finally, Tonya's reflections stir a consideration of the eternal perspective that Christianity offers. It challenges both the believer and skeptic to think beyond the immediate pain to the promises of Christianity about eternal life, inviting a reflection on how earthly experiences of pain and joy relate to eternal realities.

These themes underscore a narrative deep with theological inquiry and human emotion, illustrating how existential questions about suffering, life's meaning, and the afterlife continue to resonate deeply, pushing individuals to explore their faith and beliefs more profoundly.

Prayer

Heavenly Father, In moments of doubt and uncertainty, we turn to You, the author and perfecter of our faith. We bring before You our questions, our fears, and our struggles, knowing that You understand the depths of our hearts. Grant us the courage to confront our doubts, to wrestle with them honestly, and to seek Your truth with open hearts and minds. Strengthen our faith, O Lord, and deepen our trust in Your promises, even in the face of uncertainty. May our faith be strengthened through the testing of doubt, emerging refined like gold purified in the fire. May we cling to Your promises with unwavering trust, knowing that You are faithful and that You will never leave us nor forsake us. In Jesus' name, we pray. Amen.

34

Wrestling with Faith

Cole slouched in his chair, the dim hospital room casting shadows across his weathered face. Malcolm, the chaplain, sat beside him, listening to the weight of Cole's words.

"You know, Chaplain," Cole began, his voice heavy with the burden of his confession, "I know I'll be with God in heaven, but I feel like such a failure. Like I've wasted so much time in my life on things that don't matter, on stuff that hurt people."

Malcolm nodded, understanding the depth of Cole's remorse. "It's never too late to seek forgiveness and make amends," he said gently.

Cole's eyes welled with tears as he spoke of the pain he had caused his mother, the trouble he created, and the heartache he had inflicted upon her. "I hope she's forgiven me," he murmured. "Because I know I'll see her again after I die."

Malcolm reached out, placing a comforting hand on Cole's shoulder. "God's love is greater than any mistakes we've made," he assured him. "And forgiveness is always available to those who seek it."

But Cole's past sins weighed heavily upon him, suffocating him with a sense of inadequacy and remorse. He wondered aloud whether he should simply let go of his regrets or pray fervently for redemption.

"Sometimes praying doesn't make much sense to me," he confessed, his voice barely above a whisper. "And I don't know if it'll make me a better person in this life."

Malcolm listened in silence, letting Cole's words hang in the air, knowing that sometimes the answers to life's hardest questions weren't easily found.

In the weeks that followed, Cole wrestled with these existential questions, grappling with the demons of his past and the uncertainties of his future. His face bore the marks of his inner turmoil, a reflection of the tumultuous storm raging within his soul.

Despite their efforts, Malcolm couldn't shake the feeling that Cole never found the resolution he sought. But in their moments together, they prayed fervently for him to find solace and peace in his final days, hoping that in the end, he would find the healing he so desperately longed for.

Christian Themes and Values

Cole's story in the hospital room, laden with reflections on his past mistakes and the quest for forgiveness, encapsulates several profound Biblical themes. These themes explore the nature of sin, redemption, forgiveness, and the search for peace in the face of death.

Acknowledgment of Sin and Regret: Cole's admission of his past errors and the impact they had on others, especially his mother, aligns with the Biblical theme of confession. The Bible encourages confession as a step toward redemption, as seen in 1 John 1:9: "If we confess our sins, he is faithful and just and will forgive us our sins and purify us from all unrighteousness." Cole's openness about his failures reflects this call for honesty with oneself and with God.

Desire for Forgiveness: The longing for forgiveness, especially from his mother, and ultimately from God, ties into the Biblical theme that emphasizes forgiveness as central to the Christian faith. Jesus teaches extensively about forgiveness, indicating that it is not only something to be received but also something to be given, as in the Lord's Prayer: "And forgive us our debts, as we also have forgiven our debtors" (Matthew 6:12).

The Uncertainty of Redemption: Cole's struggle with the effectiveness of prayer and his doubts about becoming a better person underscore the theme of redemption and the often difficult path it entails. The Biblical narrative is filled with stories of individuals who grapple with doubt and redemption, such as the apostle Peter, who denied Christ three times yet was forgiven and restored (John 21:15-17).

Wrestling with Faith: Cole's confession that "sometimes praying doesn't make much sense to me" mirrors the Biblical accounts of individuals wrestling with their faith. Examples include Job, who questioned God amidst his suffering, and Thomas, who doubted the resurrection of Jesus. These stories highlight that faith can be tested, but these moments of doubt are also opportunities for growth and deeper understanding.

Seeking Peace: Cole's quest for solace and peace in his final days resonates with the Biblical promises of peace that surpasses all understanding, which God offers to those who seek Him. Philippians 4:7 notes, "And the peace of God, which transcends all understanding, will guard your hearts and your minds in Christ Jesus." This theme is pivotal as it offers hope that beyond the turmoil of this life, there is peace available through spiritual reconciliation and trust in God.

End-of-Life Reflection and Hope: Finally, the narrative touches on the theme of eschatological hope—the hope concerning death, judgment, and the final destiny of the soul and of humankind as a whole. Cole's mention of seeing his mother again points to a belief in an afterlife where reunions are possible, a concept that is comforting and pivotal in many Christian doctrines about heaven and eternal life.

Cole's story is an exploration of the complexities of faith, sin, and redemption, offering a vivid illustration of the Biblical themes that underscore the human condition and the transformative power of divine grace and forgiveness.

Prayer

Dear God, As we come before You today, we acknowledge the wrestling within our souls, the struggle of faith and doubt that often consumes us. We confess that there are times when we find it difficult to trust in Your goodness and Your plans for us. You are the God who wrestles with us in the depths of our being, who meets us in our doubts and questions. Help us to embrace this wrestling as a part of our journey of faith, knowing that it is through struggle that we often find deeper intimacy with You. Grant us the courage to face our doubts honestly, to lay them before You, and to seek Your truth with humility and sincerity. Strengthen our faith, O Lord, and deepen our trust in Your promises, even when they seem far off or difficult to understand. Guide us in our wrestling with faith, illuminating Your Word and speaking to our hearts. Help us to discern Your voice amidst the doubts and confusion that surround us. May Your presence bring us peace and assurance, reminding us of Your faithfulness and Your unchanging character. In Jesus' name, we pray. Amen.

35

Wrestling with God

Ben lay in his hospital bed, his gaze fixed on the ceiling as if searching for answers in the blank expanse above. Chaplain Rhonda sat nearby, attentive to his words.

"I really, in my heart, don't feel the need for God," Ben confessed, his voice tinged with resignation. "I'm tired of making excuses to my family about my, so-called, theology."

Rhonda nodded, understanding the weight of Ben's words. "It's okay to wrestle with your beliefs, Ben," she said gently. "Many people find themselves questioning their faith, especially in times of difficulty."

Born and raised in the Jewish faith, Ben had long grappled with questions of faith and doubt. But now, in his early fifties and battling advanced prostate cancer, he found himself confronting his beliefs with a newfound clarity.

"If God wants me so bad, he'll make a way for me," he continued, his tone tinged with defiance. "And if he's not there or won't make a way for me, that's okay, too."

Rhonda listened as Ben poured out his frustrations and uncertainties. Ben spoke of crying out to the Lord, like the Psalmists, of grappling with the silence that often greeted his prayers.

"I'm not a patient man, Chaplain," he admitted, his voice heavy with frustration. "And I'm tired of asking God for favors."

Rhonda reached out, placing a comforting hand on Ben's arm. "Sometimes it's not about asking for favors, Ben," she said softly. "It's about finding peace in surrender, in accepting that we can't always control the outcomes."

As Rhonda listened to Ben's words, she couldn't help but admire the honesty and courage with which he confronted his doubts and fears. In his vulnerability, he embodied the essence of the human condition—searching, questioning, and ultimately finding peace in the acceptance of life's inherent mysteries and contradictions.

Christian Themes and Values

Ben's heartfelt confession and struggle with faith amid life-threatening illness presents several biblical themes that resonate deeply with the human experience, particularly in times of crisis.

Wrestling with God: Ben's admission of grappling with his belief in God mirrors the biblical story of Jacob wrestling with God (Genesis 32:22-32). This story is often interpreted as a metaphor for engaging in profound doubts and coming to terms with one's spirituality. Ben's challenges echo this struggle, highlighting a raw and honest confrontation with faith, akin to Jacob's all-night struggle until the break of dawn.

Prayer and Silence: The Psalms are replete with instances where the authors cry out to God amidst suffering, questioning His presence and pleading for deliverance—Psalms like Psalm 22 and Psalm 88 exemplify this. Ben's experience of crying out and facing silence aligns with these moments, reflecting the often painful reality of unanswered prayers and the solitude it can engender. His frustration and weariness in prayer underscore a common biblical theme where followers find themselves in the depths of despair yet continue to seek divine intervention.

Questioning Divine Justice and Presence: Ben's doubts about God's existence or His willingness to intervene reflect themes found in the Book of Job, where Job questions God's justice and His reasons for human suffering. Ben's defiant stance, "If God wants me so bad, he'll make a way for me," echoes Job's bold challenge to God's fairness and his demand for an audience with Him to discuss his suffering.

Human Patience and Divine Timing: Ben's impatience with asking God for favors touches on the biblical principle of divine timing being different from human expectations. Scripture often encourages believers to wait on the Lord and His perfect timing, as seen in verses like Psalm 27:14 ("Wait for the Lord; be strong and take heart and wait for the Lord."). Ben's struggle with this concept is emblematic of a broader human impatience with the unseen plans of God.

Faith and Doubt Coexistence: The narrative encapsulates the tension between faith and doubt within a believer's life. This theme is portrayed in the Gospels through the figure of Thomas, who doubts the resurrection of Jesus until he sees physical proof (John 20:24-29). Ben's simultaneous challenge to and reliance on divine response illustrates this complex dynamic of belief peppered with skepticism.

Acceptance of Mortality and Mystery: Ultimately, Ben's journey toward accepting life's mysteries, without definitive answers to his spiritual questions, aligns with Ecclesiastes' reflections on the enigmas and inherent uncertainties of life (Ecclesiastes 3:1-14). This book of the Bible suggests that finding peace often involves embracing the limitations of human understanding and the unpredictable nature of life's course.

Ben's candid exploration of his faith amidst terminal illness brings these biblical themes into a contemporary context, offering a raw and honest depiction of a person's confrontation with the divine amidst personal crises. His story is a reminder of the complex relationship between faith, doubt, and the human condition.

Prayer

Heavenly Father, In the depths of our souls, we come before You with hearts heavy with the weight of our struggles and doubts. We acknowledge that there are times when we find ourselves wrestling with You, questioning Your ways and Your plans for our lives. Grant us the strength to confront our doubts, to face our fears, and to seek Your face with boldness and humility. May we be like Jacob, who wrestled with You at Peniel and emerged with a new name and a deeper understanding of Your purposes. Holy Spirit, guide us through our wrestling, illuminating Your Word and speaking to our hearts. Help us to discern Your voice amidst the chaos of our doubts and fears. May Your presence bring us comfort and assurance, reminding us of Your unfailing love and faithfulness. May our wrestling with You lead us to a deeper faith, a stronger trust, and a greater love for You. And may we emerge from this struggle with a renewed sense of purpose and a deeper intimacy with You, our God and our Redeemer. In Jesus' name, we pray. Amen.

36

Redemption and Forgiveness

James sat at the edge of the pier, his eyes fixed on the horizon where the sun slowly settled into the sea, casting hues of gold and crimson across the sky. The air was cool, laden with the salty scent of the ocean and the cries of distant seagulls. It had been years since he'd allowed himself the luxury of simply watching a sunset, years since he'd done much of anything that didn't revolve around his work or his numerous personal failings.

Once a man of fierce ambition and even fiercer temper, James had burned many bridges in his relentless pursuit of success. He'd stepped over friends, alienated his family, and lost the love of his life, Maria, who had walked away when his obsessions became too much for her gentle heart to bear. He had gained the world, so to speak, but at what cost? Now, at fifty, he found himself alone, wealthy, and utterly miserable.

The gentle lapping of the waves against the pier's sturdy pillars was a soft, rhythmic sound that reminded him of church hymns from his childhood. His mother had taken him to church, had instilled in him the stories of Christ's love and redemption, but somewhere along the way, he'd lost sight of those lessons. He'd become cynical, hardened by life's disappointments and his own relentless drive.

That morning, a letter had arrived, postmarked from a small town in Italy. Maria, it seemed, had kept track of him through mutual friends. She had written not out of bitterness or to rekindle anything lost, but out of concern. In her neat, flowing script, she spoke of forgiveness and of the peace she had found in her faith. "Remember, James," she had written, "that no one is beyond redemption. Not even you. It is never too late to seek forgiveness, to start anew."

It was that single line that had driven him to the pier, which had him staring out into the vastness of the ocean and contemplating the vastness of God's love. Maria had found something he had not—peace. She had forgiven him, perhaps, but had he forgiven himself?

As the sun dipped lower, casting the world into twilight, James felt a stirring in his heart. The beauty of the sunset, so like the paintings he'd once loved before he'd deemed them unimportant, seemed to speak of possibility and hope. Maybe, just maybe, he thought, there was a chance for him yet—a chance to find the redemption Maria spoke of.

In the fading light, he made a decision. He would go to Italy, not to disrupt her life, but to find the peace she described. He wanted to see the world through her eyes, to understand the love and forgiveness that had changed her so profoundly. He wanted, at last, to bridge the chasm that he had allowed to widen between himself and God.

James stood, feeling the first real sense of purpose in years coursing through him. He wasn't sure what awaited him, but the thought of seeking forgiveness, of embracing a long-forgotten faith, filled him with a tentative hope. As he walked back to his car, the stars began to appear, one by one, like beacons guiding him on his newfound path toward redemption and love.

Christian Themes and Values

James' story at the pier, reflecting on his life's choices and the letter from Maria, draws deeply on several key biblical themes, particularly redemption, forgiveness, and the transformative power of love and faith.

The Parable of the Prodigal Son: James' life mirrors the story of the prodigal son in Luke 15:11-32, where a young man squanders his inheritance and returns home, repentant and humbled, only to be warmly welcomed by his father. Like the prodigal son, James realizes the emptiness of his pursuits and contemplates returning to a simpler, more meaningful way of life that aligns with his earlier teachings about Christ's love and redemption.

Forgiveness and Redemption: The central message of Maria's letter and the biblical narrative is that no one is beyond redemption, echoing the teachings of Christ about forgiveness. The Bible is replete with stories of individuals who turn back to God after periods of sin or disbelief, such as King David (Psalm 51) and Peter (Luke 22:54-62, John 21:15-17). James' reflection on his need for self-forgiveness and his decision to seek redemption are pivotal moments that highlight this theme.

Transformation through Faith: James' contemplation of Maria's peace and forgiveness underlines the theme of transformation through faith. This change is often depicted in the Bible through the lives of characters who experience profound shifts in their values and lifestyles after encountering the love and mercy of God, such as Saul's conversion to Paul the Apostle (Acts 9:1-19).

Seeking God's Love: The metaphor of the vast ocean and the sunset that James watches symbolize the infinite nature of God's love and the beauty of His creation, reminding readers of Romans 1:20, which speaks of understanding God's invisible qualities through what has been made. This setting prompts James to reconsider the beauty of life and God's love that he had ignored in his pursuit of worldly success.

New Beginnings: The theme of new beginnings is underscored by James' decision to travel to Italy, not to rekindle an old romance but to discover the peace and faith that transformed Maria. This echoes biblical promises that it's never too late to turn back to God and start anew, as highlighted in Lamentations 3:22-23 about God's mercies being new every morning.

Hope and Guidance: As James walks back to his car, guided by the stars appearing one by one, this scene symbolizes the biblical theme of hope and divine guidance. Just as the stars guided the Wise Men to Jesus after His birth (Matthew 2:1-12), the stars for James represent hope and the guidance he seeks on his new path toward spiritual recovery and redemption.

In summary, James' reflective and transformative journey by the pier is steeped in rich biblical themes, illustrating a powerful narrative of self-realization, repentance, and the search for deeper spiritual meaning in life.

Prayer

Dear God, We come before You, grateful for the gift of redemption and forgiveness that You offer us through Your Son, Jesus Christ. We confess that we are unworthy of Your mercy, yet You freely give it to us out of Your great love. Lord, You have promised to forgive us of our sins and to cleanse us from all unrighteousness when we confess them to You. We thank You for the assurance of Your forgiveness, which gives us hope and peace in the midst of our brokenness. Help us to fully embrace Your forgiveness, Lord, and to extend it to others as You have extended it to us. Grant us the humility to acknowledge our faults and the courage to seek reconciliation with those we have wronged. Empower us to live lives worthy of the forgiveness we have received, walking in obedience to Your will and reflecting Your grace and mercy to the world around us. May Your forgiveness transform our hearts and minds, Lord, making us vessels of Your love and instruments of Your peace. May we be quick to forgive others as You have forgiven us, and may Your love flow through us, bringing healing and reconciliation to a broken world. In Jesus' name, we pray. Amen.

37

The Simple Need for Companionship

I met Malik in the dimly lit confines of the hospice inpatient unit, where the soft scent of flowers mingled with the hushed whispers of nurses and other caregivers. As a hospice chaplain, my encounters with Muslim patients were rare, their spiritual needs often tended to by their own Imams and family members.

Introducing myself as the hospice chaplain, I sought to gauge Malik's spiritual and emotional needs and prepared to assist him in finding appropriate religious guidance, if needed. But Malik, with his gentle demeanor and warm smile, surprised me with his response.

"I just want to talk to a spiritual guide," he said, his words soft but resolute. "It doesn't matter what religion you happen to be."

I nodded, understanding the universal need for companionship and comfort in the face of life's final journey. I assured him that I met all individuals where they were on their hospice journey, regardless of their religious affiliation or lack thereof.

Malik's eyes twinkled with inquisitiveness as he asked if I had ever read the Quran. I admitted that I had read parts of it, finding it both compelling and at times perplexing.

"You're honest," he chuckled, his laughter echoing through the room. "Yes, it is compelling, but it is not confusing for the believer."

His words struck a chord within me, resonating with a truth that transcended religious boundaries. I acknowledged his perspective with a nod of understanding.

"We don't need to talk about the Quran at this time," he continued, his voice softening with sincerity. "I just need a calm, human voice, a real person to sit with me for a while. And then I will kick you out so that I may pray to Allah on my knees." Malik smiled.

I smiled, too, grateful for the opportunity to share in Malik's journey, even if only for a brief moment. And as I sat beside him, enveloped in the quiet stillness of his room, I realized that sometimes, the greatest comfort we can offer is simply the presence of a kindred soul.

Christian Themes and Values

The chaplain's interaction with Malik in the hospice setting highlights several profound biblical themes, reflecting the universal aspects of spiritual care and human connection.

Interfaith Respect and Understanding: Your openness to engaging with Malik, despite the differences in religious backgrounds, echoes the biblical theme of love and respect for one's neighbor, which transcends religious boundaries. This is akin to the parable of the Good Samaritan (Luke 10:25-37), where Jesus emphasizes the importance of showing mercy and kindness across cultural and religious divides.

The Ministry of Presence: The simple act of being present and offering companionship to Malik underscores the Christian practice of "bearing one another's burdens" (Galatians 6:2). This theme is evident throughout the Bible, where followers of Christ are called to offer support, comfort, and empathy to others, reflecting Christ's compassion and empathy for all people.

Spiritual Companionship Beyond Religious Labels: Malik's request for a "calm, human voice" and a "real person to sit with me" highlights the universal need for connection and comfort in times of suffering, which resonates with the biblical assurances found in Psalms that God is near to the brokenhearted and saves those who are crushed in spirit (Psalm 34:18). It shows that spiritual care often transcends doctrinal differences and focuses on the shared human experience of seeking comfort and understanding.

Humility in Service: Your role as a chaplain, serving and listening without imposing your own beliefs, exemplifies the biblical principle of humility. Philippians 2:3-4 encourages believers to value others above themselves and not to look to their own interests but each to the interests of others. This humility is fundamental in providing effective pastoral care.

Dialogue and Learning: Your honest admission of having read parts of the Quran and finding it both compelling and perplexing showcases a willingness to learn and engage in dialogue, which is crucial in interfaith interactions. This reflects the biblical theme of seeking wisdom and understanding, as seen in Proverbs 4:6-7, which advises not to forsake wisdom, as it will protect and watch over you.

Respecting Individual Worship Practices: Malik's gentle insistence on praying alone to Allah after your visit highlights the respect for individual religious practices and personal space, echoing the biblical respect for individual expressions of faith. This is similar to Jesus's teaching on prayer, where he encouraged private communion with God (Matthew 6:6).

These themes demonstrate that true spiritual care in a hospice setting involves empathy, respect, and an openness to understand and support the patient's spiritual and emotional needs, regardless of their faith background. Your encounter with Malik serves as a beautiful example of how spiritual care providers can bridge differences and offer solace through presence, conversation, and mutual respect.

Prayer

Heavenly Father, In the quiet moments of our hearts, we come before you, recognizing our simple need for companionship. You created us for relationship, to walk alongside one another in love and support. Grant us the grace to find meaningful connections with those around us. Help us to be open to the friendships and companionships you bring into our lives, knowing that they are gifts from your hand. We pray for those who feel alone and isolated, that you would surround them with your comforting presence and bring people into their lives who will uplift and encourage them. Teach us to love one another as you have loved us, sharing in both joys and sorrows, supporting each other through every season of life. In Jesus' name, we pray. Amen.

38

Grappling with Emotions

In the solemn hush of the intensive care unit, where sorrow often hung heavy in the air, Chaplain Bob grappled with emotions threatening to spill over like water over a dam. His colleague's words from his clinical pastor education days echoed in his mind, a reminder to maintain professional composure even in the face of profound grief.

"Don't get emotionally involved," she had cautioned, her voice tinged with wisdom. "Stick a plug in it."

Bob nodded, understanding the necessity of keeping his emotions in check, of maintaining those elusive boundaries that separated the personal from the professional. But try as he might, there were moments when the sorrow of others seeped into his soul, overwhelming him with its intensity.

Giving last rites was always a test of his resolve, especially when faced with the loss of a young hospice patient or a soul he had grown fond of. He clung to his faith, seeking solace in the prayers he offered, but sometimes, even the most steadfast beliefs faltered in the face of such profound loss.

It was the moments when a mother had given birth to a stillborn child that tested him the most. To see that mother hold her dead baby, to witness the raw anguish etched upon her face, to feel the weight of her grief pressing down upon him—it was almost unbearable.

Yet, in those moments of shared sorrow, Bob realized the true measure of his calling. For if he could no longer feel the pain of another, if he could no longer let it show, then perhaps it was time to seek another path.

But for now, he remained rooted in his purpose, grounded both spiritually and technically, as he sought to offer whatever comfort and solace, he could to those whose souls had been torn apart by loss. And though the tears may fall, and the emotions may overflow, he knew that it was in those moments of shared humanity that the truest form of healing could be found.

Christian Themes and Values

The story of a chaplain grappling with the emotional weight of providing spiritual care in an intensive care unit delves into deep biblical themes related to compassion, empathy, professional duty, and personal faith. These themes reflect the complex interplay between one's spiritual calling and the human response to grief and suffering.

Compassion and Empathy: The chaplain's emotional involvement with patients, especially during moments like giving last rites or comforting a mother with a stillborn child, embodies the biblical injunction to "weep with those who weep" (Romans 12:15). This shows a profound level of empathy and compassion, which are central to Christian teachings about loving one's neighbor as oneself (Mark 12:31).

Professional Boundaries vs. Personal Compassion: The advice to "stick a plug in it" and keep a professional composure reflects the biblical theme of self-control, which is a fruit of the Spirit (Galatians 5:22-23). However, the chaplain's struggle to maintain these boundaries while being emotionally present for patients highlights the tension between professional duties and personal empathy, a balance often explored in biblical narratives through figures like Jesus, who showed deep compassion while also withdrawing at times to pray and reflect (Mark 1:35).

The Role of Faith in Suffering: The chaplain's reliance on faith and prayer during emotionally challenging times speaks to the biblical understanding that faith provides solace and strength in times of distress. This is akin to the Psalmist's reliance on God during times of deep emotional turmoil (Psalm 42:11).

The Power of Shared Humanity and Healing: The chaplain's recognition that true healing can be found in moments of shared humanity aligns with the biblical theme of communal support and love in healing. The New Testament church was marked by a strong sense of community and mutual aid, reflecting the idea that sharing in each other's burdens is a way to fulfill the law of Christ (Galatians 6:2).

The Struggle with Profound Loss: Facing the profound loss of a young patient or a stillborn child tests the chaplain's faith, reminiscent of Job's struggles with loss and suffering in the Bible. Job's story is a profound exploration of faith under pressure and addresses the question of how to find meaning and trust in God amid inexplicable suffering (Job 23:10).

Call to Ministry: Lastly, the chaplain's contemplation of his calling — questioning whether to continue if he can no longer feel the pain of others — echoes the biblical theme of vocational calling. The prophets and apostles often grappled with their callings, especially when faced with daunting challenges. This includes Jeremiah, who lamented his role as a prophet but found that he could not hold back from speaking what God had commanded him to say (Jeremiah 20:9).

These biblical themes underscore the chaplain's narrative as a powerful testament to the challenges and spiritual dimensions of caregiving in settings marked by intense suffering and loss. It highlights the delicate balance between professional boundaries and personal empathy, the sustaining power of faith, and the profound impact of shared human experiences in fostering healing and hope.

Prayer

Heavenly Father, In the simplicity of our need for companionship, we come before You, recognizing that You created us for relationship, both with You and with one another. We thank You for the gift of companionship, for the friends and loved ones You place in our lives to walk alongside us in our journey. You understand our longing for companionship, for someone to share our joys and sorrows, our triumphs and struggles. You promised to never leave us nor forsake us, and we find comfort in Your constant presence with us. Help us to cherish the relationships You have given us, Lord, and to nurture them with love, kindness, and patience. Grant us the wisdom to be good friends and companions to others, offering them the same love and support that You give to us. May we never take for granted the gift of companionship, Lord, but always be grateful for the friends and loved ones You have placed in our lives. And may we always find our ultimate companionship in You, our faithful and ever-present God. In Jesus' name, we pray. Amen.

39

The Need for Reconciliation

Joanne's words hung heavy in the air, each syllable laden with the weight of a lifetime's worth of regret and longing. She sat on her bed, her hands trembling as she spoke, her voice choked with emotion.

"I know I'm going to die," she began, her words barely more than a whisper. "And I know it's going to be soon."

Brianna, the nurse's aide, listened quietly, her heart going out to Joanne as she poured out her soul. She sat beside her, offering a supportive presence in the dimly lit room.

Marc, Joanne's son, was a ghost that haunted her every thought, a specter of regret that tore at her heartstrings with relentless fervor.

"He tears my heart out," Joanne confessed, her voice breaking with anguish. "I haven't seen him in years, and I don't have the energy for him anymore."

Brianna reached out, placing a comforting hand on Joanne's trembling shoulder. "You have so much love in your heart, Joanne," she said softly. "Maybe it's time to let go of the pain and reach out to him."

Joanne's shoulders slumped with the weight of her burden, her hands trembling as she covered her face, seeking solace in the darkness.

"Do you think God hears my prayers?" she asked, her voice filled with uncertainty. "My pleas for reconciliation, for forgiveness?"

Brianna nodded, her own faith giving her strength to reassure Joanne. "Joanne," she said softly, "God hears every prayer, especially those spoken from a heart filled with remorse and longing."

Their eyes met, a glimmer of hope flickering in Joanne's, like a beacon in the darkness.

"Thank you," she whispered, her voice barely audible above the steady rhythm of her own heartbeat.

And in that moment, Brianna knew that even in the darkest of times, there was still room for redemption, for forgiveness, for love. As Joanne closed her eyes, her breathing slow and steady, Brianna offered up a silent prayer, trusting that God's grace would prevail in the end.

Christian Themes and Values

Joanne's emotional story, filled with longing, regret, and a quest for reconciliation, resonates with several deep biblical themes.

Forgiveness and Reconciliation: One of the central themes in Joanne's story is her desire to reconcile with her estranged son, Mark, before she dies. This mirrors the biblical emphasis on forgiveness and reconciliation both with God and with one another. In Matthew 5:23-24, Jesus emphasizes the importance of reconciling with others before offering gifts at the altar, highlighting the value placed on interpersonal relationships in spiritual life.

The Prodigal Son: Joanne's yearning for her son's return and her readiness to make peace can be seen as a reflection of the parable of the Prodigal Son (Luke 15:11-32). In the parable, the father's unconditional love and readiness to forgive his returning son mirrors Joanne's own feelings towards her son, emphasizing the themes of grace and redemption.

Prayer and Divine Listening: Joanne's question, "Do you think God hears my prayers?" touches on the biblical assurance that God hears the prayers of the faithful. Scriptures such as Psalm 34:17 ("The righteous cry out, and the Lord hears them; He delivers them from all their troubles.") provide comfort and assurance that God is attentive to the pleas of those who seek Him earnestly.

God's Unconditional Love and Forgiveness: The reassurance given to

Joanne that "God loves you and accepts you just as you are" reflects the biblical theme of God's unconditional love and forgiveness. Ephesians 2:8-9 teaches that it is by grace through faith that individuals are saved, not by their own efforts, highlighting the gift of God's grace independent of human merit.

Hope and Redemption: The glimmer of hope in Joanne's eyes, in response to being told of God's forgiveness, aligns with the biblical theme of redemption and hope found through faith. Romans 15:13 speaks of God filling believers with joy and peace as they trust in Him, so that they may overflow with hope by the power of the Holy Spirit.

The Power of Presence and Comfort: The chaplain's presence and comforting words to Joanne underscore the biblical call to "mourn with those who mourn" (Romans 12:15) and to offer comfort to others as God comforts us (2 Corinthians 1:3-4). This act of spiritual and emotional support is fundamental in Christian ministry and pastoral care.

These themes collectively highlight the spiritual depth of Joanne's struggle and the pastoral response that seeks to affirm her worth, alleviate her anguish, and reinforce her faith in God's mercy and love. Her story is an illustration of the transformative power of forgiveness, the hope of reconciliation, and the comforting presence of faith even as life draws to a close.

Prayer

Heavenly Father, We come before You with hearts burdened by the need for reconciliation. We acknowledge the brokenness in our relationships, the hurt we have caused, and the wounds we carry from others. You are the God of reconciliation, who has reconciled us to Yourself through the blood of Your Son, Jesus Christ. We thank You for the forgiveness and grace You offer us, and we pray for the courage and humility to extend that forgiveness and grace to others. Soften our hearts and the hearts of those with whom we need to reconcile. Give us the words to speak and the actions to take that will bring about healing and restoration. May Your presence be felt in every step of the reconciliation process, guiding us toward forgiveness, understanding, and peace. Lord, we pray for reconciliation in our families, in our communities, and in our world. Help us to bridge the divides that separate us, to build bridges of understanding and empathy, and to work toward reconciliation with humility and love. In Jesus' name, we pray. Amen.

40

Kingdom of God on Earth

Bonita sat across from me, her eyes probing, her mind sharp as a dagger. She was a woman of intellect, with a stack of degrees to match, and she didn't shy away from asking the tough questions. As a chaplain, I was accustomed to offering solace and comfort, but Bonita wasn't interested in platitudes. She wanted truth, raw and unfiltered.

"So," she began, her voice cutting through the air like a whip, "if I don't want to die to get into heaven, what are my options for the here and now?"

Her question hung in the air, pregnant with meaning, and I paused, considering my response carefully. Bonita knew her scripture, perhaps better than I did, and she wasn't looking for empty words. She wanted substance, something real to sink her teeth into.

"Doesn't Jesus say a lot about the Kingdom of Heaven on Earth?" she continued; her gaze unwavering.

I nodded, grateful for the lifeline she'd thrown me. "Yes," I replied, "He does."

And so, we delved into the teachings of Jesus, exploring the concept of the Kingdom of God as a present reality, not just a distant promise for the afterlife. We talked about the Beatitudes, the Lord's Prayer, and the parables that illustrated the transformative power of God's Kingdom here on earth.

As we spoke, I watched the lines of tension ease from Bonita's face, her eyes alight with understanding. She wasn't just seeking knowledge; she was searching for meaning, for a way to live out her faith in the here and now.

And in that moment, I realized that perhaps Bonita had answered her own question. In her quest for truth, she had found a glimpse of the Kingdom of God right here, in our midst. And together, we embarked on a journey to uncover its mysteries, one question at a time.

Christian Themes and Values

Bonita's probing questions and the ensuing dialogue about the Kingdom of God present in this world highlight several key Biblical themes.

Kingdom of God on Earth: Bonita's inquiry into the possibility of experiencing the Kingdom of Heaven on Earth directly aligns with Jesus' teachings about the Kingdom of God. Throughout the Gospels, Jesus discusses the Kingdom not just as a future reality but as a present experience. In Luke 17:21, Jesus says, "nor will people say, 'Here it is,' or 'There it is,' because the kingdom of God is in your midst." This reflects the theme that the divine realm of God's rule can be experienced here and now through the lives of believers who follow Jesus' teachings.

The Beatitudes: Discussing the Beatitudes as part of this dialogue ties into the theme of living out the principles of the Kingdom of God in everyday life. These teachings from the Sermon on the Mount (Matthew 5:1-12) outline the attitudes and behaviors that characterize the citizens of God's Kingdom, emphasizing qualities like meekness, righteousness, mercy, and peacemaking as pathways to experiencing and manifesting God's Kingdom on Earth.

The Lord's Prayer: By bringing up the Lord's Prayer, the conversation touches on the petition "Thy Kingdom come, Thy will be done, on Earth as it is in Heaven" (Matthew 6:10). This request in the prayer that Jesus taught His disciples emphasizes the believer's role in invoking and facilitating the reign of God's Kingdom values in the earthly realm.

Parables of the Kingdom: Exploring parables that describe the Kingdom of God highlights Jesus' method of teaching about the Kingdom's nature through stories and similes. Parables like the mustard seed and the leaven (Matthew 13:31-33) illustrate how the Kingdom starts small within the hearts of individuals and grows expansively, influencing greater society.

Transformative Power of Faith: Bonita's shift from seeking knowledge to searching for meaning and how to practically live out her faith reflects the transformative power of the Gospel. It emphasizes that true understanding of Biblical teachings leads to personal transformation and practical application, which is a core theme of the New Testament teachings.

Seeking and Finding Truth: The story embodies the theme from Matthew 7:7, "Ask and it will be given to you; seek and you will find; knock and the door will be opened to you." Bonita's approach to seeking the truth about God's Kingdom on Earth demonstrates that earnest seeking leads to profound discoveries and deeper faith.

This conversation not only provides intellectual stimulation but also spiritual direction, showing that understanding Biblical themes can lead to practical implications for living out one's faith daily. It serves as an example of how theology can be intensely practical and personally transformative, aligning one's life with the principles of the Kingdom of God.

Prayer

Heavenly Father, We come before You with hearts full of hope and longing for Your Kingdom to come on earth as it is in heaven. We acknowledge that Your Kingdom is one of righteousness, peace, and love, and we yearn to see Your will done here on earth as it is in heaven. You have called us to be ambassadors of Your Kingdom, to spread Your love and light to the world around us. Help us to live as citizens of Your Kingdom, seeking first Your righteousness and working to bring about Your Kingdom values in our homes, our communities, and our world. Empower us to be agents of Your Kingdom, filling us with Your presence and guiding us in Your ways. Help us to bear witness to Your Kingdom values through our words and actions, so that others may come to know You and experience the transformation that Your Kingdom brings. In Jesus' name, we pray. Amen.

41

Communion and Spiritual Nourishment

Sheila's once radiant beauty from the 1970s had surrendered to the relentless march of illness, leaving behind a shadow of her former glory. Fred, her stalwart companion and husband of fifty-seven years, navigated the narrow corridors of their suburban home, maneuvering Sheila's wheelchair with practiced ease.

The once elegant dining room, now stripped of its finery, had morphed into a hospice sanctuary—a shrine to Sheila's battle against cancer. The commode stood front and center as a reminder of changing body needs. A pile of medicine bottles littered the top of the dining room table.

Each cough that wracked Sheila's frail form served as a grim reminder of the adversary that lurked within. In moments of quiet desperation, she turned her gaze heavenward, her voice a whispered entreaty to the Divine.

"Take me now, Jesus," she implored, her outstretched arm a frail offering to a power beyond her control.

Fred's eyes, a mosaic of sorrow and resignation, met hers with silent resignation as he offered her a meager meal. The weight of impending loss hanging heavy in the air.

Despite the relentless assault on her appetite, Sheila found comfort in the familiar ritual of smoking—a small rebellion against the encroaching darkness that threatened to engulf her. The act, a relic of decades past, offered a fleeting reprieve from the suffocating grip of her illness. How ironic.

"Here's your soup, Sheila," Brianna, the nurse's aide, said softly as she set the bowl down on the table.

"Thank you, Brianna," Sheila replied weakly, her voice barely above a whisper.

Amidst the tumult of her affliction, Sheila sought solace in communion, brought to her once a month by the hospice chaplain, a sacred act with the Divine Presence that transcended the confines of her failing body. Despite the choking fit that seized her with each swallow of the sacred morsel, her smile remained steadfast, a testament to her unyielding faith and indomitable spirit.

As the sun dipped below the horizon, casting long shadows across the room, Sheila's plea echoed softly in the stillness. With a quiet resolve that belied her frailty, she whispered a supplication to the heavens above.

"Take me, Jesus," she murmured, her voice a fragile whisper in the gathering darkness—a silent plea for peace and deliverance.

Fred sat by her side, holding her hand, his own silent prayer joining hers in the fading light.

Christian Themes and Values

Suffering and Redemption: Sheila's battle with cancer symbolizes the suffering and trials that humans endure in life. Like Job in the Bible, she faces physical affliction and turns to God in her distress (Job 30:16-20). Her plea, "Take me now, Jesus," reflects a desire for deliverance from her suffering, echoing Job's cries for relief.

Faith in the Midst of Adversity: Sheila's reliance on her faith, even in the face of illness and impending death, mirrors biblical examples of trusting God in difficult circumstances. Despite her struggles, she maintains her belief in God's presence and power to bring comfort and peace (Psalm 23:4; Isaiah 41:10).

Communion and Spiritual Nourishment: Sheila finds solace in the act of communion, representing her spiritual connection with God. Just as Jesus shared bread and wine with his disciples as a symbol of his sacrificial love

(Matthew 26:26-28), Sheila partakes in communion as a reminder of God's presence and love during her suffering.

Hope in the Midst of Darkness: Sheila's whispered plea, "Take me, Jesus," reflects a longing for peace and deliverance from her pain. This echoes biblical themes of hope and trust in God's promises, even in the midst of darkness and uncertainty (Psalm 27:13-14; Romans 15:13).

Love and Support in Relationships: Fred's steadfast presence by Sheila's side embodies the biblical theme of love and support within marriage. Just as Christ's love for the church is sacrificial and enduring (Ephesians 5:25), Fred cares for Sheila with dedication and compassion, despite the weight of impending loss.

In summary, the story of Sheila and Fred explores themes of suffering, faith, communion, hope, and love, reflecting the complexities of human experience and the enduring truths found in Scripture.

Prayer

Heavenly Father, As we gather around the table of communion, we thank You for the spiritual nourishment You provide us through this sacrament. We recognize that as we partake of the bread and the cup, we are reminded of Your sacrifice for us and the sustenance You offer to our souls. Grant us a deeper understanding of the significance of communion, Lord, and help us to approach it with reverence and gratitude. May this time of communion be a means of drawing closer to You and to one another, as we remember Your love and sacrifice for us. Open our hearts to receive the spiritual nourishment You offer us through communion. Fill us with Your presence and Your peace, and empower us to go forth as Your disciples, sharing Your love and grace with the world. In Jesus' name, we pray. Amen.

42

Vulnerability and Healing

Peter lay in his hospital bed, his once strong frame now confined by the cool bland surroundings of the rehabilitation facility. The sunlight filtered through the curtains, casting a soft glow on the linoleum floor. He stared out the window, his gaze fixed on the world beyond, a world that seemed to have moved on without him. His very elderly father was now in a hospice facility close to death.

"I don't think I can take this much longer," Peter said, his voice barely above a whisper. His hand absently traced the lines of his healing leg, a tangible reminder of his vulnerability.

I sat beside him, my presence a silent anchor in the storm of his emotions. Peter was not one to wear his heart on his sleeve, but the cracks in his façade were becoming increasingly evident.

"I feel so useless," he continued, his words heavy with self-doubt. "And I'm now experiencing a lot of fears and emotions I haven't felt since Suzanne (his wife of forty years) died. Where the hell did all that stuff come from?"

His eyes searched mine, a mix of confusion and desperation reflected in their depths. I understood his struggle, his reluctance to confront the pain that lay buried beneath the surface.

"You know, Pete," I began, my voice steady despite the weight of his words. "All those feelings, emotions, and hard memories don't just go away and vanish forever."

I paused, choosing my words carefully as I navigated the delicate terrain of his heartache.

"Sometimes they hide for years in holes that you dug for them," I continued, "and then they pop out like whack-a-moles to bite at your soul."

Peter listened intently; his brow furrowed in contemplation. It was clear that my words struck a chord, resonating with the hidden truths he had long tried to ignore.

"Maybe you never really dealt with your feelings when Suzanne died," I suggested gently. "I sure don't know if that's so, but you've always told me that you had a hard time with your feelings. I'd say that what you're feeling now is normal and natural, even if it's very painful. Especially those emotions regarding your dad's decline and even your own injuries."

I reached out, placing a reassuring hand on his shoulder, a silent gesture of solidarity in the face of his pain.

"Let's spend some time on this stuff," I offered, my voice a beacon of hope in the darkness of his despair. "I'm listening."

Christian Themes and Values

Peter's story highlights biblical themes that touch on the human condition, faith, suffering, and mortality.

Vulnerability and Healing: Peter's struggle with his vulnerability and recovery from physical injury brings to light biblical themes of healing and restoration. The Bible often speaks of God as a healer, not just physically but emotionally and spiritually, as seen in Psalm 147:3, "He heals the brokenhearted and binds up their wounds."

Confronting Emotional Pain: Peter's unaddressed grief and the resurgence of emotions related to his wife's death illustrate the biblical understanding that emotional pain must be confronted and dealt with, rather than ignored. This is similar to the Lamentations where profound grief is expressed openly as a step towards healing.

Support and Community: The chaplain's role as a supportive presence for Peter underlines the biblical theme of bearing one another's burdens

(Galatians 6:2). The chaplain's encouragement to address deep-seated emotions highlights the importance of community and fellowship in the healing process.

Resilience and Hope: Finally, the chaplain's offer to help Peter work through his emotions and the acknowledgment that this pain is both "normal and natural" ties into the biblical themes of resilience and hope in the face of trials. Scripture often encourages believers to maintain hope and faith through difficult times, as in Romans 5:3-5, which talks about suffering producing perseverance, character, and hope.

In summary, Peter's story illustrates how biblical themes can provide a framework for understanding and navigating the complexities of human suffering, the search for meaning in pain, and the quest for spiritual and emotional healing.

Prayer

Heavenly Father, We come before You with hearts open and vulnerable, acknowledging our need for healing and restoration. We confess that we are broken and wounded, and we long for Your healing touch to bring wholeness to our lives. You are the Great Physician, who heals the brokenhearted and binds up their wounds. We thank You for Your promise of healing and restoration, and we surrender our pain and brokenness into Your loving hands. Grant us the courage to be vulnerable before You, Lord, and to allow Your healing light to shine into the darkest corners of our hearts. Help us to lay down our defenses and to trust in Your power to bring healing and transformation. May Your healing touch bring restoration to our relationships, our bodies, and our spirits, Lord. May we experience the depth of Your love and the power of Your healing grace in every area of our lives. In vulnerability, may we find strength. In brokenness, may we find healing. And in You, may we find our true identity and purpose. In Jesus' name, we pray. Amen.

43

Assurance of Salvation

"I ain't dead yet," Bert bellowed from his hospital bed as I entered the room, his voice echoing with a touch of defiance.

"Are you the chaplain or the undertaker?" he quipped, a mischievous glint in his eye.

I chuckled, shaking my head at his irreverence. "Do I look like an undertaker?" I retorted, gesturing to my casual attire of flannel shirt and jeans.

Bert grinned, his eyes squinting to see me clearly.

"Well, you might be one of them streetwise priests, wanting to 'save' me, but I don't need saving."

I raised an eyebrow, intrigued by his assertiveness. "I had no intention of talking about your salvation, especially if that's a topic you don't want to discuss."

Bert nodded, his expression firm. "I'm saved, and I know it, and that settles that."

I respected his conviction, choosing not to press further on the topic. "Do you want to talk about cars or sports?" I asked, eager to engage in further conversation.

Bert's face lit up at the mention of cars, his enthusiasm palpable. "I used to be a taxi driver," he began, launching into tales of his days behind the wheel. "Had a medallion, drove fifty thousand miles a year. Made a good living, and now I'm not worth a pot of spit."

He paused, his tone turning somber. "I need to have my cataracts done, and the doc says I probably need another damn hernia operation, too. Now, that's another pain in the ass."

"You sound angry," I remarked, noting the edge in his voice. "Do you want to talk about your feelings, your anger, or anything you want?"

Bert hesitated for a moment before changing the subject. "Yeah, let's talk about cars. Do you know anything about Mustangs? What about the 1955 Thunderbird?" He grinned mischievously. "But don't tell me about salvation, because I know I'm saved."

Bert's encounter with the chaplain in the hospital reflects a variety of biblical themes, often expressed in his candid, spirited dialogue and his reflections on life, illness, and faith.

Christian Themes and Values

Assurance of Salvation: Bert's firm statement, "I'm saved, and I know it, and that settles that," echoes the biblical theme of assurance in one's salvation. This concept is highlighted in scriptures like John 5:24, where Jesus speaks about eternal life for those who hear his word and believe in God who sent him, asserting that they will not be judged but have crossed over from death to life. Bert's confidence in his salvation aligns with this assurance that faith in Christ secures eternal life.

Human Dignity and Value in Old Age: As Bert discusses his past as a taxi driver and his current health struggles, he touches on the theme of human dignity and worth beyond one's economic productivity or physical health. This reflects Psalm 71:9, which pleads, "Do not cast me away when I am old; do not forsake me when my strength is gone." Despite his current ailments and feeling of worthlessness ("now I'm not worth a pot of spit"), the biblical perspective upholds the intrinsic value of every individual regardless of their physical condition or societal status.

Endurance Through Suffering: Bert's experience with ongoing health issues and his straightforward acknowledgment of his frustrations illustrates the theme of enduring suffering, which is prevalent throughout the Bible.

James 1:12 offers encouragement in this regard: "Blessed is the one who perseveres under trial because, having stood the test, that person will receive the crown of life that the Lord has promised to those who love him." Bert's willingness to discuss his challenges, albeit with a hint of resistance, underscores a common human response to suffering and the process of finding resilience.

Rejection of Further Spiritual Discussion: Bert's rejection of further talk on salvation, despite his acceptance of his saved status, highlights a theme of spiritual independence and personal conviction, akin to the New Testament narratives where individuals affirm their faith but may resist deeper theological discourse or external interpretations (Acts 26:28-29 where Paul discusses faith with King Agrippa).

Community and Conversation: Finally, Bert's eagerness to shift the conversation to more familiar and comfortable topics like cars illustrates the biblical theme of community and communication. Just as Jesus engaged with people where they were, discussing matters they cared about (John 4 with the Samaritan woman about water and daily life), the chaplain navigates towards topics that resonate with Bert, building rapport and community in the midst of his hospital stay.

Bert's story, while unique in its details, underscores broad biblical principles about the dignity of the individual, the reality of human suffering, the assurance of faith, and the importance of meeting people where they are in their spiritual journey.

Prayer

Heavenly Father, We come before You with grateful hearts, thankful for the assurance of salvation that You have given us through Your Son, Jesus Christ. We praise You for the gift of eternal life and for the hope that we have in Him. We confess that there are times when doubts and fears creep into our hearts, causing us to question our salvation. But Your Word assures us that those who believe in Jesus will have eternal life, and we hold fast to this promise. Grant us the peace that surpasses all understanding, Lord, as we rest in the assurance of Your love and grace. Help us to live each day with confidence, knowing that nothing can separate us from Your love. May the assurance of our salvation fill us with joy and gratitude, Lord, and may it compel us to live lives that honor and glorify You. In Jesus' name, we pray. Amen.

44

Peace, Solitude, and the Presence of God

Josephine sat quietly on the porch of her small, weathered house, watching the sun's final display of orange and pink before it dipped below the horizon. The years had etched deep lines into her face, each one a marker of seasons passed, and hardships weathered. Alone now, in the twilight of her life, she found her days stretching out like the endless prairie that surrounded her humble home.

Once, the house had pulsed with the laughter of children and the steady rhythm of shared existence. But her children had long since moved to distant cities, chasing their own futures, and her husband, Michael, had passed quietly one winter morning five years prior. The silence that filled her days was profound, punctuated only by the whisper of the wind through the grasses and the occasional creak of her rocking chair.

Yet, Josephine was not lonely. She felt the presence of Jesus in the quiet hours of the morning, heard His voice in the rustling leaves, and saw His face in the myriad expressions of nature's beauty. Her faith had deepened as she aged, each wrinkle a testament to a life fully lived and a spirit still vibrant with hope and love.

She had learned to see the beauty in her solitude, finding companionship in the quiet conversations with Jesus, her guide and confidant. He walked with her in her garden, His lessons in every blooming flower and every falling leaf—reminders of the cycles of life, of death and rebirth.

Each morning, Josephine rose with the sun, her prayers a soft murmur blending with the dawn chorus. "Guide me in wisdom," she would ask, feeling the weight of her years as a cloak draped softly around her shoulders, not as a burden but as a comfort.

In the evenings, she read her Bible by the light of an old lamp, her fingers gently tracing the worn pages as she absorbed the words of Christ. His teachings soothed her soul, the parables and psalms as familiar as the lines on her own hands, each one a reminder that she was not truly alone.

Sometimes, when the night was particularly still, Josephine felt as if she could hear the heartbeat of the earth itself, a vast and rhythmic pulse that connected her to every living thing. It was these moments that she cherished the most—when the veil between this world and the next seemed thin and permeable, and she could almost feel the warmth of her husband's hand in hers, could almost hear the laughter of her children echoing back to her through time.

Josephine knew her journey on this earth was nearing its end, but she was unafraid. With Jesus as her guide, she had come to understand that aging was not a march toward obscurity but a progression toward a new horizon, a different kind of beginning. As she rocked gently in her chair, watching the stars take their places in the velvet night sky, she felt a profound peace.

"Thank you," she whispered into the quiet night, a simple prayer of gratitude for the years she'd been given, for the journey still to come. Her heart was full, her spirit unbroken, and her resolve as steady as ever. In the vast expanse of existence, she was but a single point of light, yet she burned with the fire of radical acceptance and the unshakeable certainty that she was, indeed, never alone.

Christian Themes and Values

Josephine's story, woven with moments of reflection, solitude, and communion with nature and the divine, highlights several profound biblical themes that resonate through her experiences.

Presence of God: Josephine feels the presence of Jesus in her daily life, a reflection of the biblical promise that God is omnipresent and always near to those who call on Him. This is similar to Psalm 139:7-10, where the psalmist speaks of God's presence being inescapable, a comforting assurance for those who feel alone.

Peace and Solitude: The solitude that Josephine experiences is portrayed not as loneliness but as a peaceful, fulfilling presence that fills her days. This echoes Jesus' own practices as described in the Gospels, where He often withdrew to lonely places to pray (Luke 5:16), suggesting that solitude can be a profound source of strength and communion with God.

Wisdom and Aging: Josephine's prayer for guidance and wisdom in her advancing years aligns with biblical values that respect and venerate the wisdom of age. Scriptures such as Proverbs 16:31 view gray hair as a "crown of splendor" and are attained by a righteous life. Her approach to aging as a journey toward a new beginning reflects a biblical understanding that with age comes wisdom and an ever-closer relationship with the divine.

Reflection on Mortality: Her acknowledgment of nearing the end of her earthly journey with peace and not fear touches on the biblical theme that death is not an end but a transition to eternal life for believers. This is echoed in Philippians 1:21, where Paul states, "For to me, to live is Christ and to die is gain," suggesting that death brings Christians closer to Christ and eternal joy.

Communion with Nature: Josephine's connection with nature and seeing God's hand in the environment reflects the biblical theme of God's revelation through His creation. Romans 1:20 states, "For since the creation of the world God's invisible qualities—his eternal power and divine nature—have been clearly seen, being understood from what has been made, so that people are without excuse." Her communion with nature is a daily reminder of these truths.

Eternal Perspective and Hope: Finally, Josephine's nighttime reflections and her sense of being part of a larger cosmic order illustrate the biblical theme of hope and eternal perspective. It resonates with the Christian hope in Revelation 21:1-4, where a new heaven and a new earth are promised, where there will be no more death or mourning.

Josephine's experiences and reflections offer a rich tapestry of biblical themes that illustrate a life well-lived in faith, marked by a profound understanding of and peace with the cycles of life and the promise of eternal companionship with the divine. Her story is a testament to the depth of spiritual peace and assurance that faith in God can provide.

Prayer

Heavenly Father, In the midst of the chaos of this world, we seek Your peace and the solitude of Your presence. We come before You, longing to be still and know that You are God, to find rest for our souls in Your loving embrace. Grant us the grace to quiet our minds and hearts, Lord, that we may find solace in Your presence. Help us to set aside the distractions of this world and to focus our attention on You alone. May the peace of God, which transcends all understanding, guard our hearts and minds in Christ Jesus. May we experience Your presence as a constant source of strength and comfort, even in the midst of trials and challenges. In the solitude of Your presence, may we find rest for our weary souls, Lord, and may Your peace reign in our hearts forevermore. In Jesus' name, we pray. Amen.

45

Vulnerability and Faith

Carl's once formidable presence now seemed diminished, his towering stature eclipsed by the shadow of illness. For decades, he had stood as a pillar of strength in his community, revered for his wisdom and leadership. But now, faced with the harsh reality of his own mortality, Carl grappled with a profound sense of vulnerability.

As he lay in his hospice bed, Carl's thoughts turned inward, grappling with the unsettling notion of relinquishing control. The prospect of surrendering to the care of others struck at the very core of his identity, challenging his deeply ingrained sense of independence.

"I won't be cleaned and wiped like some helpless infant," he declared to his wife Barbara, his voice tinged with defiance. Yet beneath his bravado lay a wellspring of fear—a fear of losing control and agency, of relinquishing the reins of his own destiny.

In the quiet confines of his room, Carl poured out his frustrations to me, his weariness palpable in every word. Together, we navigated the turbulent waters of his spiritual struggle, seeking solace amidst the tumult of uncertainty.

Weeks turned into months, and gradually, Carl began to find acceptance in the midst of his vulnerability. Through the tender ministrations of his family and the hospice team, he discovered a profound truth—that strength lay not in the ability to stand alone, but in the willingness to lean on others in times of need.

In the gentle touch of a caregiver's hand and the compassionate gaze of a Loved one, Carl found a reflection of Divine Love—a Love that transcended the boundaries of fear and uncertainty. And in that moment of surrender, he glimpsed the presence of Jesus, walking alongside him in the midst of his frailty.

As the final chapters of Carl's life unfolded, he found peace in the embrace of community, his journey marked by moments of grace and profound connection. And though his physical strength waned, his spirit remained steadfast, anchored in the unwavering Love that surrounded him until the end.

Christian Themes and Values

Carl's journey through vulnerability and illness, and ultimately his acceptance of dependence and community support, brings to light several biblical themes that are central to the understanding of life, suffering, and grace.

Vulnerability and Strength: Carl's initial resistance to accepting help highlights the biblical theme that true strength is found in acknowledging one's weakness. This is akin to Paul's insight in 2 Corinthians 12:9-10, where God says, "My grace is sufficient for you, for my power is made perfect in weakness." Paul concludes that he will boast all the more gladly about his weaknesses, so that Christ's power may rest on him.

Surrender and Trust: Carl's struggle with surrendering control mirrors the biblical call to trust in God's plan, even when it contradicts our own desires for independence and control. Proverbs 3:5-6 advises, "Trust in the Lord with all your heart and lean not on your own understanding; in all your ways submit to him, and he will make your paths straight." Carl's eventual surrender to receiving care exemplifies this trust and submission to a plan beyond his own.

The Role of Community: The support Carl receives from his family and hospice caregivers illustrates the biblical theme of community and bearing one another's burdens, as found in Galatians 6:2, "Carry each other's burdens, and in this way, you will fulfill the law of Christ." The Christian community is called to support and uplift its members, especially in times of weakness and need.

Presence of Christ in Suffering: Carl's perception of Jesus' presence walking alongside him in his frailty ties into the promise of Emmanuel, "God with us" (Matthew 1:23), assuring believers of God's presence in every situation. This theme is crucial in comforting believers, reinforcing that they are never alone, even in the darkest moments.

Transformation through Suffering: Carl's journey from independence to accepting help and finding peace in reliance on others reflects the transformative power of suffering, a concept echoed throughout Scripture. Romans 5:3-5 speaks to suffering producing perseverance, character, and hope, a process that clearly manifests in Carl's life as he grows in character and spiritual depth through his experiences.

Divine Love and Compassion: The tender care Carl receives and his recognition of it as a reflection of divine love highlight the theme of God's love being manifest through human actions. John 13:34-35 commands believers to love one another as Christ has loved them, a mandate fulfilled in the compassionate care Carl experiences.

Carl's story is a reminder of the deep theological truths regarding human frailty, divine strength, and the power of community and compassion. It underscores the profound impact of biblical principles in real-life situations, especially at the end of life.

Prayer

Heavenly Father, In our moments of vulnerability, we turn to You, the source of our strength and our faith. We come before You with open hearts, acknowledging our weaknesses and our need for Your grace. You understand our struggles and our doubts, and You invite us to bring them to You in prayer. Help us to trust in Your faithfulness, even when we feel vulnerable and uncertain. Grant us the courage to be vulnerable before You and before others, knowing that Your power is made perfect in our weakness. Strengthen our faith, O Lord, and deepen our trust in Your promises. Help us to believe that You are working all things together for our good, even when we cannot see the outcome. May our vulnerability be a place where Your grace shines brightest, where Your love is most clearly seen. In Jesus' name, we pray. Amen.

46

Fear, Death, and Mortality

Roz lay in her bed, her eyes tracing the cracks in the ceiling, her thoughts unspooling like the delicate threads of a spider's web. I took my seat beside her, the weight of her words hanging heavily in the air between us.

"I'm not ready for death," she repeated, her voice steady but tinged with a vulnerability that cut through the silence like a knife. "And I'm especially not ready to die."

Her words echoed in the musty living room where she now slept, a stark reminder of the fragility of life and the inevitability of its end. I shifted uncomfortably in my chair, my gaze drifting downwards, searching for answers and philosophical patterns in the carpet beneath my feet.

"It's a sentiment many feel," I said, my voice breaking the heavy silence. "But you're confronting it head-on, Roz. That's something not everyone can do."

She turned to me, her eyes reflecting a mixture of fear and determination. "I don't want to leave this world," she admitted. "There's still so much I want to do, so much I want to see."

As a chaplain, I knew that my role was not to provide answers, but to bear witness to the journey of the soul. I was merely a guide, a companion on the path towards acceptance and understanding.

"Well, Roz," I said softly, leaning closer to her. "Please tell me how you feel about death and dying. It's your feelings that really matter, and it's your feelings that will be your soul guide."

Her gaze shifted from the ceiling to meet mine, her eyes filled with a quiet resolve. "I'm scared," she admitted, her voice trembling. "But I'm also ready to face whatever comes next. I don't want to leave, but I know I have to."

In that moment, I saw the bravery in Roz, the strength of her convictions shining through her fear. And as we sat together in the dimly lit room, I knew that she was prepared to confront death with courage and dignity.

Christian Themes and Values

Roz's deep contemplation of her own mortality and her struggle with the fear of death is a profound human experience that touches upon themes addressed in scripture. Roz's candid confrontation with her mortality and the existential dialogue with the chaplain evoke several biblical themes central to understanding human existence, fear, and faith:

Fear of Death and Mortality: Roz's admission, "I'm not ready for death," reflects the common human fear of death and the unknown. This fear is addressed in Hebrews 2:14-15, where it is said that Jesus shared in humanity so that by his death he might break the power of him who holds the power of death—that is, the devil—and free those who all their lives were held in slavery by their fear of death. Roz's struggle is a universal dilemma, highlighting the tension between earthly life and the afterlife.

Vulnerability and Human Frailty: Roz's vulnerability as she faces her imminent death resonates with the biblical reflections on human frailty. Psalms 90:12 asks God to "teach us to number our days, that we may gain a heart of wisdom." This plea acknowledges human fragility and the wisdom required to live life fully aware of its impermanence.

The Role of Spiritual Guidance: The chaplain's role as a listener and a guide mirrors the biblical theme of spiritual shepherding, where leaders are called to guide their flock with empathy and understanding. This is akin to the pastoral role described in 1 Peter 5:2-4, where elders are urged to shepherd the flock of God willingly and eagerly, serving as examples to the flock.

Courage and Faith in Facing Death: Roz's eventual acceptance and readiness to discuss her feelings about death illustrate the courage to face one's own mortality, a theme evident in the Apostle Paul's reflections in Philippians 1:21-23, where he expresses a conflict between desiring to depart and be with Christ, which is better by far, and staying in the flesh, which is more necessary for the sake of his followers. Roz's courage to face death echoes this complex interplay between personal desire for relief and the existential reality of death.

Acceptance and Peace: Roz's shift from fear to a quiet resolve to face death brings to mind the peace that the Bible says surpasses all understanding (Philippians 4:7). This peace comes from a deep trust in God's plan and presence, even in life's most challenging moments.

Eternal Perspective: The story subtly nudges toward the Christian hope in eternal life, as seen in John 11:25-26, where Jesus states, "I am the resurrection and the life. The one who believes in me will live, even though they die; and whoever lives by believing in me will never die." Roz's contemplative readiness suggests a move towards embracing this eternal perspective.

Roz's story is an exploration of the fears, vulnerabilities, and ultimate spiritual acceptance that many face as they contemplate the end of their earthly journey. Through her dialogue with the chaplain, we see a reflection of the biblical assurances that aim to comfort and guide believers through their most profound existential trials.

Prayer

Heavenly Father, In the face of fear, death, and the reality of our mortality, we turn to You, our rock and our refuge. We come before You with hearts heavy with the weight of our mortality and the uncertainty of what lies beyond. You are the God who conquered death through the resurrection of Your Son, Jesus Christ. We thank You for the hope of eternal life that You offer us through Him, and we cling to the promise of Your presence with us, even in the darkest of times.

Richard Gordon Zyne

Grant us the courage to face our fears, Lord, knowing that You are with us always, even in the valley of the shadow of death. Help us to trust in Your love and Your faithfulness, even when we cannot see the way ahead. May we live each day with the assurance of Your love and the hope of eternal life, Lord, knowing that You have overcome the power of death and that You hold us in the palm of Your hand. In Jesus' name, we pray. Amen.

47

Suffering and Perseverance

Ellie's husband, Irv, bore the burden of a rare neurological affliction, a cruel twist of fate that struck with the stealth of a silent predator. Progressive supranuclear palsy, they called it—a disorder so obscure, it seemed plucked from the realms of science fiction. Yet, for Irv and the select few like him, it was a grim reality, a relentless adversary that waged war on the body and the brain from within.

I knew a thing or two about PSP myself, having once managed an organization dedicated to its understanding and alleviation. We labored tirelessly, offering advocacy to those ensnared in its grasp, striving for a cure that remained elusive as ever. We spoke of its fatal nature, but in truth, life itself bore that same mark—a realization that softened our language, lest it add to the weight of the afflicted.

Irv, however, was not one to succumb to despair. Stoic and resolute, he drew strength from his Jewish faith, his God in the Burning Bush, his unwavering belief a beacon in the darkness that threatened to engulf him. With Ellie by his side, and the unwavering support of their children, he faced each day with a courage that defied comprehension.

He found solace in the ancient wisdom of the Book of Job, its tales of suffering and redemption a mirror to his own trials. But it was in the verses of Walt Whitman that he discovered true spirituality, the poet's words a balm to his weary soul.

Irv's journey was not an easy one, marked by pain and loss, but through it all, he remained steadfast in his conviction that Love, and faith would see him through. And in the end, as he succumbed to the ravages of aspiration pneumonia, it was that same Love that cradled him in his final moments, a testament to the enduring power of the human spirit.

In Irv and Ellie, I found not only inspiration but a profound lesson in the resilience of the human heart. They taught me that even in the face of unimaginable adversity, there is beauty to be found, and strength to be drawn from the bonds that unite us all.

Christian Themes and Values

Irv's journey through progressive supranuclear palsy (PSP) and the support from his wife, Ellie, showcase several significant biblical themes, which are woven into the narrative of his life and struggle.

Suffering and Perseverance: Irv's experience with PSP echoes the biblical narrative found in the Book of Job. Like Job, Irv encounters profound suffering but maintains his faith throughout his trials. Job's story is fundamentally about unwavering faith amid extreme personal loss and physical suffering, reflecting Irv's own stoic and resolute approach to his illness.

Faith Amid Adversity: Irv's steadfast belief in his Jewish faith and his reference to "God in the Burning Bush" symbolize a strong, unbreakable faith that guides him through his suffering. This parallels Moses' encounter with God through the burning bush in Exodus 3, which is a pivotal moment of divine calling and reassurance of God's presence and support. Irv's reliance on his faith provides him with a similar source of strength and perseverance.

Redemption and Hope: Just as the Book of Job explores themes of suffering and eventual redemption, Irv finds a sense of spiritual redemption through his engagement with both religious texts and poetry, particularly the works of Walt Whitman. This reflects the biblical promise of comfort and redemption through faith, which is often realized through personal revelation and spiritual exploration.

Community and Support: The unwavering support Irv receives from Ellie and their children underscores the biblical theme of community and familial bonds as sources of strength and comfort (as seen in Acts 2:42-47 where the early Christians share their lives and resources). This theme is crucial in demonstrating how the spiritual and emotional support from loved ones can significantly impact one's ability to cope with illness.

Love and the Human Spirit: The narrative highlights the power of love as a sustaining force through Irv's final moments, echoing the biblical assertion of love as the greatest of all virtues (1 Corinthians 13:13). The love shared between Irv and Ellie exemplifies how deep, committed relationships can provide profound comfort and peace, even in the face of death.

Endurance and the Promise of Legacy: Irv's journey leaves a lasting impression on the narrator, pointing to the biblical theme of legacy and enduring impact (Proverbs 13:22). The story serves as a testament to the enduring power of the human spirit, influenced by love and faith, which continues to inspire and teach even after physical life ends.

These themes provide a tapestry that illustrates how biblical principles can be lived out and witnessed in modern struggles, offering lessons of faith, resilience, and the indomitable human spirit in the face of severe adversity.

Prayer

Heavenly Father, In the midst of suffering and trials, we come before You, acknowledging our need for Your strength and grace. We confess that there are times when the weight of our burdens feels too heavy to bear, and we struggle to find hope and perseverance. You are the God who walks with us through the valley of the shadow of death, who comforts us in our affliction, and who gives us strength to persevere. We thank You for Your promise that You will never leave us nor forsake us, even in the midst of our suffering. Grant us the perseverance to endure, Lord, and the faith to trust in Your goodness and Your sovereignty. Help us to see beyond our present circumstances and to fix our eyes on the eternal glory that awaits us. May our suffering be transformed into a testimony of Your grace and Your faithfulness, Lord. May we find joy in the midst of our trials, knowing that You are at work in all things for our good. In Jesus' name, we pray. Amen.

48

Faith amidst Adversity

I never cared much for that nursing home near the library. It had a sour stench that clung to the walls, and its reputation was nothing to write home about. The turnover rate among staff was high, and there were only a handful of nurses I trusted to provide decent care. But despite all that, I couldn't turn down a call from the medical social worker to visit lonely or depressed residents.

Harriet was one of those residents. I'd seen her once before, but this time she looked worse for wear. She wasn't officially on hospice care, but her decline was evident. As part of the Eldercare Program, she had options for palliative or hospice as her condition continued to decline.

"How's your daughter?" I asked, knowing her daughter's troubled history with drugs and jail time. Harriet's response was a resigned shrug, but then she pulled out a photo of her new grandson, beaming with pride. "This is my new baby," she said, her smile genuine despite the worry etched in her eyes. "I gotta keep him safe from all that mess downtown. Chaplain, would you pray with me for his safety and health? I worry, but I know Jesus is watching over him."

We bowed our heads in prayer, and afterward, she offered me a mint from her pocket. "I feel better now," she said, and we sat in comfortable silence as the mint dissolved on my tongue. Despite the bleak surroundings, in that moment, there was a glimmer of peace—a reminder that even in the darkest corners, light can still find its way through.

Christian Themes and Values

The story of Harriet in the nursing home embodies several biblical themes that highlight the spiritual and emotional dimensions of human experience, especially in contexts of aging, illness, and familial concern.

Faith in the Midst of Adversity: Harriet's request for prayer over her grandson despite her own declining health and her daughter's troubled past reflects a deep-seated biblical theme of trusting in God's protection and provision, even in difficult times. This is akin to the faith exhibited by many biblical figures who trusted in God amidst their trials, such as Daniel in the lion's den (Daniel 6) or David during his escape from Saul (Psalms 59).

Prayer as Comfort and Connection: The act of praying together in the nursing home setting underscores the comfort and community connection that prayer can provide, a theme central to many biblical teachings. James 5:16 emphasizes the power of prayer, encouraging believers to "pray for each other so that you may be healed. The prayer of a righteous person is powerful and effective."

Generational Concern and Legacy: Harriet's concern for her grandson's well-being highlights the biblical theme of generational legacy and the desire to see one's descendants thrive and be kept safe from harm, much like Abraham's concern for his future generations in the book of Genesis.

Presence of God in Suffering: Harriet's conviction that "Jesus is watching over" her grandson even in the midst of her own and her daughter's troubles reflects the biblical reassurance of God's omnipresence and care, particularly in times of distress. Psalm 23, for example, speaks of God as a shepherd who guides and comforts in difficult times.

Light in Darkness: The narrative conclusion, where a moment of peace shines through the grim setting of the nursing home, echoes the biblical theme of light prevailing over darkness. This is a central message of the Gospel, encapsulated in John 1:5: "The light shines in the darkness, and the darkness has not overcome it."

Hope and Renewal: Harriet's simple act of sharing a mint, creating a moment of peace, symbolizes hope and renewal—key biblical themes that suggest no situation is beyond God's reach for transformation and grace.

This story captures the essence of how faith, prayer, and a hope for future generations permeate the lives of believers, offering solace and strength even in the less ideal circumstances, and demonstrating that spiritual warmth can thrive even in environments that may seem cold and uninviting.

Prayer

Heavenly Father, In the midst of adversity, we turn to You, the anchor of our faith and the source of our strength. We come before You with hearts filled with hope and trust, knowing that You are always with us, even in the darkest of times. You are our refuge and our fortress, a very present help in trouble. We thank You for the assurance of Your presence and Your promise to never leave us nor forsake us, no matter what challenges we may face. Grant us the faith to trust in Your sovereignty, Lord, even when life's circumstances seem overwhelming. Help us to believe that You are working all things together for our good and Your glory, even when we cannot see the way forward. Strengthen us in our times of trial, filling us with Your peace and Your presence. Help us to keep our eyes fixed on Jesus, the author and perfecter of our faith, and to stand firm in the promises of Your Word. May our faith shine brightly amidst the darkness of adversity, Lord, pointing others to Your love and Your grace. May we be steadfast in our trust in You, knowing that You are faithful, and Your love endures forever. In Jesus' name, we pray. Amen.

49

The Need for Sabbath and Rest

Weekends brought a welcome break from the relentless pace of hospice life. The ebb and flow of new patients and farewells to those who passed on was a ritual as predictable as the rising sun. Sandie's wife often reminded him, "Don't check your phone on Saturdays or Sundays. You're not obligated to be on call every day." She had a point, and he knew she was right—unless, of course, he was scheduled for on-call duty, a routine part of the job.

Being on call, especially on weekends, could be taxing. The anticipation of a distress call or an urgent message hung heavy in the air, a constant reminder of the fragility of life and the inevitability of death. But today, it was Sunday, and Sandie wasn't on call. So, when his phone rang, a wave of apprehension washed over him, expecting the worst.

Sandie picked up his phone, his heart sinking slightly as he saw the message. It was from the triage nurse. He opened it, fearing the worst news possible, but to his surprise, it wasn't an urgent plea for assistance. The nurse simply informed him that his patient had passed away, and they didn't require chaplain support at the moment. A pang of sadness washed over him, as it always did when he learned of a patient's passing. But there was also a subtle sense of relief—a respite from the weighty responsibility of providing comfort in the face of death.

With a heavy heart and a sigh of relief, Sandie settled onto the couch, grateful for the opportunity to unwind. He flipped on a movie, letting the familiar scenes wash over him, momentarily distracting him from the somber reality of his work. For now, at least, he could push thoughts of dying and death to the back of his mind and simply enjoy the quiet stillness of the weekend.

Christian Themes and Values

The story of the Sandie's weekend experience touches on several biblical themes that reflect the spiritual and emotional complexities of dealing with life, death, and rest:

Sabbath and Rest: The biblical theme of Sabbath rest is central to this narrative. The concept of Sabbath, a day of rest as commanded in Exodus 20:8-11, is echoed in the chaplain's experience of not being on call and attempting to rest from his laborious duties. This rest is not just physical but also emotional and spiritual, providing necessary rejuvenation for continued service.

The Inevitability of Death: The notification of a patient's death on a day off highlights the ever-present nature of mortality, a constant theme in the Scriptures. Ecclesiastes 3:1-2 posits that there is a time for everything, including a time to be born and a time to die. The chaplain's role and his reception of such news even during his downtime underscore the omnipresence of life's fleeting nature.

Emotional Resilience and Compassion: The mixed feelings of sadness and relief upon hearing of the patient's passing reflect the biblical understanding of compassion and empathy. Paul's letters often address bearing one another's burdens (Galatians 6:2) and mourning with those who mourn (Romans 12:15). The chaplain's internal conflict between personal relief and professional sadness mirrors these teachings, showing the deep emotional engagement required in his work.

Detachment and Engagement: The story also explores the theme of balance between engagement with the world's pain and necessary detachment for personal well-being. This can be paralleled with Jesus' own practice of withdrawing to solitary places to pray and restore himself (Luke 5:16), suggesting that even those who serve others need times of withdrawal for personal spiritual health.

Call to Ministry and Service: Despite being officially off-duty, the chaplain's reaction to the unexpected call demonstrates his deep commitment to his ministry, reflecting the biblical theme of dedication to one's calling.

Just as the disciples were called to leave their nets and follow Jesus (Mark 1:17-18), the chaplain is continually drawn back to his duties, even when officially off the clock.

Peace and Assurance: Lastly, the chaplain's ability to find some peace and relaxation, even amidst the realities of his profession, touches on the biblical promise of peace that surpasses all understanding (Philippians 4:7). This peace is crucial for sustaining those who work in emotionally demanding fields like hospice care.

This story weaves together these themes, presenting a realistic and compassionate picture of the challenges and spiritual dynamics faced by those in pastoral care, especially in contexts like hospice where the realities of mortality are ever-present.

Prayer

Heavenly Father, In the busyness of our lives, we come before You recognizing our need for Sabbath and rest. We acknowledge that You created us to work and to rest, to find refreshment in Your presence and to restore our souls in Your peace. Lord, You commanded us to remember the Sabbath day and keep it holy, setting aside time to rest from our labors and to focus on worshiping You. Help us to honor this commandment, Lord, and to prioritize time for Sabbath rest in our lives. Holy Spirit, guide us in our pursuit of Sabbath rest, helping us to create space in our lives for rest and rejuvenation. Fill us with Your peace and Your presence as we rest in You and help us to experience the true Sabbath rest that comes from abiding in You. May our Sabbath rest be a time of renewal and refreshment, Lord, strengthening us to face the challenges of life with faith and resilience. And may we always remember that true rest is found in You alone. In Jesus' name, we pray. Amen.

50

The Problem of Evil and Suffering

Esther's home was a modest place, filled with memories and echoes of a past scarred by the horrors of history and especially The Holocaust. When I first crossed its threshold, I felt a weight in the air—a heaviness that lingered, like a shadow cast by the ghosts of the past.

As we sat in her living room, I explained my own complex religious background, offering to connect her with a rabbi for spiritual guidance. But Esther waved off the suggestion with a dismissive shake of her head.

"Nah, I don't need a rabbi," she said, her voice tinged with a hint of bitterness. "And I'm not sure I ever will."

I nodded, sensing the underlying tension in her words. It was clear that Esther harbored a deep-seated mistrust of religious leaders, a sentiment I had encountered before in others scarred by their personal histories and experiences.

I probed gently, asking if there was something specific she wanted to discuss about her own religious upbringing or her feelings toward clergy. Her response was measured, tinged with a hint of resignation.

"I had a good rabbi once," Esther said, her gaze drifting to a photograph of her parents on the bedside table. "But he didn't last long. He was too liberal for the congregation, too outspoken about injustice. They broke his spirit, and he walked out and then died."

There was a sadness in her voice as she spoke of the rabbi who had dared to challenge the status quo. And yet, beneath the sadness, there was also a steely resolve—a refusal to be swayed by the hypocrisy of those who claimed to speak for God.

"I'm not a religious person," Esther continued, her tone firm. "And I don't believe in a God who stands idly by in the face of suffering. Where was he during the Holocaust? Where was he when we needed him most?"

It was a question that had haunted Esther for years, a question to which she had never received a satisfactory answer. And yet, despite her doubts, there was a glimmer of hope in her eyes—a hope that perhaps, one day, she might find peace in the midst of the unanswered questions.

As I left Esther's home that day, I couldn't shake the heaviness of her words—the weight of a faith tested by the trials of history. And yet, amidst the darkness, there was also a flicker of resilience—a Light of defiance that refused to be extinguished.

Christian Themes and Values

Esther's story, filled with reflections on her traumatic past and her struggles with faith and religious authority, touches on several profound biblical themes:

The Problem of Evil and Suffering: Esther's question, "Where was God during the Holocaust? Where was he when we needed him most?" echoes the biblical theme of lamentation found in books like Job and Lamentations. These scriptures explore the human struggle to understand God's presence (or perceived absence) in times of extreme suffering and injustice. This theme challenges believers to reconcile the existence of a loving, omnipotent God with the reality of human suffering.

Prophetic Justice: Esther's recollection of her progressive rabbi who was ostracized for his outspoken views aligns with the biblical prophets who often stood in opposition to their own communities, calling out injustices and advocating for righteousness. This can be seen in figures like Jeremiah and

Amos, who criticized the social injustices of their time and faced significant opposition for their messages.

Faith and Doubt: Esther's declaration that she is not religious and her doubts about God's presence in suffering reflect the biblical theme of wrestling with faith. This is akin to the story of Doubting Thomas (John 20:24-29) and other scriptural instances where figures express doubt or need reassurance about God's plans and presence.

Human Resilience and Defiance: Despite her challenging past and her disillusionment with institutional religion, Esther's story is marked by a certain resilience and a light of defiance that refuses to be extinguished. This can be compared to the resilience of biblical characters like Ruth or Esther, who, despite personal and communal crises, exhibit remarkable strength and determination.

The Search for Meaning: Esther's hope that she might one day find peace amid unanswered questions highlights the existential biblical theme of searching for meaning in life's experiences. Ecclesiastes, for instance, delves into the search for understanding and the meaning of life, ultimately finding peace in reverence for God and adherence to His commands, regardless of life's enigmas.

Unanswered Questions and Faith Journey: Esther's ongoing journey with her questions about faith without clear answers reflects the theme that faith is often a complex and personal journey rather than a destination with clear signposts. This theme is evident throughout the Bible, where individuals' relationships with God evolve in the context of their life experiences and in response to the divine mysteries they encounter.

Esther's narrative is an exploration of these themes, providing a window into the soul of someone grappling with the harshest realities of human existence while still nurturing a flicker of hope for understanding and peace.

Richard Gordon Zyne

Prayer

Heavenly Father, In the face of the problem of evil and suffering, we come before You with hearts heavy with questions and doubts. We confess that there are times when we struggle to understand why there is so much pain and suffering in the world. You are a God of love and compassion, and You deeply grieve with us in our suffering. We thank You for Your promise to be near to the brokenhearted and to comfort those who mourn. Holy Spirit, comforter of the afflicted, be with us in our times of suffering, bringing us Your peace and Your presence. Help us to cling to Your promises and to find hope in Your unfailing love. May our suffering be transformed into a testimony of Your grace and Your faithfulness, Lord. May we experience Your comfort and Your healing in the midst of our pain, and may Your name be glorified through it all. In Jesus' name, we pray. Amen.

51

Living Authentically with Regret

In the quiet of the morning, before the sun had fully declared its presence, Daniel sat on the worn wooden steps of his cabin, looking out over the water that mirrored the gray of the early sky. The lake was calm, barely a ripple disturbing its surface, yet Daniel's heart was anything but quiet.

His hands, strong and scarred from years of labor, were still now, resting on his knees. He had lived a life marked by hardships; each one weathered with a stoic acceptance that surprised even himself at times. Daniel wasn't a man of many words, preferring the solitude of his thoughts and the steady hum of nature around him.

The diagnosis had come as a quiet devastation, a silent storm that threatened to unmoor him from his life's simple rhythms. The doctor's words were clinical, detached, yet they carried a weight that pressed deep into Daniel's soul. Cancer, they said, with a timeline that felt both too slow and terrifyingly swift.

Yet, as he sat there watching the dawn creep across the water, Daniel felt an odd sense of peace. It was as if the lake itself whispered acceptance into the chilly air. He thought about his life, about the paths he had walked and the ones he had avoided. There were regrets, of course, there were always regrets. But there was also a deep, abiding sense of having lived authentically, true to the quiet internal compass he had always followed.

In his pocket, Daniel carried a small, well-worn Bible—a gift from his mother that he had never fully embraced until now. He pulled it out and opened it to a bookmarked page. The words spoke of divine love, of a light that shone even in the darkest of times. Daniel wasn't sure he had always believed in that light, but now, in the face of his own darkening path, he found comfort in the possibility.

His eyes lifted from the page to the horizon where the gray was giving way to the first hints of blue. It was a transformation, slow but relentless, the night yielding to the day. Daniel felt that same transformation within himself—a shift towards acceptance, a surrender not to the darkness but to the light that promised guidance even through the shadow of death.

He closed the Bible and stood up, his joints protesting softly. He had work to do, a day to live. There might not be as many days ahead as there were behind, but Daniel knew that each one was a gift, a precious opportunity to reflect the light he was slowly learning to see.

With a deep breath of crisp morning air, he stepped off the porch, his boots crunching on the gravel path. Each step was an act of faith, a humble acceptance of whatever lay ahead, guided not by his own strength but by a light that, once dim, now seemed to illuminate everything it touched.

Christian Themes and Values

Daniel's story, as he reflects on his life and confronts his mortality, is rich with biblical themes that resonate deeply with the spiritual journey many undertake in facing life's ultimate challenges:

Peace in Trials: Daniel's experience of finding peace despite his devastating diagnosis reflects the biblical promise of peace that surpasses all understanding, which God offers to those who are facing trials. This is highlighted in Philippians 4:7, where it is written that the peace of God, which transcends all understanding, will guard the hearts and minds of those in Christ Jesus.

The Sovereignty of God in Suffering: As Daniel contemplates the serenity of the lake and finds acceptance in his diagnosis, it reflects the biblical theme of recognizing God's sovereignty even in suffering. Job's story is particularly resonant here, as Job acknowledges God's sovereignty despite immense personal losses and suffering (Job 1:21).

Light in Darkness: The imagery of dawn breaking over the lake as Daniel reads his Bible speaks to the theme of God's light shining in darkness, a recurring motif in the Bible. John 1:5 notes, "The light shines in the darkness, and the darkness has not overcome it," suggesting hope and divine presence that persists even in the most challenging times.

Living Authentically with Regret and Acceptance: Daniel's reflection on his life, acknowledging both his regrets and his efforts to live authentically, mirrors the biblical wisdom about living a life reflective of one's beliefs and values, as seen in Ecclesiastes 12:13-14, where the conclusion of the matter after all has been heard is to fear God and keep His commandments.

Divine Guidance and Protection: Daniel's reliance on the words of the Bible during his time of trial and the comfort he derives from them illustrate the theme of divine guidance and protection. Psalms 23 is particularly relevant, portraying God as a shepherd who guides and comforts in times of difficulty.

Acceptance and Surrender: The transformation Daniel experiences from night to day, and his acceptance of each day as a gift, underscore themes of surrender and acceptance which are evident in Christ's prayer in the Garden of Gethsemane (Luke 22:42), where He submits to God's will, even in the face of death.

The Promise of Eternal Guidance: The closing scene, with Daniel embracing each day as a gift and walking in light, captures the biblical promise of eternal guidance and presence, reminiscent of Psalms 119:105, "Your word is a lamp for my feet, a light on my path."

Daniel's story is a compelling narrative of finding spiritual solace and acceptance in the face of life's inevitable end, showcasing how biblical themes can provide comfort and guidance, helping individuals navigate their darkest moments with hope and faith.

Richard Gordon Zyne

Prayer

Heavenly Father, As we come before You, we bring our regrets and mistakes, laying them at Your feet. We acknowledge that we have fallen short and made choices that we deeply regret. Yet, we trust in Your boundless mercy and grace, knowing that You offer forgiveness and redemption to all who come to You in humility and repentance. Lord, help us to live authentically with our regrets, acknowledging our failures and seeking Your guidance and strength to move forward. Grant us the courage to face our mistakes honestly, to learn from them, and to grow in wisdom and grace. Holy Spirit, guide us in living authentically with our regrets, leading us to make amends where possible and to find healing and restoration in You. Help us to trust in Your promise that You can make all things new, even the mistakes of our past. May we find freedom in Your forgiveness, Lord, and may our lives be a testament to Your grace and mercy. May we live each day with authenticity, humility, and gratitude, knowing that You are with us, guiding us, and transforming us into the likeness of Your Son. In Jesus' name, we pray. Amen.

52

Suffering and the Search for Relief

The hospital room was quiet, devoid of the usual chatter and commotion that filled its space. As I stepped inside, my eyes scanned the room, searching for the familiar sight of two patients sharing the space. But there was only one figure sitting up in bed—Toby, a middle-aged woman with a weary expression etched on her face.

I approached her bed, my footsteps echoing softly against the tiled floor. Toby glanced up at me, her gaze shifting briefly to the empty bed beside her. Without preamble, she spoke, her words tinged with a hint of indifference.

"She died this morning," Toby said matter-of-factly, her chubby fingers clutching a pillow tightly against her abdomen. "We didn't really get along, but she was sort of nice."

I nodded in affirmation, silently acknowledging the loss that hung heavy in the air. But Toby seemed unfazed by the absence of her former roommate, her attention focused on the discomfort that plagued her own body.

"Are you in any pain?" I asked, my voice gentle as I began my usual spiritual assessment. But Toby's response was blunt, tinged with bitterness.

"All the time," she replied, her smirk betraying a hint of sarcasm. "Life is just one big pain in the ass, day after day. Isn't it obvious?"

I paused, taken aback by her candidness. But Toby's words were a stark reminder of the harsh reality she faced—a reality defined by physical discomfort and emotional detachment.

"Tell me about your pain," I prompted, my tone clinical as I attempted to address her concerns. But Toby's response caught me off guard, her words laced with a raw honesty that struck a chord.

"It's in my ass, those damned hemorrhoids," she said gruffly, her tone devoid of pretense. "It's really in my ass."

In that moment, I realized that Toby's pain was more than just a metaphorical expression of her disillusionment with life. It was a tangible reality—a physical ailment that demanded attention and care.

"Let me call your nurse," I said, my voice gentle as I moved to address her needs. And as I reached for the call button, I couldn't help but feel a pang of empathy for Toby—a woman whose pain extended far beyond the confines of her hospital room.

Christian Themes and Values

The story of Toby in the hospital presents several biblical themes that can offer a deeper spiritual perspective on her experiences and reflections:

Human Suffering and the Quest for Comfort: Toby's experience with physical pain and her dismissive attitude towards her former roommate's death highlight the biblical theme of human suffering and the search for comfort. This theme is prevalent throughout the Bible, particularly in the Book of Job, where Job faces immense suffering and seeks understanding and relief from his afflictions.

Compassion and Caregiving: The chaplain's response to Toby's discomfort, and his efforts to address her needs, align with the biblical injunctions to care for the sick and suffering. This reflects Jesus' teachings on compassion and service, as seen in Matthew 25:36, where caring for the sick is portrayed as a duty of the faithful.

The Reality of Mortality and Coping Mechanisms: Toby's indifferent reaction to her roommate's death and her focus on her own physical pain illustrate how individuals cope differently with mortality and suffering.

Ecclesiastes discusses the inevitability of death and the importance of finding meaning and solace in life's realities.

Isolation and Community: The setting of Toby being alone in the room after her roommate's death can reflect the biblical theme of isolation versus community. Scriptures often emphasize the importance of community and fellowship, as seen in Hebrews 10:24-25, which encourages believers to meet together and support one another.

The Role of Faith in Facing Life's Challenges: While not explicitly discussed in this snippet, the presence of the chaplain and his readiness to help suggests the underlying theme of faith's role in providing strength and consolation in difficult times. Psalms are replete with instances of turning to God for relief from pain and distress.

Empathy and Understanding: The chaplain's empathetic approach towards Toby, despite her outward bitterness, embodies the Christian call to bear one another's burdens and to approach each other with kindness and understanding, a principle taught in Galatians 6:2.

This story, while centered on a very human and earthly scenario, touches on profound spiritual themes that resonate with the biblical understanding of suffering, care, and the human condition in the face of life's inevitable difficulties.

Prayer

Heavenly Father, In the midst of suffering and the search for relief, we come before You, recognizing that You are our refuge and our strength, a very present help in trouble. We lift up to You all who are experiencing pain, whether physical, emotional, or spiritual, and we ask for Your comfort and healing touch to be upon them. We know that You are intimately acquainted with suffering. We thank You for the promise of Your presence in our times of need and for the assurance that You will never leave us nor forsake us. Grant us the strength to endure, Lord, and the faith to trust in Your sovereign will, even when we cannot understand it. Help us to find relief in Your presence, knowing that You are with us in our suffering and that You are working all things together for our good. May Your grace abound in the midst of suffering, Lord, and may Your love be a source of comfort and strength to all who are in need. In Your name, we pray. Amen.

53

Faith in Healing

Sometimes I wish I could summon Jesus like calling for room service—just ring a bell, and he'd appear, ready to work his miracles. But it doesn't quite work like that. Instead, I find myself grappling with the complexities of faith and healing, trying to navigate the murky waters of human suffering.

There are moments when I feel the weight of my role, as if I'm expected to have all the answers, to possess the power to ease the burdens of those who come seeking solace and healing. But Jesus reminds me that the power lies within me, that I have been entrusted with the ability to perform miracles.

Yet, despite this assurance, I still struggle. I find myself yearning for tangible signs of Divine intervention, wishing for the ability to transform the ordinary into the extraordinary with a mere wave of my hand. Hey, Jesus, can you change this lousy bottle of Merlot into a fine Cabernet Sauvignon?

But Jesus gently reminds me that miracles are not conjured through magic or wishful thinking. They are born from faith, from the unwavering belief that all things are possible with God.

And so, I press on, knowing that my role is not to perform miracles, but to bear witness to them—to walk alongside my patients as they journey through their trials and tribulations, offering whatever comfort and support I can along the way.

For in the end, it is not my hands that hold the power to heal, but the grace of God working through me, guiding me as I strive to fulfill my calling with humility and compassion.

Christian Themes and Values

The story touches on several deep biblical themes related to faith, miracles, and the role of a spiritual care provider.

The Nature of Miracles: The narrator's musings on the nature of miracles reflect a central biblical theme. In the Bible, miracles often serve as signs of God's power and presence (John 2:11). The story underscores that miracles are not merely supernatural interventions but are manifestations of faith and expressions of divine will in everyday life.

The Role of Faith in Healing: The idea that "miracles are born from faith" aligns with numerous biblical narratives where Jesus heals those who show faith (Mark 5:34, where Jesus tells the woman, "Your faith has healed you"). This theme highlights the belief that faith itself is integral to witnessing and experiencing God's work in the world.

Humility and Service: The narrator's role as a caregiver who walks alongside patients, rather than as a miraculous healer, underscores the biblical values of humility and service. This is similar to Jesus' teaching in Mark 10:43-45 about servant leadership, where He explains that "whoever wants to become great among you must be your servant."

Human Limitations and Divine Power: The story illustrates the tension between human desire for control and the ultimate divine authority over miracles and healing. This reflects Paul's discourse in 2 Corinthians 12:9, where God says, "My grace is sufficient for you, for my power is made perfect in weakness," emphasizing that human limitations are an opportunity for showcasing divine power.

Persistence in Faith Amid Doubt: The narrator's internal conflict and desire for tangible signs of divine intervention echo the biblical encounters where disciples and followers of Jesus grapple with doubt and understanding (e.g., Thomas in John 20:24-29). The story portrays the journey of faith as one that involves persistence and continued trust in God's plan, despite not always seeing immediate or clear results.

Divine Guidance in Spiritual Ministry: The reminder that it is "not my hands that hold the power to heal, but the grace of God working through me" reflects a biblical understanding of divine guidance in ministry. This theme is central to Christian theology, which holds that spiritual work is ultimately empowered and directed by God, not by human effort alone.

These themes enrich the narrative, providing a nuanced reflection on the complexities of faith, the pursuit of spiritual understanding, and the humble acceptance of one's role in the divine plan of care and healing.

Prayers

Heavenly Father, We come before You with faith in Your healing power, knowing that You are the God who makes all things new. We lift up to You those who are in need of healing, whether it be physical, emotional, or spiritual, and we ask for Your divine touch to bring restoration and wholeness to their lives. Lord, we believe that You are the ultimate healer, and we trust in Your promise that by Your wounds, we are healed. Strengthen our faith, Lord, and help us to believe wholeheartedly in Your power to heal, even when circumstances seem dire. Grant wisdom and skill to those who provide medical care, Lord, and may they be instruments of Your healing grace. Lord Jesus, You went about healing all who were oppressed, and You commissioned Your disciples to do the same. We pray for Your healing touch to be upon all who are sick and suffering, and we ask for Your presence to bring comfort and strength to them and their loved ones. May our faith in Your healing power be a testimony to Your goodness and Your grace, Lord, and may Your name be glorified as we witness Your miraculous works in the lives of those who are in need. In Jesus' name, we pray. Amen.

54

Servanthood and Sacrifice

In the sacred halls of the hospice, in the bedrooms of a thousand homes, amidst the hushed whispers of pain and sorrow, there exists a silent army of angels—our nurses, aides, social workers, staff and volunteers. Day in and day out, they walk the corridors of suffering, their hearts heavy with the weight of human frailty.

With skills honed through years of experience, they tend to the needs of the dying, their hands gentle yet firm as they soothe fevered brows and administer medication to ease the ache of existence.

But their work extends beyond the physical realm. They are also the guardians of the soul, offering comfort and solace to those teetering on the brink of eternity. They listen patiently to the ramblings of the delirious and the lamentations of the grieving, their presence a balm to wounded spirits.

And yet, amidst the chaos and the despair, they remain steadfast, their resolve unshaken by the enormity of the task before them. They clean up vomit and attend to incontinence with grace and dignity, their compassion unwavering in the face of suffering.

But their burdens do not end when their shift is over. They carry with them the weight of the stories they have heard, the pain they have witnessed, and the lives they have touched. And yet, they return each day, ready to face whatever challenges lie ahead.

So let us not forget to honor these unsung heroes, to recognize the sacrifices they make and the love they give. Let us offer them our gratitude, our support, and our respect. And let us never underestimate the importance of a dozen donuts in the break room, a kind word, or a moment of recognition for those who walk the path of compassion in the darkest of times.

Christian Themes and Values

The narrative encapsulates several profound biblical themes related to service, compassion, and the human condition:

Servanthood and Sacrifice: The role of nurses, aides, and other staff as caregivers who serve tirelessly mirrors the biblical call to servanthood. Jesus Christ exemplifies this in the Gospel of Mark 10:45, where He states, "For even the Son of Man did not come to be served, but to serve, and to give His life as a ransom for many." The selflessness and dedication of these caregivers reflect this core Christian principle of serving others, especially those in need.

The Good Samaritan: The story parallels the parable of the Good Samaritan (Luke 10:25-37), where care is given without reservation to a stranger. Like the Samaritan who tends to the wounded man without hesitation, hospice workers provide compassionate care across all barriers, embodying this scriptural call to love and assist those who are suffering.

Bearing One Another's Burdens: The caregivers in the story not only address physical needs but also engage deeply with emotional and spiritual pain, reflecting Galatians 6:2: "Carry each other's burdens, and in this way, you will fulfill the law of Christ." Their work involves empathetic engagement with the emotional states of their patients, embodying this biblical injunction through their daily actions.

Compassion and Mercy: The continual return of these workers to their challenging roles highlights the biblical theme of mercy and relentless compassion. Lamentations 3:22-23 speaks to God's mercies never ceasing, being renewed every morning, much like the daily renewal of commitment by these caregivers despite the hardships they face.

Light in Darkness: The presence of caregivers as a source of comfort and solace in the darkest times of life reflects the biblical imagery of light in darkness (John 1:5 - "The light shines in the darkness, and the darkness has not overcome it"). Their role in alleviating suffering and providing support in the final moments of life showcases how human actions can bring light to the darkest situations.

Recognition and Reward: The call to acknowledge and honor the work of these silent heroes resonates with Matthew 25:40, where Jesus says, "Truly I tell you, whatever you did for one of the least of these brothers and sisters of mine, you did for me." Recognizing and appreciating the hard work of caregivers is akin to honoring Christ Himself, as they serve the most vulnerable and needy in society.

This story highlights how the principles taught in the Bible about compassion, service, and humanity are lived out through the daily acts of dedicated hospice workers, making them modern-day embodiments of these timeless truths.

Prayer

Heavenly Father, We come before You with hearts open to Your call of servanthood and sacrifice. We recognize that You have called us to follow the example of Jesus Christ, who came not to be served, but to serve. Lord, help us to embrace the call to servanthood, to put the needs of others before our own, and to serve with humility and love. Grant us the grace to follow in the footsteps of Jesus, who washed the feet of His disciples and laid down His life for the sake of others. Teach us to see the opportunities for service that You place before us each day, Lord, and give us the courage to act upon them. May we be willing to sacrifice our time, our resources, and even our comfort for the sake of Your kingdom and the well-being of others. Holy Spirit, empower us to serve with joy and enthusiasm, knowing that our labor is not in vain in the Lord. Fill us with Your love and Your grace, and guide us in the ways of true servanthood. May our lives be a living sacrifice, Lord, pleasing and acceptable to You, as we seek to serve others in Your name. And may Your kingdom come and Your will be done on earth as it is in heaven. In Jesus' name, we pray. Amen.

55

God's Timing and Sovereignty

David slouched in his frayed armchair, evening shadows stretching like long fingers across the room. At ninety-four, he wore his years like a heavy overcoat, each ache and pain a reminder of a life well-lived but worn thin.

"I pray every night that God will take me in my sleep," he muttered, his voice worn but resolute. His eyes, clouded with age, held a glimmer of longing for peace, for release from the burdens of existence.

"Why in your sleep?" I asked, intrigued.

"Because at least I'll be lying down," he replied, a bitter edge to his laughter. David had grown tired of doctors, medicines, and the ceaseless cycle of treatments that offered little respite from time's relentless march.

"I'm through with it all," he declared, defiance ringing in his voice. "I'll never step foot in that hospital again. It's all a racket, you know."

His words poured out like a flood, decades of frustrations and disappointments bubbling to the surface. He cursed insurance companies, government red tape, and the cruel passage of years that had stolen his vitality.

But amid his tirade, there was a glimmer of vulnerability, a crack in his armor of bravado. "Sometimes I feel like a foolish old man," he confessed, barely above a whisper.

I nodded, offering a sympathetic smile. "But God still loves you," I said, trying to offer solace in the gathering gloom. "And maybe, just maybe, He's not quite ready for you in heaven yet."

David's eyes met mine, gratitude shining in their depths. "Thank you for listening," he murmured, emotion thick in his voice.

As I offered him communion, a simple gesture of grace amidst his weariness, I marveled at the resilience of the human spirit, even as it weathered life's inevitable storms.

Christian Themes and Values

This story about David and his reflections on life and death, tinged with humor and frustration, draws upon several biblical themes:

Longing for Eternal Rest: David's wish to be taken in his sleep reflects the biblical theme of rest in the afterlife. In the Bible, death for the believer is often depicted as a peaceful transition to eternal rest, a concept illustrated in Revelation 14:13, where it is said, "Blessed are the dead who die in the Lord from now on... they will rest from their labor."

Weary of Earthly Life: David's weariness and his disdain for the continuous cycle of medical treatments echo the biblical perspective of earthly life's fleeting and often painful nature, as seen in Ecclesiastes 12:1-7, which discusses the hardships of old age and the inevitability of returning to dust.

God's Timing and Sovereignty: David's reflection on whether God is ready for him yet touches on themes of divine sovereignty and timing. This is akin to biblical narratives where the timing of events, especially death, is portrayed as being in God's control, not ours, as Psalm 31:15 states: "My times are in your hands."

The Value and Dignity of Old Age: The story also highlights the value and dignity of old age, which the Bible upholds as a time of wisdom and honor. Proverbs 16:31 declares, "Gray hair is a crown of splendor; it is attained in the way of righteousness."

Frustration with Earthly Systems: David's frustration with healthcare systems and bureaucracy reflects a broader biblical theme of the imperfections of earthly governance and institutions, contrasted with the perfect justice and righteousness of God's kingdom, as found in Revelation 21:4, where God promises a future without pain, sorrow, or suffering.

Presence and Comfort of God: Lastly, the chaplain's reassurance of God's love and the act of offering communion are reminders of God's continual presence and comfort in times of distress, reflecting promises found throughout scriptures like Matthew 28:20, "And surely I am with you always, to the very end of the age."

These themes interweave to form a narrative that not only addresses the hardships and realities of aging but also offers a biblical perspective on enduring faith and the comfort available through spiritual support and the promise of eternal life.

Prayer

Heavenly Father, We come before You with hearts that trust in Your timing and Your sovereignty. We acknowledge that Your ways are higher than our ways, and Your timing is perfect, even when we cannot understand it. Help us to surrender our plans and desires to You, trusting that Your timing is always best. Grant us the patience to wait on You, knowing that You are always working behind the scenes for our good and Your glory. Teach us to trust in Your sovereignty, Lord, even when circumstances seem uncertain or overwhelming. Help us to believe that You are in control of all things and that nothing can happen apart from Your will. May we find peace in Your sovereignty, Lord, and may Your timing be our timing as we surrender our lives to You. In every season and circumstance, may Your will be done on earth as it is in heaven. In Jesus' name, we pray. Amen.

56

Life, Aging and Grace

Pat reclined on her worn-out couch, Herman the cat nestled beside her, a makeshift cooler filled with soda cans perched on the side table. With a deft twist, she popped open a can and took a sip, the fizz tickling her throat as she reminisced about her old habits.

"I used to mix this stuff with whiskey or rum," she remarked, a hint of nostalgia in her voice.

"Sounds like quite the concoction," I replied, offering a wry smile. "But maybe just the whiskey straight is the healthier option."

Pat chuckled, a raspy sound that echoed through the room. "Yeah, maybe. But these days, even this stuff makes me choke sometimes. Can't swallow like I used to. Can't chew like I used to. Can't crap like I used to. You get the picture."

I nodded, understanding her sentiment. Aging had a way of humbling even the strongest of us.

Suddenly, Pat turned to me with a question that caught me off guard. "What's your favorite Bible verse?"

I paused, considering her question. "Well, I don't know if I have a favorite, but one that's always resonated with me is 2 Corinthians 12:9. 'My grace is sufficient for you.' It's a reminder that I don't have to carry the weight of the world on my shoulders, that I can lean on God's grace when I'm feeling weak."

Pat's eyes softened, a glimmer of recognition flickering within them. "I like that," she murmured. "I wish I had known about God's grace years ago, when I was too busy running from it."

With a quiet reverence, she bowed her head and offered a simple prayer,

203

thanking Jesus for the grace she had finally come to understand. And as the afternoon sun filled the room in a warm glow, I couldn't help but feel a sense of peace settle over us, like a gentle embrace from above.

Christian Themes and Values

The story of Pat and her reflections on life, aging, and grace contains several biblical themes that resonate deeply with Christian teachings.

Transformation and Redemption: Pat's reflection on her past lifestyle and her acknowledgment of how she has moved away from harmful habits is emblematic of the biblical theme of transformation and redemption. This is seen in scriptures like 2 Corinthians 5:17, which states, "Therefore, if anyone is in Christ, he is a new creation. The old has passed away; behold, the new has come."

Grace: The theme of grace is central to the conversation, particularly when the chaplain quotes 2 Corinthians 12:9 ("My grace is sufficient for you, for my power is made perfect in weakness"). This highlights the concept of divine grace as a sustaining force, emphasizing that God's support is available not because of what individuals deserve but because of His generous nature.

Aging and Human Frailty: Pat's candid remarks about the physical challenges of aging reflect the biblical understanding of human frailty. The Bible often discusses the ephemeral nature of human life and the physical decline that comes with aging, as seen in Ecclesiastes 12:1-7, which poetically describes the realities of growing old.

Spiritual Awakening: Pat's expression of wishing she had understood God's grace earlier in life points to a theme of spiritual awakening. This theme is often explored in the Bible, where individuals come to a deeper understanding or recommitment to faith later in life. Luke 15:11-32, the Parable of the Prodigal Son, is a clear example of how individuals can return to faith and be warmly received.

Prayer and Connection to God: The story concludes with Pat praying, an act that signifies her personal connection to God and her acceptance of His grace. Prayer as a theme is ubiquitous in the Bible, highlighted as a means for individuals to communicate directly with God, express gratitude, and seek guidance.

Peace and Divine Presence: The final note of peace that settles over the scene as Pat prays is reflective of the biblical promise of peace that surpasses all understanding (Philippians 4:7), which believers may experience through their faith and trust in God.

These themes collectively paint a picture of spiritual maturity, the ongoing relevance of faith throughout one's life, and the comforting role that divine grace plays in human existence, especially as one confronts the inevitable challenges of aging.

Prayer

Heavenly Father, In the journey of life, as we age and face the passing of time, grant us the grace to embrace each moment with faith and hope. Help us to see the beauty in every stage of life, knowing that each season is a gift from You. As our bodies grow weary and our minds may falter, may Your strength sustain us and Your love surround us. Let us find solace in Your promises, trusting that Your plans for us are always good. Grant us wisdom to cherish the memories of our youth, the experiences of our middle years, and the lessons learned in our older age. Help us to pass on our wisdom and faith to those who come after us, leaving a legacy of love and grace. Guide us, O Lord, as we walk through the twilight years of our lives. May we shine with the light of Your love, reflecting Your glory to the world around us. In Jesus' name we pray, Amen.

57

Independence and Reliance

Susan sat in her worn armchair, her fragile frame trembling as she adjusted the cannula that tethered her to the oxygen tank beside her. Each labored breath seemed to echo the weight of her suffering, and I couldn't help but feel a pang of sympathy for her plight.

"COPD is a bitch," she muttered, her voice strained as she struggled for air. "Feels like I'm drowning on dry land."

I watched helplessly as she grappled with her illness, her hands shaking as she fidgeted with the tubing. It was clear that she was in pain, both physically and emotionally.

Summoning the nurse, I waited anxiously as they made adjustments to Susan's oxygen levels, hoping to bring her some measure of relief. Her son, Joe, arrived soon after, his concern etched deeply into the lines of his face.

Joe was Susan's rock, her protector, but his attempts to convince her to move into an assisted living facility fell on deaf ears. Stubborn as ever, Susan refused to relinquish her independence, even as her health continued to decline.

But Joe knew that living alone was no longer an option, and he made the difficult decision to move her into one of the area's top facilities. It was a move born out of Love, albeit tinged with frustration and desperation.

As Susan tearfully voiced her desire to simply end her suffering, I promised to work with her nurse and social worker to ensure her comfort and dignity in the days ahead. We held hands in prayer, seeking peace and comfort in the belief that God's plan, however mysterious, would guide us through the darkness.

In the end, Susan's decline was swift, but in the quiet halls of the assisted living facility, she found a measure of peace. And as she slipped away, I couldn't help but believe that she had finally found her place in the grand design of things, her faith unwavering in the face of life's most challenging trials.

Christian Themes and Values

The story of Susan deals with several profound biblical themes that are woven into the narrative of her struggle with chronic illness and her journey toward the end of life.

Suffering and Comfort: Susan's experience with COPD and her description of feeling like she's "drowning on dry land" evoke biblical discussions of suffering, such as those found in the Book of Job, where the protagonist endures great physical and emotional pain. The Bible often addresses suffering not just as a trial but also as a conduit for divine comfort and mercy (2 Corinthians 1:3-4).

Independence vs. Reliance: Susan's resistance to giving up her independence reflects a human desire to maintain control over one's life, which is contrasted in the Bible with the call to depend not solely on oneself but also on God and the community of believers for support and strength (Galatians 6:2).

The Role of Family and Love: Joe's dedication to his mother and his struggle to make the best decisions for her care illustrate the biblical mandate to honor and care for one's parents (Exodus 20:12). His actions are driven by love and responsibility, themes central to Christian ethics.

End-of-Life Ethics and Dignity: Susan's expression of wanting to end her suffering touches on the biblical respect for life but also introduces the complexity of preserving dignity in suffering. Christianity often grapples with these issues, emphasizing compassionate care and the sanctity of life while also recognizing the profound challenges posed by terminal illnesses.

Prayer and Divine Guidance: The scene where they hold hands and pray together highlights the comfort and guidance sought through prayer, which is a central practice in Christianity for seeking peace and understanding God's will, especially in times of crisis (Philippians 4:6-7).

Peace in Faith: Susan's peaceful passing in the facility, surrounded by care and comfort, aligns with the Christian hope and belief in a peaceful transition to eternity, where there is no more suffering or pain (Revelation 21:4).

These themes collectively explore the intersections of faith, the human condition, and the trials of life and death, providing a deep reflection on how spirituality can provide meaning and comfort even in the most difficult circumstances.

Prayer

Heavenly Father, As we navigate the journey of life, grant us the wisdom to understand the balance between independence and reliance on You. Help us to embrace the independence You have given us, while recognizing that our true strength comes from depending on Your grace and guidance. Give us the courage to take bold steps, to pursue our dreams, and to use the gifts and talents You have bestowed upon us for Your glory. May we walk confidently in the paths You have set before us, trusting in Your provision and protection. Help us to surrender our pride and self-sufficiency at Your feet, knowing that Your strength is made perfect in our weakness. May we find freedom in relying on Your unfailing love and grace, knowing that You are always with us, guiding us through every trial and triumph. In Jesus' name we pray, Amen.

58

Guidance and Providence

Olivia stood on the edge of the dock; her gaze lost in the expanse of the vast bay stretching infinitely before her. The early morning mist still clung to the water, making the horizon appear as if it were an endless merging of sky and sea. The chilly air was filled with the briny scent of the sea, mixed with the faint smell of the old wood under her feet.

Her father had been a fisherman on the bay, and Olivia had spent countless mornings like this one, watching him disappear into the dawn. Now, years after his small boat had been anchored for the last time, she came here seeking a connection not just to him but to something greater, something eternal that she felt in the vastness before her.

Today was different, though. Today, Olivia carried with her more than the memory of her father; she carried a decision that felt as heavy as the ocean itself. The university in the city had offered her a scholarship, a gateway to a world far from the sleepy coastal town she called home on the eastern shore. It was everything she had worked for, everything she thought she wanted.

As she watched the first rays of sunlight pierce through the mist, Olivia thought about the prayer she had whispered last night, a plea for guidance and insight, a hope that she could carry the essence of her small town—the closeness, the simplicity, the divine presence she felt in every wave and whisper of wind—with her into this new life.

The sun climbed higher, and the mist began to lift, slowly revealing the dark outline of a small boat making its way toward the shore. It was Joe, the fisherman who had taken her father's place. Olivia watched as he skillfully navigated the swells, his figure steady and sure against the shifting sea.

In that moment, Olivia felt a surge of something powerful and profound—an anticipation not of leaving, but of returning. She realized that no matter how far she traveled, the essence of this place, the deep, unspoken understanding of life's ebbs and flows, would always be with her. She was not leaving her home; she was extending its boundaries, carrying its truths with her.

The boat reached the dock, and Joe nodded to her, a silent acknowledgment of the journey ahead. Olivia stepped forward, her heart full of gratitude and resolve. She understood now that her spirituality, her connection to the divine, wasn't tied to one place or one moment; it was a part of her, as vast and profound as the sea before her.

With a deep breath of salty air, Olivia felt ready. She was ready to navigate the complexities of a new life, grounded in the wisdom that the divine essence is everywhere, permeating all things. And with this realization, she felt a lightness, a clarity that she carried with her as she turned from the pier and walked towards her future.

Christian Themes and Values

The story of Olivia contains several deep biblical themes. These themes collectively paint a picture of a life lived in awareness of and reliance on divine guidance, the importance of community and origin, and the eternal perspective that faith provides, navigating life's changes with a spiritually grounded understanding of one's path and purpose.

Guidance and Providence: Olivia seeks guidance through prayer, reflecting biblical teachings on seeking divine direction in times of decision (Proverbs 3:5-6). Her contemplation at the pier symbolizes a moment of seeking God's will, akin to many biblical figures who sought God's guidance in critical life moments.

Faith and Trust in God: Olivia's trust in feeling a connection to something greater—something eternal—echoes the biblical theme of faith in an unseen, omnipresent God who guides and sustains through life's journeys (Hebrews 11:1).

Stewardship and Calling: The scholarship and the decision to move to the city represent a calling for Olivia, a chance to use her talents and opportunities wisely, as encouraged in biblical teachings (1 Peter 4:10). Her decision-making process shows her stewardship of her own life's path.

Sense of Belonging and Community: The closeness and simplicity of life in her coastal town, and her desire to carry these qualities with her, underscore the biblical theme of community and belonging, which are central to Christian teachings about the Church as a community of believers (Acts 2:42-47).

Continuity and Change: Olivia's realization that she carries her home and its values with her wherever she goes speaks to the biblical understanding of continuity amidst change. This theme is often illustrated in the Bible through the journey of the Israelites, carrying their faith and practices with them even in exile.

Eternal Perspective: Olivia's connection to the vastness of the ocean and the divine presence she feels therein reflect an eternal perspective, recognizing God's omnipresence and the deeper spiritual reality that underpins physical existence (Romans 1:20).

Return and Renewal: Olivia's anticipation of returning, even as she leaves, reflects the biblical theme of renewal and the promise of return, akin to the prodigal son's journey (Luke 15:11-32). Her story is one of leaving to grow and returning enriched, a cycle of renewal that reflects spiritual growth and maturity.

Prayer

Heavenly Father, In the complexities of life, we often find ourselves in need of guidance and reassurance. We come before You now, seeking Your wisdom and Providence to light our path and lead us forward. Grant us, O Lord, the discernment to recognize Your voice amidst the noise of the world. Help us to listen attentively to Your gentle whispers, guiding us in the way we should go. May Your Word be a lamp to our feet and a light to our path, illuminating the way ahead. As we journey through life, may Your hand be upon us, directing our steps and shaping our destinies according to Your perfect will. Let us not lean on our own understanding, but in all our ways acknowledge You, knowing that You will make our paths straight. In Your mercy and grace, we place our lives, our hopes, and our futures. Guide us, protect us, and lead us ever closer to Your heart. In Jesus' name we pray, Amen.

59

Gifts and the Use of Talents

Frankie, with his weathered hands, held the clarinet as if it were an extension of his very being. His fingers, once nimble and deft, now moved with a certain hesitancy, a testament to the passage of time and the toll of age and disease.

He had been a musician, once upon a time, his clarinet a vessel through which he poured his soul into the rhythms of jazz. They said he played like Benny Goodman but looked like Jimmy Durante. His melodies weaving through the air with a grace and elegance that belied his humble beginnings.

But fame and fortune eluded him, slipping through his fingers like sand, and Frankie found himself back in his hometown, his dreams of stardom replaced by the mundane rhythms of everyday life.

Yet, even as the years passed, and his wife Selma died, and his memory began to fade, there was one thing that remained constant: his Love for music. Despite the encroaching fog of Alzheimer's, Frankie could still conjure a few melodies of his youth, his fingers dancing up and down the keys with a familiarity born of a lifetime of practice. He Loved Artie Shaw's Begin the Beguine and it still sounded smooth and clear.

And so it was that I found myself drawn to his bedside, a silent witness to the magic of his music. We shared moments of communion, both spiritual and musical, finding joy in the melodies that transcended the boundaries of time and space.

For Frankie, music was more than just a hobby; it was a lifeline, a tether to a past that threatened to slip away into the abyss of forgotten memories. And in those fleeting moments of clarity, when the notes flowed effortlessly from his fingertips, I saw the essence of his soul laid bare, a testament to the enduring power of art to uplift and inspire.

As I watched him play, I couldn't help but marvel at the resilience of the human spirit, the way it could find beauty and joy even in the face of decline and adversity. And in Frankie's music, I found a glimpse of something sacred, a reminder that, no matter how dark the night may seem, there is always a melody waiting to be heard, a song of hope and redemption echoing through the corridors of our souls.

Christian Themes and Values

The story of Frankie and his clarinet intertwines several biblical themes, illustrating the profound nature of human life, the persistence of gifts and passions, and the transcendent power of music, which are reminiscent of many spiritual messages found throughout the Bible.

The Gift and Use of Talents: Frankie's life as a musician highlights the biblical theme of using one's talents for joy and fulfillment, akin to the parable of the talents (Matthew 25:14-30), where individuals are encouraged to use their gifts wisely and not waste them.

Endurance and Perseverance: Despite the setbacks in his career and personal life, Frankie's continuation to play music, even as Alzheimer's takes hold, underscores the theme of perseverance through trials, as found in James 1:12, which praises those who persevere under trial.

Memory and Identity: The story reflects on the nature of memory and identity, particularly how Frankie clings to his identity as a musician even as his other memories fade. This resonates with the biblical understanding of personal identity being anchored in something greater than earthly experiences and achievements—found in the idea that humans are created in the image of God (Genesis 1:27) and have inherent value.

Solace and Comfort in Suffering: The comfort Frankie derives from music in his declining years speaks to the biblical theme of finding solace in God's gifts during times of suffering. This mirrors the Psalms, where music is often a refuge and a means to communicate with the divine (Psalm 71:22-23).

The Power of Art to Transcend: The transcendent quality of music, which reaches beyond Frankie's cognitive decline, illustrates the biblical theme of eternal truths being expressed through earthly means. This is similar to Jesus' use of parables to convey spiritual truths through everyday stories and objects.

Legacy and Continuity: Frankie's continued engagement with music is a testament to the enduring impact of one's life work and passions, resonating with the idea that what we create and how we influence others can have lasting effects beyond our physical presence, akin to the biblical theme of a spiritual legacy (2 Timothy 4:7).

Redemption and Hope: The notion that there is always a melody waiting to be heard, even in the darkest times, mirrors the biblical message of redemption and hope—that no matter the trials, there is always the promise of renewal and salvation available (Romans 8:24-25).

Overall, Frankie's story is a reminder of the beauty and complexity of human life, the resilience of the spirit, and the profound connections between our earthly experiences and our spiritual beliefs.

Prayer

Heavenly Father, You are the giver of every good and perfect gift, and we come before You with hearts full of gratitude for the talents and abilities You have bestowed upon us. Help us, Lord, to recognize these gifts as blessings from Your hand, entrusted to us for Your glory and the benefit of others. Grant us the wisdom to steward these gifts faithfully, using them to serve You and build up Your kingdom here on earth. May we not hide our talents out of fear or selfishness, but instead, may we invest them boldly and creatively, knowing that You have equipped us for every good work. Lord, show us how to multiply our talents for Your kingdom, just as the faithful servants did in the parable. May we be diligent and faithful stewards, eagerly anticipating the day when we hear Your voice saying, "Well done, good and faithful servant." In His name we pray, Amen.

60

Remembrance and Joy

Arnold sat in his modest living room, his haggard appearance telling the story of his struggles. His thin frame was wrapped in oversized clothing, a physical testament to the weight of his illness. Despite this, there was a warmth in his smile as he welcomed me, offering a cup of instant coffee with a gesture of hospitality.

Perched on his threadbare couch, I listened as Arnold poured out his frustrations, his voice a mixture of anger and resignation. He lamented the passing of time and cursed the complexities of modern life. Butch, his grizzled canine companion, lay beside him, offering silent companionship, his wet nose nudging my hand.

Amidst the cacophony of Arnold's complaints, there was a moment of tranquility—a glimpse into the past when life was simpler, and joy was easier to find. He spoke fondly of Sarah, his late wife, and their adventures in Baltimore. Together, they had savored the sights of the Inner Harbor and relished the taste of fresh crabs.

As the evening wore on, I offered a silent prayer for Arnold, a plea for comfort and strength in the face of his struggles. With a heavy heart, I said my goodbyes, unsure of what the future held but finding solace in the belief that God alone held the answers to life's mysteries.

"Take care, Arnold," I said, my voice soft with empathy.

He nodded, a tired smile on his lips. "Thanks, Richard. And thanks for listening."

I squeezed his hand gently before making my way out into the fading light of evening, Butch's tail thumping softly against the floor in farewell.

Christian Themes and Values

The story of Arnold and his struggles with illness and change, punctuated by moments of reflection on happier times, incorporates several biblical themes that resonate with core spiritual messages:

Hospitality and Community: Arnold's gesture of offering coffee, despite his own hardships, echoes the biblical call to hospitality and caring for one's neighbor, as seen in Hebrews 13:2, "Do not forget to show hospitality to strangers, for by so doing some people have shown hospitality to angels without knowing it."

The Burden of Suffering: Arnold's physical and emotional weight reflects the biblical theme of human suffering and the endurance required to face life's challenges. This is similar to the message in 2 Corinthians 12:9, where Paul discusses strength in weakness through God's grace.

Companionship and Comfort: The presence of Butch, Arnold's dog, as a source of comfort and companionship, highlights the biblical theme of God's provision of companionship in our times of need, reminiscent of God's statement in Genesis 2:18 that "It is not good for the man to be alone."

Remembrance and Joy: Arnold's recollection of good times with his late wife, Sarah, ties into the biblical theme of remembering past blessings as a source of comfort during trials, as suggested in Lamentations 3:21-23, which speaks about recalling to mind and therefore having hope.

Faith and Uncertainty: Arnold's story concludes on a note of uncertainty but also faith, aligning with the biblical acknowledgment that life is often unpredictable and beyond human understanding, but trust in God provides a grounding force. This theme is echoed in Proverbs 3:5-6, which advises trusting in the Lord rather than one's own understanding.

Prayer and Intercession: The chaplain's silent prayer for Arnold highlights the theme of intercessory prayer and the power of spiritual intervention on behalf of others, which is a key aspect of Christian practice as encouraged in 1 Timothy 2:1, urging that "requests, prayers, intercession, and thanksgiving be made for all people."

These themes collectively illustrate the complex interplay between human frailty and spiritual resilience, showcasing how biblical teachings can provide comfort and guidance in navigating the vicissitudes of life.

Prayer

Heavenly Father, As we gather before You, we remember Your faithfulness throughout the ages. You have been our Rock, our Redeemer, and our constant source of joy. We thank You for the countless blessings You have bestowed upon us, both big and small, and for the gift of Jesus Christ, who brings us eternal hope and joy. In the midst of our busy lives, help us to pause and reflect on Your goodness. May we remember Your mighty acts of salvation, Your unfailing love, and Your constant presence in our lives. As we recall Your faithfulness, fill our hearts with gratitude and joy that transcends our circumstances. Help us, Lord, to spread Your joy to those around us, sharing Your love and grace with a world in need. May our lives be a testament to Your goodness, drawing others into relationship with You. In Jesus' name we pray, Amen.

61

Simple Presence and the Ministry of Comfort

Entering the room was stepping into a battlefield of emotions. No playbook, no rehearsed lines—just raw humanity laid bare. Sue and Fran stood by their brother Paul's bedside, their faces etched with lines of pain and their eyes weary with resignation. Machines beeped in a relentless symphony of life and death. Yet amidst the chaos, a silent plea for connection lingered in the air.

I approached with measured steps, a silent observer in their world of suffering. There were no words, no platitudes to offer. Only presence—my silent witness to their struggle.

Sue's shoulders sagged as she reached out to adjust the blanket over Paul's frail form. "He's so weak," she whispered, her voice thick with tears.

Fran nodded; her hand clasped tightly around Sue's. "I don't know how much longer he can hold on," she murmured, her voice trembling with fear.

I stood beside them, offering a gentle squeeze of support. There was no need for words; the weight of their worry hung heavy in the air.

In the quiet of the room, amidst the whirlwind of emotions, we forged a connection—a bond born of shared humanity. And as I left, I carried with me their stories, their pain, their hopes—etched forever in my memory.

Outside the room, Sue turned to me, her eyes brimming with tears. "Thank you for being here, Richard," she said, her voice barely above a whisper.

I offered her a weak smile, my own heart heavy with the weight of their suffering. "Of course, Sue. We're all here for Paul and the family."

Fran joined us, her expression a mix of exhaustion and determination. "We have to stay strong for Paul," she said, her voice trembling with emotion.

Together, we stood in the hospital corridor, our silent solidarity a beacon of hope in the darkness of uncertainty. And as we parted ways, each of us carried a piece of the other's burden, united in our shared journey through the storm.

Christian Themes and Values

The story of the chaplain's encounter in a hospital room, rich with emotional and spiritual complexity, reflects several profound biblical themes.

Presence and Ministry of Comfort: The chaplain's presence, serving as a silent witness to suffering, embodies the biblical theme of comfort in times of distress. This mirrors the promise found in 2 Corinthians 1:3-4, where God is described as the "Father of compassion and the God of all comfort, who comforts us in all our troubles." The chaplain's role is akin to that of a comforting presence, similar to how the Holy Spirit is described as the Comforter or Advocate in John 14:16.

Shared Humanity and Bearing Burdens: The shared connection and understanding that transcends words between the chaplain and the patients align with Galatians 6:2, "Carry each other's burdens, and in this way you will fulfill the law of Christ." The act of bearing witness to the patients' struggles reflects the Christian call to empathize with and support others in their pain.

The Power of Silent Support: The effectiveness of the chaplain's silent presence highlights the biblical theme of supporting others not always with words but through being there — reminiscent of the story of Job's friends who initially sat with him in silence, sharing in his suffering without speech (Job 2:13).

Human Fragility and Divine Strength: The scene vividly illustrates human fragility, a central theme in many biblical passages that discuss human life's transitory nature and the need for divine strength. Psalms 103:15-16 talks about how man's days are like grass, and 2 Corinthians 12:9 emphasizes that God's power is made perfect in weakness, resonating with the story's depiction of human vulnerability and the spiritual strength derived from shared empathy.

Reflection and Memory: The chaplain carrying away the stories, pain, and hopes of the patients ties into the biblical importance of remembering and reflecting upon human experiences and God's role within them. Just as the Israelites were often reminded to remember the acts of God and their own history, the chaplain retains these encounters as part of their spiritual and emotional journey, which can be seen as a form of bearing witness or testimony.

These themes collectively suggest a deeply spiritual encounter where the chaplain's simple, quiet presence brings a measure of peace and connection to those enduring great pain, illustrating how biblical principles of compassion, presence, and shared humanity are vital in ministry and caregiving contexts.

Prayer

Heavenly Father, In the midst of life's storms and struggles, we find solace in Your simple presence. You are our refuge and strength, a constant source of comfort and peace. We thank You for the ministry of comfort You provide, comforting us in our times of need and guiding us through the darkest valleys. Lord, help us to recognize Your presence in the simple moments of life – in the warmth of a gentle breeze, in the beauty of a sunrise, and in the quiet moments of solitude. May we find comfort in knowing that You are always with us, holding us close in Your loving embrace. Lord, in times of grief and loss, may Your comforting presence be like a gentle balm to our souls, soothing our hearts and bringing us peace that surpasses all understanding. We thank You, Father, for Your unwavering love and for the comfort You provide in every season of life. May Your presence be our constant refuge, and may we share Your comfort with others, shining Your light in the darkness. In Jesus' name we pray, Amen.

62

Servant Leadership

Jake, an old friend of mine from my days in clinical pastoral education, truly practiced the art of compassionate care, the kind that went beyond mere religious words, and fully demonstrated empathy as he delved deeply into the hearts of suffering patients. He was always somewhat of a hero of mine; a model to follow and to learn from. His skill set had been honed over years of service, a response born from his own experiences of loss and grief.

As he made his way through the wards, Jake couldn't help but notice the harried expressions of the doctors and nurses he passed. They moved with urgency, their focus on tasks at hand, but he could sense the weight of their burden, the toll that caring for the sick and dying took on their spirits.

It was then that Jake realized the potential for chaplains and to play a more active role in teaching compassionate care to other healthcare professionals. He saw himself as a bridge, a role model who could show them the way to navigate the emotional complexities of their work.

In the quiet moments between patient visits, Jake regularly began to reach out to his colleagues, offering a listening ear and a gentle word of encouragement. He shared stories of his own experiences, illustrating the power of compassionate care to bring healing and comfort in the face of suffering.

Slowly but surely, Jake's efforts began to bear fruit. He noticed a shift in the atmosphere of the nursing home where he worked, a softening of hearts and a deepening of connections among staff and patients alike. The once frenetic pace began to slow—just a bit—replaced by a sense of calm and purpose.

As Jake continued his work, he knew that the impact of compassionate care extended far beyond the walls of the nursing home. It was a ripple effect, spreading out into the world and touching the lives of all those in need. And in that simple truth, Jake found even more purpose and direction in his calling.

Christian Themes and Values

Jake's story as a chaplain in a healthcare setting resonates with multiple biblical themes that underscore the essence of Christian ministry and compassionate care.

Servant Leadership: Jake embodies the concept of servant leadership, a theme central to the teachings of Jesus Christ. In Mark 10:45, Jesus explains, "For even the Son of Man did not come to be served, but to serve," which Jake mirrors through his commitment to serving both patients and healthcare staff with empathy and compassion.

The Good Samaritan: Jake's approach to compassionate care reflects the parable of the Good Samaritan (Luke 10:25-37), where care and assistance are provided across traditional boundaries. Jake acts as a neighbor to those in need, not only through direct pastoral care but also by educating and nurturing a spirit of compassion among the healthcare professionals.

Bearing One Another's Burdens: Galatians 6:2 instructs believers to "bear one another's burdens, and so fulfill the law of Christ." Jake's efforts to ease the emotional load of the healthcare staff and improve their ability to offer empathetic care align with this directive.

The Ripple Effect of Good Works: The impact of Jake's compassionate actions demonstrates the biblical principle found in Matthew 5:16: "Let your light shine before others, that they may see your good deeds and glorify your Father in heaven." His work not only improves the immediate environment but also serves as an example that influences the broader community.

Spiritual Sustenance and Renewal: Jake's role and the deepening connections he fosters at the nursing home reflect Isaiah 40:31, where it is said, "But those who hope in the Lord will renew their strength. They will soar on wings like eagles; they will run and not grow weary; they will walk and not faint." This theme highlights the rejuvenating power of spiritual support in challenging environments.

Through these actions, Jake's story illustrates how biblical principles can be applied to enhance the care provided in healthcare settings, emphasizing the importance of empathy, servant leadership, and community in Christian theology. His life exemplifies the powerful impact that one individual, guided by faith and compassion, can have on a community, fulfilling the Christian call to service and love.

Prayer

Heavenly Father, You have called us to follow the example of Your Son, Jesus Christ, who came not to be served, but to serve. Teach us, Lord, the true meaning of servant leadership – to lead with humility, compassion, and selflessness. Help us to see leadership as a sacred trust, a responsibility to steward Your gifts and talents for the benefit of others. Give us the heart of a servant, willing to put the needs of others before our own, and to serve with love and grace in all that we do. Grant us wisdom to lead with integrity and courage, standing firm in Your truth and righteousness. May we be guided by Your Holy Spirit, following Your will and seeking Your glory above all else. In Jesus' name we pray, Amen.

63

Bearing Burdens

In the realm of the chaplain's duties, the spotlight often strays from the patient and falls instead upon the family—the silent witnesses to the suffering, the bearers of their own burdens. Theirs is a quiet anguish, a burden borne in the shadow of illness and uncertainty.

It's a familiar refrain—the estranged son, the fractured relationship, the weight of regret and unspoken apologies. Words hang heavy in the air, laden with the weight of missed opportunities and unresolved conflicts. "I haven't seen Peter in years," they lament, the bitterness of past grievances still fresh in their minds. "We had a falling out," they confess, the wounds of the past reopening with each passing day.

For Wanda, the burden of caring for her ailing husband, Gregory, weighed heavily upon her shoulders. Her days were spent in a haze of regret, remorse, and guilt, each passing moment a reminder of her perceived failures. The strain of her responsibilities drove her to the brink of despair, prompting her to flee in search of healing, only to find herself consumed by anger and guilt upon her return.

In moments of desperation, the chaplain and social worker offered a lifeline—a glimmer of hope amidst the darkness. Together, they forged connections to support services and therapists, providing Wanda with the tools she needed to navigate the treacherous waters of her emotions.

Through it all, the chaplain remained a steadfast presence, offering guidance and solace in the face of uncertainty. With gentle words and a compassionate ear, they helped Wanda rediscover a semblance of peace, guiding her back to the faith she had once known.

In the end, there may be no easy answers or swift resolutions, but for Wanda, there is a path forward—a beacon of hope amidst the turmoil. And though the road ahead may be fraught with challenges, she walks it with newfound strength, supported by the unwavering presence of those who stand by her side.

Christian Themes and Values

The story of Wanda and her journey through her husband Gregory's illness highlights several biblical themes that resonate deeply with Christian teachings and the chaplaincy's role in providing spiritual and emotional support.

Bearing Burdens: This theme is central to Christian teachings, particularly reflected in Galatians 6:2, "Bear one another's burdens, and so fulfill the law of Christ." The chaplain's role in supporting Wanda underscores the biblical call to help lighten the loads of others through empathy and action.

Forgiveness and Reconciliation: The story touches on themes of unresolved conflicts and the need for forgiveness, reminiscent of Matthew 5:24, "Leave your gift there before the altar and go; first be reconciled to your brother, and then come and offer your gift." The narrative suggests a journey towards forgiveness and healing, both within oneself and in relationships with others.

Restoration and Healing: The assistance provided to Wanda by the chaplain and social worker reflects the biblical promise of restoration found in Psalm 23, "He restores my soul." This theme is vital as it points to the hope and renewal available through faith and community support, even during life's darkest times.

Compassion and Loving Kindness: Demonstrated through the chaplain's unwavering support and patient listening, these values echo the teachings of Jesus about loving one's neighbor as oneself, as found in Mark 12:3 The chaplain's actions embody this commandment, showing deep care for the emotional and spiritual well-being of the family.

The Peace of God: As Wanda begins to find peace amidst turmoil, it reflects Philippians 4:7, "And the peace of God, which surpasses all understanding, will guard your hearts and your minds in Christ Jesus." This peace is portrayed as a transformative force that helps individuals cope with the challenges they face.

Through these themes, the story illustrates the complex interplay of faith, forgiveness, and the human condition within the context of illness and family dynamics. It highlights the chaplain's role not just in addressing the needs of the patient but also in supporting the family members, who are often in need of as much care and guidance as the patient themselves.

Prayer

Heavenly Father, You have called us to bear one another's burdens, just as Jesus Christ, bore the weight of our sins on the cross. We come before You, Lord, recognizing the heavy burdens that weigh upon us and those around us. Grant us the strength and compassion to carry the burdens of others with love and grace. Help us to be a source of comfort and support to those who are struggling, offering a shoulder to lean on and a listening ear to hear their cries. Lord, we lift up to You all who are carrying heavy burdens today – those who are overwhelmed by grief, burdened by illness, or weighed down by worries and fears. May Your presence bring them comfort and peace, and may Your strength sustain them in their time of need. Teach us to bear one another's burdens not out of obligation, but out of genuine love and concern for our brothers and sisters. Help us to share in their struggles, to intercede for them in prayer, and to walk alongside them with compassion and empathy. Give us the wisdom to know when to offer help and when to simply be present, trusting in Your grace to guide us in every situation. May our love for one another reflect Your love for us, shining brightly in a world filled with darkness and despair. In Jesus' name we pray, Amen.

64

Endurance and Hope

Thomas and I sat on the back porch, the kind of place where the evening light stretches long over the fields and the world seems to pause for a breath. He'd been quiet for a good while, watching the sun dip below the horizon, his hands wrapped around a cup of coffee that had gone cold hours ago.

"I do believe that illness, for good or bad, transforms us," he said finally, breaking the silence with a certain gravity in his voice. There was an assurance there, born of facing something you can't outrun.

Thomas shifted in his chair, his body frail but his eyes still sharp, burning with a mixture of determination and resignation. "We're not here on this earth to be like turnips." He chuckled softly, a sound that seemed to hold more sorrow than humor. "God wants us to change, and if we don't do it ourselves, He will make it happen."

He leaned forward, pressing his hands firmly on his Bible, which lay open on his lap, worn pages fluttering slightly in the evening breeze. "I know I'm on the road to the cross," he continued, his voice steady, his fingers tracing the edges of the paper as if drawing strength from the words written there.

Thomas looked up at me, his face etched with lines of pain and wisdom. "Terminal illness can do special things to people," he said, and I sensed the depth of his own journey in those words. "I guess at some point in our lives we all go through that period where terminal illness will transform us whether we want it or not, and no matter how or what we believe."

A spasm of pain flickered across his face, and he clenched his jaw tight, eyes closing for a moment. "Oh, God, it's painful," he murmured, and when he opened his eyes again, they were moist but fierce.

I knew he was in pain, the kind that weaves itself into your bones—the kind that's a combination of physical, emotional, and spiritual, all rolled up into one consuming fire.

"And there you are," he continued, his voice dropping to a whisper as he stared off into the fading light, "on your own personal road to the Cross, looking out for someone to give you a little water while all the while you know that when you get there your feet will be all bloody and you won't have the energy to look up to where you think God might be."

We sat together in silence; the only sound was the rustling of the leaves and the distant call of a night bird. The darkness settled around us like a blanket, thick and soft.

In that moment, sitting beside a man confronting his final journey, I felt a profound shift—a stark and powerful reminder of our fragility and our strength. Thomas's journey was his own, but in his words, I saw the universal path we all walk in one form or another, the transformation that comes, invited or not.

As the first stars appeared in the night sky, I understood a little more about what it meant to be transformed, to be broken and rebuilt, to walk a road marked by shadows but headed towards something that might just be light.

Christian Themes and Values

The story of Thomas confronting his terminal illness while reflecting on his spiritual journey embodies several profound biblical themes, especially those found in Christian teachings about suffering, transformation, and redemption:

Transformation Through Suffering: Thomas's belief that illness transforms us echoes the themes that suffering can lead to personal growth and spiritual deepening, similar to the refining fire described in 1 Peter

1:6-This scripture speaks of suffering as a test of faith that, though painful, results in praise, glory, and honor.

The Road to the Cross: Thomas explicitly references his own suffering as a journey on "the road to the cross," drawing a direct parallel to Jesus' journey to Golgotha. This imagery is rich in Christian theology, symbolizing the idea of bearing one's cross (Luke 14:27), which suggests enduring suffering or challenges with the faith and courage exemplified by Jesus.

Redemptive Suffering: The notion that Thomas's terminal illness could have a purpose or result in a profound spiritual state reflects the theme of redemptive suffering found in the Bible. This theme is often associated with the belief that suffering can bring us closer to God and is a key element of many Christian interpretations of the Passion of Christ.

Compassion and Support in Suffering: The desire for companionship and support in his suffering ("looking out for someone to give you a little water") resonates with the Christian call to compassion and service to others, as Jesus showed in his ministry, especially in moments of others' need (Matthew 25:35-40).

Endurance and Hope: Despite the pain and hardship, Thomas's story is tinged with an undercurrent of hope—a central tenet of Christian faith. His journey reflects the biblical promise that those who endure will be rewarded and that there is a greater purpose and hope beyond the present suffering (Romans 5:3-5).

Encounter with the Divine in Suffering: Thomas's reflection on the nature of God and the human condition in the face of terminal illness touches on the mysterious ways in which people encounter and wrestle with the divine presence during times of extreme hardship, reminiscent of Job's experiences.

This narrative captures the essence of Christian beliefs surrounding the meaning and purpose of suffering, the redemptive potential of pain, and the profound journey of faith that often accompanies life's most challenging moments.

Prayer

Heavenly Father, In the midst of trials and tribulations, You are our steadfast hope and refuge. We come before You, seeking Your strength and endurance to persevere through the challenges we face. Lord, grant us the endurance to run the race set before us with perseverance, keeping our eyes fixed on Jesus, the author and perfecter of our faith. When we grow weary and faint-hearted, renew our strength and empower us to press on, knowing that You are with us every step of the way. Lord, we lift up to You all who are facing trials and hardships – those who are battling illness, grieving loss, or feeling overwhelmed by life's challenges. May Your presence bring them comfort and peace, and may Your hope sustain them in their time of need. Teach us, O Lord, to find joy in the midst of suffering, knowing that our trials produce endurance, and endurance produces character, and character produces hope. Help us to trust in Your plan and to believe that You will bring beauty from ashes. In Jesus' name we pray, Amen.

65

Sacrificial Love

The season was changing, a steady rain falling outside Ruth's hospice room as if the sky itself were trying to wash away the pain of those within. The room smelled faintly of antiseptic and flowers—a futile attempt to mask the starker scents of illness and decline. Ruth lay in her bed, a thin blanket pulled up to her chin, a smile playing around the edges of her mouth as she listened to her nephew, Chuck, talk about his future.

Ruth was a good mother, or so everyone said. She had raised Chuck almost as her own after his parents passed away early, pouring into him all the aspirations she had once held for herself. Chuck was now graduating college, and his anticipation was a bright flame in the dim light of the room.

"I guess my oncologist just wants to torture me a little more so that I can come back on hospice care and then really die," Ruth joked, her voice light but her eyes reflecting the weight of her reality. She was tired, her body frail but her spirit still flickering strong.

Chuck smiled, though his heart ached with the kind of pain only partially softened by the routine of impending loss. "Maybe I'll even get my doctorate in nursing practice, and then you'll have to call me Doctor."

Ruth's laugh was weak but genuine. "I'll call you doctor any time you want."

Ruth had been in hospice care before, the previous year, and had rallied unexpectedly. For a short while, she had fooled herself and everyone else into thinking the beast inside her was retreating. But cancer is often a cruel monster, and now it had returned with a vengeance, spreading its dark fingers deep into her bones.

This time, she wasn't thinking about leaving hospice. She had accepted the end was near, the conversations with her doctors more about comfort than cure. The morphine and other painkillers were constants by her bedside, close companions in her final journey.

"I really want to see him graduate, march down the aisle, and receive that wonderful diploma... and then go and insert a Foley catheter in some old lady," she said with a chuckle, her humor untouched by her ordeal.

Chuck held her hand, feeling the delicate bones beneath the skin, a stark contrast to the strength it had once wielded. "You'll see it, Aunt Ruth. I promise." His voice was thick, his own battle against despair not as successful as he would have liked.

The day of Chuck's graduation came. Ruth was too weak to attend, but the hospice arranged for a live Zoom feed in her room. Chuck, in his cap and gown, found the camera before the ceremony began and waved, blowing a kiss in her direction. Ruth watched from her bed, morphine in a syringe, but her mind was sharp, her heart swollen with pride.

When Chuck's name was called, and he walked across the stage to collect his diploma, Ruth's room was silent except for the soft sobbing of joy from an old woman who had been a mother, a friend, a mentor.

"You see, my dear, you've done it. Doctor Chuck," she whispered to the empty room, a tear rolling down her cheek.

Days later, when Chuck returned, diploma in hand, he found Ruth quieter, her body finally succumbing to the relentless tide of her disease. He sat by her bed; the diploma placed where she could see it.

"Doctor Chuck," she murmured, her voice a fading echo of the life she had once lived so vibrantly.

"Yes, Aunt Ruth. Thanks," he replied, squeezing her hand gently.

Ruth smiled, her eyes slowly closing, her breaths shallow but peaceful. Outside, the rain had stopped, the clouds parting as if in deference to the quiet dignity of her passing. In the clean, fresh air after the storm, the world seemed to pause, holding its breath for a woman who had changed the life of at least one young man forever.

Christian Themes and Values

The story of Ruth and Chuck unfolds with several profound Biblical themes, deeply resonant with Christian teachings on suffering, hope, caregiving, and the cyclical nature of life and death.

Suffering and Redemption: Ruth's experience with terminal cancer reflects the Biblical perspective on suffering—not as a meaningless ordeal but as a part of the human condition that can lead to spiritual growth and deeper relationships. Her suffering allows her to impart final lessons of love and strength to Chuck, reminiscent of how Biblical figures often gain insight or redemption through their trials.

Sacrificial Love: Ruth's dedication to raising Chuck after his parents' death echoes the Biblical theme of sacrificial love, similar to that of Christ's. She puts his needs and future before her own, sacrificing her aspirations to ensure he has opportunities, paralleling the scriptural call to love others selflessly.

Hope Amidst Despair: Even as Ruth faces the inevitability of her death, she maintains a sense of humor and hope—particularly in her desire to see Chuck graduate. This hope amidst despair mirrors the Christian belief in the resurrection and the hope of eternal life, offering comfort and motivation even in the darkest times.

Faith and Acceptance: Ruth's acceptance of her impending death, coupled with her faith in seeing Chuck's success, demonstrates a deep biblical theme of trusting in God's plan. Her acceptance resonates with the idea that faith involves surrendering to God's will, finding peace even when the path is fraught with pain.

Legacy and Influence: The impact Ruth has on Chuck's life highlights the Biblical theme of legacy—how one's faith and actions reverberate beyond their own life. Like the spiritual legacies left by Biblical patriarchs and matriarchs, Ruth's teachings and love live on in Chuck's accomplishments and character.

Communion and Community: The support from the hospice staff in setting up a Zoom feed for Ruth to witness Chuck's graduation underscores the theme of community in Christianity. The communal support reflects the Biblical call to bear one another's burdens and to celebrate each other's successes, emphasizing that no one should face life's greatest challenges alone.

Transition and Eternity: Ruth's passing after achieving her last earthly desire to see Chuck graduate symbolizes the transition from earthly existence to eternal life, a central Christian belief. Her peaceful departure, set against the backdrop of a clearing storm, metaphorically suggests the Christian hope of heaven—a place free from pain and suffering.

Through these themes, the story not only portrays the challenges and beauties of human life but also intertwines them with deep spiritual truths about the nature of suffering, the power of love, and the eternal impact of our lives on others.

Prayer

Heavenly Father, Your love for us is sacrificial and boundless. Teach us, Lord, to love one another with the same sacrificial love that You have shown us. Help us to lay down our own desires, ambitions, and comforts for the sake of others. May we be willing to sacrifice our time, resources, and even our own lives, if necessary, to demonstrate Your love to those around us. Lord, forgive us for the times when we have been selfish and self-centered, thinking only of our own needs and desires. Fill us with Your Spirit, that we may have the same attitude of humility and selflessness that was in Christ Jesus. Show us, O Lord, the opportunities to love sacrificially in our daily lives – to serve the poor, to comfort the grieving, to uplift the oppressed, and to share the gospel with those who are lost. May our actions be a reflection of Your love, drawing others to You. Help us to love even those who may not deserve it, just as You have loved us while we were still sinners. May our sacrificial love be a testimony to Your grace and mercy, shining as a light in a world filled with darkness. In Jesus' name we pray, Amen.

66

Acceptance of Mortality

The chaplain made his rounds with a list folded neatly in his pocket. It was a quiet morning, the kind where the sunlight seemed to pause respectfully at the windows of the hospice wing. When he stepped into Dory's room, she greeted him with a brightness in her eyes that belied her nearly one hundred years.

"Nice to meet you, chaplain," Dory said with a raspy but spirited voice. "I hear you have a great bedside manner and a very calming style. You do have a soft voice, but you might have to talk a little louder. I'm very hard of hearing."

The chaplain smiled, moved his chair closer, and complied, raising his voice just enough for comfort. "How are you feeling today, Dory?"

"Oh, about as well as one can at my age," Dory chuckled. "I'm almost a century old, can you believe it? It doesn't really matter, though. I'm ready for the Lord anytime, but" her eyes twinkled mischievously, "I wouldn't mind making it to a hundred. Just to round things out nicely, you know?"

The chaplain nodded, finding himself drawn into the warmth of her spirit. "So, a big birthday coming up. Any special plans?"

Dory shrugged, a gentle pull at the corner of her mouth. "I suppose they'll throw some sort of party here. Cake, maybe some music. That'd be nice. But it's all the same to me. I'm just passing the time until the Good Lord decides it's time to go."

They talked about Dory's life, wandering through memories like they were pages of an old, well-loved book. She spoke of her father and mother, victims of the 1919 flu, and her friends and brothers who returned from the Great War, only to find a different kind of battle waiting at home.

237

"It's strange, isn't it?" Dory mused. "How life throws these things at us. Now there's this Covid thing. Makes you wonder."

The chaplain listened, nodding, his presence a steady calm. He did not venture into theology or philosophy, merely companionship and an open ear. As the conversation lulled, a question, simple yet deep, seemed right.

"What kind of frosting would you like on your birthday cake?"

Dory laughed, a clear, ringing sound that filled the room. "Oh, chaplain, you do ask the important questions. Chocolate. It's got to be chocolate. Nothing beats that."

"I'll make sure they know," the chaplain promised, his words etching a pact between them.

As he stood to leave, Dory held his gaze, her voice softening. "Thank you, chaplain. For the talk, and for listening to an old lady ramble."

"Anytime, Dory. And it's never rambling. It's your story, and it's been a privilege to hear it."

Stepping out into the hallway, the chaplain felt the weight and the lightness of his role intertwine. Each room held a story, each person a journey. In Dory's case, it was a journey nearly a century in the making, marked by a clarity and readiness for whatever came next, but still with room for a slice of chocolate cake. It was, after all, these small joys that often made the grand story of life feel complete.

Christian Themes and Values

The story featuring the chaplain and Dory touches on several Biblical themes that resonate deeply within the Christian tradition.

Acceptance of Mortality and Hope in Resurrection: Dory's readiness to meet the Lord anytime reflects a profound acceptance of mortality, a central theme in Christianity which emphasizes the transient nature of earthly life and the hope of eternal life. This belief is rooted in Scriptures such as John

11:25-26 where Jesus speaks about the resurrection and the life, promising eternal life to those who believe in Him.

Value of Each Individual Life: The chaplain's visit and his attentive listening to Dory's stories underscore the Biblical principle of the inherent value and dignity of each individual life, as seen in Psalm 139:13-16, where it is said that God formed each person uniquely in the womb. The chaplain treating Dory's life history as a precious narrative reflects this sanctity attributed to individual lives.

Community and Companionship: The interaction between Dory and the chaplain highlights the Christian theme of fellowship and community as vital components of spiritual life. In Hebrews 10:24-25, believers are encouraged to meet together and encourage one another. The chaplain's role as a listener and his pastoral presence exemplifies the pastoral care aimed at nurturing spiritual fellowship and emotional support.

Joy and Contentment in Simplicity: Dory's anticipation of simple pleasures, like her birthday cake with chocolate frosting, echoes the Biblical encouragement to find contentment and joy in life's simple blessings (Philippians 4:11-13). This theme is often highlighted to show that while life can be challenging and complex, there is profound joy to be found in simple, everyday moments.

Endurance and Faith Through Trials: Dory's reflection on her life, including personal losses and global crises like the flu pandemic and wars, resonates with the Biblical theme of enduring faith through trials. James 1:12 praises those who persevere under trial, promising the crown of life to those who have stood the test.

Servant Leadership: The chaplain's gentle and attentive approach to his pastoral duties embodies the Biblical theme of servant leadership, as modeled by Jesus in passages like Mark 10:44-45, where true greatness comes through serving others. His role as a caregiver who prioritizes listening and responding to needs showcases the Christian call to serve one another in love (Galatians 5:13).

Overall, the story encapsulates these themes within a modern setting, offering a reflective glimpse into how Biblical principles might manifest in everyday interactions and the pastoral ministry within a community care context.

Prayer

Heavenly Father, You are the Alpha and the Omega, the beginning and the end. In Your wisdom, You have ordained the seasons of life, including our mortality. Grant us, Lord, the grace to accept the reality of our mortality and to live each day in light of eternity. Help us to remember that our time on this earth is but a fleeting moment compared to the eternity we will spend with You. May we use the time You have given us wisely, seeking to glorify You in all that we do and to fulfill the purposes You have for us. Lord, in the face of our mortality, give us a deep sense of peace and assurance in the hope of resurrection and eternal life. May we find comfort in knowing that death has been defeated, and that for those who have faith in You, death is not the end but a doorway to eternal joy in Your presence. Lord, as we face the reality of our mortality, deepen our faith and strengthen our trust in You. May we live with confidence, knowing that nothing can separate us from Your love, not even death itself. In Jesus' name we pray, Amen.

67

The Nature of Spiritual Warfare

In the hospital's behavioral unit, the walls carried a clinical sterility that could not entirely cleanse the air of its burdened past. It was a place reimaged through the years, softened in name from the stark 'psychiatric ward' to something less severe, more inclusive of the diverse conditions its corridors held: depression, dementia, substance abuse, disorders spanning the frail spectrums of the human mind.

I, as the chaplain, navigated these halls not with the sharp toolkit of medicine but with a softer, subtler craft aimed at the spirit. Here, spiritual ailments overlaid neurological and psychiatric complexities. It was an intricate dance, often as perplexing as the medical diagnoses that filled the thick folders in the nurses' station.

I preferred not to review patient charts before meetings. Fresh encounters, I believed, allowed a more genuine connection, unhindered by preconceptions. Yet, this method, while pure in intention, sometimes led me unexpectedly deep into the thorny thickets of human suffering and belief.

Julianna was one such complexity. A young Catholic woman, her face etched with the sort of weariness that spoke of battles more internal than most could fathom, she declared herself possessed. "You're the chaplain, I'm possessed, and you need to perform an exorcism," she said with a conviction that was both disturbing and heart-wrenchingly sincere.

Images from old horror films flickered unbidden into my mind, scenes of ordained men battling the supernatural, a cinematic spectacle ill-suited to the reality of our sterile, fluorescent-lit setting. I explained gently, "I'm not a Catholic priest, Julianna. I don't have the training or authority to perform an exorcism."

She looked at me, eyes searching for either contradiction or confirmation of her fears. "But I've been saved," she insisted. "Shouldn't that protect me?"

"It does," I assured her, my voice calm, attempting to anchor her to a safer, more rational shore. "If you've embraced Christ, then you are shielded by that grace. No demon can hold power over you."

Our conversation dwindled; her initial fire quelled into contemplation. Perhaps she was weighing my words, or perhaps, as I sometimes suspected with patients harboring deep internal chaos, she was merely adapting her strategy for the next engagement.

I left her room with a soft thanks and a promise to return if she wished to talk more. In the quiet of the hallway, the echo of our conversation lingered with me as I made my way to document the encounter.

Later, recounting the visit to my supervisor, a rabbi with an ample reservoir of wisdom and humor, he chuckled at the theatricality of it all. "Good job," he said, his laughter not mocking but understanding. "Go back tomorrow; I have a few more demons for you to deal with."

His jest, though light, carried the truth. Each day here was a confrontation with demons of a sort, not those of biblical lore, but the myriad torments and disorders that plagued the human mind. My role was less about casting out spirits than about offering presence, a listening ear, and perhaps, a path back to a peace that felt spiritually cleansing in its own secular, sacred way.

Christian Themes and Values

The story of the chaplain's experience in the behavioral unit of a hospital brings forth several Biblical themes that reflect the intersection of faith, mental health, and spiritual care. Here are some key Biblical themes highlighted in the narrative:

The Nature of Spiritual Warfare: The story delves into the concept of spiritual warfare, a theme found in scriptures such as Ephesians 6:12, which speaks of battling against spiritual forces of evil. Julianna's belief in being possessed and the chaplain's assurance of her protection in Christ illustrates the tension between perceived spiritual attacks and the protective shield of faith.

Compassion and Pastoral Care: The chaplain's approach to Julianna and other patients highlights the Biblical call for compassion and care for the suffering, reflecting Jesus' ministry to those in distress (Matthew 9:36). His decision to meet patients without preconceptions emphasizes a non-judgmental, compassionate approach, resonating with the Christian imperative to "bear one another's burdens" (Galatians 6:2).

Healing and Restoration: The interactions in the hospital underscore the theme of healing, a central element of Jesus' ministry on earth (e.g., Matthew 4:23-24). The chaplain's role is less about miraculous interventions and more about facilitating mental and spiritual healing through presence, listening, and offering reassurance of divine grace.

The Power of Faith: Julianna's assertion that she has been saved and should therefore be protected from demonic influences highlights the theme of salvation and its protective power, as outlined in scriptures like Romans 8:37-39, which assure believers that nothing can separate them from the love of God in Christ Jesus. The chaplain reinforces this by affirming her shielded status through her faith.

The Reality of Human Struggle and the Presence of Hope: The chaplain's encounter with Julianna and the broader context of the behavioral unit speak to the human condition's complexity and the struggles inherent in mental health challenges. This aligns with Biblical reflections on human suffering and the hope offered through faith (Psalm 34:18, which states that the Lord is close to the brokenhearted).

Interfaith Respect and Collaboration: The chaplain recounts his experience to a rabbi, his supervisor, suggesting a theme of interfaith understanding and cooperation. This reflects a broader Biblical theme of peace and respect among different peoples, reminiscent of the call to peace and unity found in passages like Romans 12:16.

Overall, the chaplain's experience in the behavioral unit illustrates how Biblical themes can be woven into the fabric of modern spiritual care, emphasizing compassion, healing, faith, and the constant presence of hope amid human suffering.

Prayer

Heavenly Father, We come before You aware of the spiritual battle that surrounds us. We recognize that our struggle is not against flesh and blood, but against the spiritual forces of darkness in the heavenly realms. Grant us, Lord, the strength and courage to stand firm in the face of this warfare. Help us to be vigilant and alert, always watching and praying, so that we may not fall into temptation. Give us discernment to recognize the enemy's tactics and the wisdom to resist his lies and deceptions. Lord, we lift up to You those who are engaged in spiritual warfare, whether they are battling personal struggles, oppression, or persecution. Strengthen them, Lord, and surround them with Your angels to protect and defend them. May Your light shine brightly in the darkness, dispelling every shadow of fear and doubt. May Your truth prevail over every lie, and Your love conquer every evil intent. Lord, we know that victory belongs to You, for You have already overcome the world. Help us to walk in the confidence of Your victory, knowing that nothing can separate us from Your love and that in You, we are more than conquerors. In Jesus' name we pray, Amen.

68

The Presence of God in Everyday Life

In the small, cluttered room where the outside world insisted on being heard, Joyce found her sanctuary. The constant hum of city life—the shouting of children at play, the harsh grumble of trucks, and the intermittent wail of sirens—filled her apartment like a cacophonous symphony. It was music to her, each sound a reminder that life, in its chaotic beauty, still surged on just beyond her reach.

When I visited Joyce, stepping into her room felt like entering a different realm—one punctuated by the incessant chatter of a television and the static-laced tunes from an old radio, both fighting to drown out the world outside. Joyce, confined to her bed, her body a map of the relentless progression of illness, seemed like an island in the middle of this storm of sounds.

Her hands, once so skilled at the piano, now lay restlessly beside her, occasionally fluttering like the wings of a caged bird. The rosary beads she'd spin on her fingers were more a toy than a tool for prayer now.

"I'm just too tired to think about Jesus," she had confessed on one quiet afternoon, her voice a whisper lost beneath the room's din. Her gaze had drifted to the window, to the glimpse of street where children's laughter rose above the urban roar.

The first few times I sat with her; the noise was unbearable. I strained to hear her soft voice, to offer words of comfort that stumbled awkwardly between us. But she didn't seem to need words, her eyes often fixed on something unseen, a private reverie amidst the tumult.

Gradually, I began to understand. The sounds that filled Joyce's room were not just white noise; they were her lifelines, essential vibrations filling her remaining days. The noises told her that the world was still there, vibrant and alive, that children still played, and people still moved, and life, in all its messy glory, persisted.

As the weeks passed, I learned to sit quietly beside her, the din no longer a barrier but a bridge. I listened, truly listened, to the jazz of the streets, the unscripted laughter of children playing—it was here I found the essence of prayer, which Joyce no longer chased. In the purity of these moments, in the sacred space of shared silence punctuated by life's chorus, I found a profound communion.

One afternoon, as the room bathed in the golden hue of a setting sun, the noises seemed to soften around us, as though the world outside acknowledged the sanctity of our silence. Joyce's breath was shallow, her eyes closed gently, a soft smile curving her lips. There were no words needed, no prayers whispered. The presence of life, in all its forms, was prayer enough.

In the quiet that followed, I understood. Sometimes, the most profound acts of love are not found in the words we speak but, in the willingness, to simply be—to sit beside another in their noise and listen to the world with them. Here, in the jumble of Joyce's last days, I learned that sometimes the greatest comfort we can offer is to just be present, to allow the world outside to speak the prayers our hearts can no longer form.

Christian Themes and Values

This narrative of the chaplain's visits with Joyce in her final day's weaves together several profound Biblical themes. Here are the key elements that are reflected in the story.

The Presence of God in Everyday Life: The story suggests that even in the bustling sounds of the city and the quieter chaos of Joyce's room, there is a manifestation of life that transcends the physical. This reflects the Biblical theme that God can be found in all aspects of life, not just in quiet, traditionally "holy" places (Acts 17:28 - "For in him we live and move and have our being.").

Peace and Comfort in God's Presence: Joyce's environment, though chaotic, provides her with a sense of connection to the living world, much like the peace that believers find in God's presence. This aligns with Philippians 4:7, which talks about the peace of God transcending understanding, guarding hearts and minds.

Value of Human Life and Dignity: Joyce's room, her illness, and her cherished connection to the outside world, despite her physical limitations, underscore the inherent value and dignity of every human life—a central theme in the Bible (Genesis 1:27 - "So God created mankind in his own image...").

Communion and Fellowship: The shared silence and attentive presence of the chaplain beside Joyce illustrate the Biblical principle of communion and fellowship with others. This resonates with passages such as Matthew 18:20 ("For where two or three gather in my name, there am I with them.").

The Ministry of Presence: The chaplain learns that ministry is not always about active speaking or doing; sometimes, it is about being present and sharing in the ambient life of the world, which can be equally healing and spiritual. This reflects Jesus' ministry, often characterized by His simple presence and attention to the marginalized and suffering (Luke 5:29-32).

Sacredness in Ordinary Moments: The narrative captures the sacredness found in ordinary, everyday noises and moments, suggesting that all of creation and every moment of existence can be imbued with spiritual significance. This echoes Psalms 19:1-4, which speaks about how the heavens declare the glory of God and the skies proclaim the work of His hands, emphasizing that God's presence is revealed through all creation.

Endurance Through Faith: Even as Joyce admits her fatigue and inability to actively engage with her faith as she once did, her connection to the life bustling around her serves as a metaphor for the endurance of faith through trying times. This can be paralleled with 2 Corinthians 4:16 ("Therefore we do not lose heart. Though outwardly we are wasting away, yet inwardly we are being renewed day by day.").

These themes collectively emphasize the holistic approach of Christianity to life and death, recognizing God's presence in all aspects of life, the importance of community and presence, and the sanctity and spirituality found in the everyday.

Prayer

Heavenly Father, We thank You for Your constant presence in our lives, a presence that is not confined to sacred spaces or special moments but permeates every aspect of our everyday existence. Help us, Lord, to be ever aware of Your presence, to recognize Your hand at work in the ordinary moments of our lives. As we go about our daily routines, may we be attentive to Your voice speaking to us through the beauty of creation, the kindness of others, and the still, small voice within our hearts. Open our eyes to see Your presence in the laughter of children, the warmth of the sun, and the embrace of loved ones. Lord, help us to cultivate a deeper intimacy with You in our daily lives, seeking Your guidance and wisdom in all that we do. May we abide in You, drawing strength and comfort from Your presence, knowing that You are with us always. Thank You, Lord, for the gift of Your presence in our everyday lives. May we never take it for granted, but cherish it always, seeking to walk in step with You each day. In Jesus' name we pray, Amen.

69

The Transience of Life

Aaron sat by the window, his gaze often drifting towards the little garden outside where his daughter Joan liked to plant her flowers. Despite the comfort of her home, there was a stiffness to him—a rigidity that spoke of his longing for his own space, for the rooms that had echoed with his wife's laughter and the walls lined with books he no longer read but loved to see.

His office days, when every decision was crucial and every paper had its place, were distant memories now, like photographs faded by the harsh light of time. The progression of technology, which he had once grudgingly embraced, had now far surpassed his ability to keep up. His frustrations with tiny screens and elusive fonts had morphed into a more pervasive confusion, a fog that occasionally cleared but mostly enveloped him.

"I used to know every statute, every case by heart," he told me once, his voice tinged with a mix of pride and loss. "Now, I can't even remember what I had for breakfast."

When Aaron's daughters convinced him to leave his home, it was as if he had stepped off the solid ground onto a perpetually swaying deck, unmoored and uncertain. The book he threw at Joan wasn't just an expression of anger; it was a futile grab for control, for the solidity of his old life.

After he moved in with Joan, I started visiting him, initially as a hospice chaplain, soon as something akin to a friend. Aaron was clear about what he wanted from our visits. "Don't try to convert me," he warned. His sharpness, dulled by illness, still had its edges.

We talked about everything and nothing—politics, weather, the books he could no longer read. He shared stories of his youth, of a time when everything seemed possible, when the law was not just a profession but a calling.

"You know Jesus was a Jew," he said more than once during our talks, a fact he punctuated as if it were a punchline to a joke, we were both in on. It wasn't defiance, not exactly. It was more of an assertion of identity, of continuity in a world where he felt increasingly disconnected.

His mind wandered and wobbled, but occasionally he'd lock onto a topic with the old fervor of his lawyering days. We'd debate, and in those moments, he wasn't a patient or a fading old man but a peer, a combatant in the arena of ideas.

But more often, he simply wanted to sit in silence, looking out at the garden. These silences weren't empty; they were filled with the weight of his thoughts, the presence of his past, and the encroaching shadows of his mortality.

As his body weakened, his moments of clarity grew rarer, but in those lucid spells, he clung to his dignity like a shipwreck survivor clinging to a piece of driftwood. "I'm still here," his eyes seemed to say, even when his voice faltered.

Aaron's life, filled with the noise and clatter of a world that no longer made sense to him, slowed down in those final months. The technological marvels that once frustrated him were no longer relevant. Instead, the simple, enduring human connections—our talks, Joan's gardening outside his window, the visits from his grandchildren—became his solace.

In the quiet of a particularly soft afternoon, when the light made the room glow as if lit from within, Aaron passed away. It was peaceful, a quiet end to a life that had been anything but. In the stillness, he seemed almost to smile, as if in his final moment, he had found some long-sought-after answer in the silence he had once resisted.

Christian Themes and Values

The story of Aaron's later years and his interactions as an elderly man dealing with the loss of his independence and cognitive decline is rich with Biblical themes. Here are some that particularly stand out:

Dignity in Old Age: Aaron's struggle to maintain his dignity and identity in the face of aging and illness reflects a Biblical respect for the elderly. Scriptures like Leviticus 19:32, which commands respect for the aged, affirm the inherent dignity of every life stage.

The Transience of Life: Aaron's reflections on his past and his loss of control over his present circumstances echo the Biblical theme of the transience of life. Psalms 103:15-16 compares human life to grass that flourishes and then withers, a reminder of the fleeting nature of earthly existence.

Wisdom and Memory: Aaron reminisces about his days as a knowledgeable lawyer, but now struggles with memory loss. This can be seen in light of Ecclesiastes 12, which describes the challenges of old age and the inevitable decline of mental and physical strength, emphasizing the importance of seeking wisdom.

Loss and Coping: Aaron's frustration, exemplified by throwing a book at his daughter, showcases the human struggle with loss — not just of loved ones but of autonomy and familiarity. This reflects the Biblical theme of coping with loss and the search for comfort, as seen in comforting passages like Psalm 23.

Community and Care: The story underlines the importance of community and care in providing comfort and dignity. The Biblical principle of bearing one another's burdens (Galatians 6:2) is lived out through the chaplain's visits and the family's care, showing the spiritual value of compassion and companionship.

Identity and Continuity: Aaron's repeated mention of Jesus being a Jew serves as a reminder of his own identity and past, which he clings to as a means of continuity in a rapidly changing world. This mirrors the Biblical emphasis on remembering one's roots and God's steadfastness (Deuteronomy 8:2).

Peaceful Endings: Aaron's peaceful passing in a moment of quiet beauty reflects the Biblical theme of finding peace with God. Philippians 4:7 talks about the peace of God, which transcends all understanding. Aaron's final moments where he appears to smile as if finding an answer in the silence suggests a spiritual peace akin to this passage.

Existence Beyond Mortality: The narrative subtly hints at the hope of continuity beyond physical life, a core Christian belief in eternal life beyond death. Aaron's death scene, imbued with a sense of peace and fulfillment, hints at a transition to a state of eternal rest and peace promised in scriptures like John 14:1-3.

Through these themes, the story deeply engages with the universal human experiences of aging, loss, and the quest for dignity, framed within a context that resonates with Christian values and Biblical teachings.

Prayer

Heavenly Father, We come before You with humble hearts, acknowledging the transience of life on this earth. You have given us the gift of life, yet it is fleeting, like a vapor that appears for a little while and then vanishes away. Help us, Lord, to number our days aright, that we may gain a heart of wisdom. As we reflect on the brevity of life, may we live each day with purpose and intention, seeking first Your kingdom and Your righteousness. Teach us to treasure the moments we have, to love deeply, forgive freely, and serve joyfully, knowing that our time here is limited. Lord, in the face of life's uncertainties and the inevitability of death, anchor our hearts in the hope we have in You. Your Word assures us that though our outer self is wasting away, our inner self is being renewed day by day. May we fix our eyes not on what is seen, but on what is unseen, for what is seen is temporary, but what is unseen is eternal. Lord, in the midst of life's transience, may we find comfort in Your unchanging nature and Your eternal promises. May we trust in Your perfect timing and rest in Your unfailing love, knowing that You hold our past, present, and future in Your hands. In Jesus' name we pray, Amen.

70

Strength in Weakness

Wilbur stood in the small courtyard of the rehab center, his eyes tracing the patterns of shadows the morning sun drew across the gravel. It was one year to the day since his last drink—a year measured in small, hard-won victories and the constant, gnawing presence of temptation. I watched him from the window, noting the set of his jaw, the way his hands, once so unsteady, now held a quiet stillness.

The other men shuffled around him, their movements subdued, as if aware of the significance of the day for Wilbur yet bound by an unspoken agreement to leave the moment unmarked. These men, scarred by war and worn by the bottle, understood better than anyone the fragile triumph of a single year sober.

"You don't beat alcoholism on an annual basis," one of them, a grizzled Vietnam vet named Carl, had muttered to me earlier. "It's a battle you fight day by day, twenty-four hours at a time." His words were seasoned with the bitter knowledge of his own relapses, each one a stark lesson in the perils of complacency.

As a chaplain, I had come to this place with a mission to heal, armed with scripture and a lifetime of guiding youth groups and church congregations, but nothing had truly prepared me for the raw, unfiltered reality of these men's lives. Their stories were not just testimonies of survival from addiction but of the horrors they had witnessed in jungles and cities half a world away. Their battles did not end when the war did; they simply changed shape.

Each day, we gathered in a circle, our chairs scraping against the linoleum floor, and shared our burdens and our hopes. The men spoke, often with reluctance, and I listened, offering words that sometimes felt woefully inadequate against the magnitude of their pain. We prayed together for strength, for guidance, for peace—prayers not just for spiritual solace but for the tangible feeling of making it through another day.

Today, Wilbur's year of sobriety hung heavy over us. I wanted to celebrate him, to acknowledge his struggle and his success, but I knew that for Wilbur and the others, there were no true victories, only respites in a continuous struggle.

In the fading light of the afternoon, I approached him. His face was lined with the roads he had traveled, each one etched deep by years of alcohol and hard living.

"Wilbur," I said, my voice low, mindful of the sanctity of the moment, "I know today is significant for you. I just want you to know how proud I am of what you've achieved."

He looked up, eyes clear but haunted by the weight of a hundred battles yet to fight. "Thank you," he said simply, but the gravity in his voice carried the weight of his journey.

"It's just another day, Chaplain," he added, turning his gaze back to the courtyard. "Just another day, but God willing, there'll be another one tomorrow."

And so, we stood, two men shadowed by the struggles of many, finding solace not in grand declarations or celebrations, but in the quiet recognition of the endurance of the human spirit and the relentless pursuit of another day.

Christian Themes and Values

The story of Wilbur's journey through sobriety in the rehab center, observed by a chaplain, is infused with deep Biblical themes, reflecting the struggles and triumphs of the human spirit in the face of adversity. Here are several prominent themes depicted in the narrative:

The Daily Battle Against Sin and Temptation: Wilbur's daily struggle with alcoholism parallels the Biblical theme of resisting sin and temptation, as depicted in passages like 1 Corinthians 10:13, which discusses the endurance of temptations and the promise of God providing a way out so that one can bear it. This ongoing battle emphasizes the need for constant vigilance and reliance on spiritual strength.

Redemption and Renewal: Wilbur's one-year sobriety milestone represents themes of redemption and renewal, reminiscent of Biblical messages of being born again or made new through Christ (2 Corinthians 5:17). Each day offers a new beginning, a theme echoed in Lamentations 3:22-23, which speaks of God's mercies being new every morning.

Community and Fellowship: The shared experiences of the men in the rehab center highlight the Biblical importance of community and fellowship in bearing one another's burdens (Galatians 6:2). The group meetings where men share their struggles and support each other resonate with the Christian practice of communal prayer and mutual encouragement.

Endurance and Perseverance: The narrative stresses the theme of perseverance in faith and life's challenges, as demonstrated by Wilbur and his peers. This aligns with scriptures like James 1:12, which blesses those who persevere under trial, promising the crown of life to those who have stood the test.

Strength in Weakness: Wilbur's journey underscores the Biblical theme that strength is often found in acknowledging one's weaknesses, a principle found in 2 Corinthians 12:9-10, where Paul discusses delighting in weaknesses because when he is weak, then he is strong through the power of Christ.

Hope and Continuous Struggle: The sober acknowledgment that each day is just another day in the ongoing battle captures the essence of hope in Christian faith—the hope for a better future and the strength to continue despite difficulties, reflected in Hebrews 11:1, defining faith as confidence in what we hope for and assurance about what we do not see.

God's Sustaining Grace: Wilbur's reliance on the possibility of another day "God willing" underscores his dependence on divine grace for endurance and survival. This echoes the reliance on God's grace seen throughout the Bible, such as in Philippians 4:13, where Paul states he can do all things through Christ who strengthens him.

Sanctity of the Individual Journey: The chaplain's respect for the sanctity of Wilbur's personal milestone, understanding its profound significance beyond a mere celebration, aligns with the Biblical theme of recognizing and honoring each person's unique journey and struggles.

Through these themes, the story illustrates how Biblical principles can provide a framework for understanding and navigating the complexities and challenges of recovery and personal transformation.

Prayer

Heavenly Father, In our weakness, You are our strength. When we are weary and burdened, You carry us. We come before You, Lord, acknowledging our frailty and our need for Your power to sustain us. Give us, O God, the grace to embrace our weaknesses, knowing that Your strength is made perfect in our weakness. Help us to see our limitations as opportunities for Your power to be displayed in our lives. When we feel overwhelmed by life's challenges, remind us that we can do all things through Christ who gives us strength. May Your Spirit empower us to persevere through every trial and tribulation, trusting in Your promise to never leave us nor forsake us. Lord, may Your strength be our refuge and our fortress, our ever-present help in times of trouble. May we walk in confidence, knowing that Your power is at work within us, enabling us to overcome every obstacle and to live victoriously in You. In Jesus' name we pray, Amen.

71

The Importance of Witness and Memory

Ralph's apartment was a time capsule, lined with relics of a life lived boldly if not always wisely. The walls, an eclectic tapestry of his own art and faded concert posters, seemed to pulse with echoes of a bygone era. It was here, among these remnants, that I found him, a figure as textured and worn as the objects that surrounded him.

He sat in an old armchair, one that might have once graced a coffeehouse where his folk group played. The nylon-string guitar rested on his lap, his fingers occasionally stirring to strum chords that were half-remembered, half-improvised. When I entered, he looked up, his face crinkling into a smile that belied the fatigue etched deep into his features.

"I used to be everywhere, man," Ralph rasped, his voice a hoarse whisper of what it once was. "Woodstock, anti-war rallies, downtown clubs. Played everywhere. Painted everything."

He showed me his paintings, his hands trembling slightly as he pointed to each one. "Thought I'd be the next Warhol," he chuckled, the sound dry and papery. "Turned out I was just another guy with a brush and too many dreams."

Despite the regrets that threaded through his words, there was a lightness to Ralph, a resilience that seemed to shimmer through the haze of his illness. He was a man who had embraced every facet of life, diving headfirst into the music and art of his youth, chasing a vision of greatness that, even unattained, had given his days a vibrant purpose.

As he talked about his past marriages and his children, his tone softened, the edges of his regret showing clearly. "Wasn't much of a family man. Too caught up in my own head, my own stuff. Now, they're all I think about."

The room was quiet for a moment, the only sound the distant hum of city traffic and the occasional wheeze from Ralph's strained lungs. He picked up the guitar again, his fingers carefully navigating the frets as he began to play "The Times They Are a-Changin'."

The music was halting at first, but soon it found its rhythm, flowing around us like a gentle river. Ralph's eyes closed, his expression one of peace, perhaps reliving moments when his voice could fill a room, when his hands danced effortlessly along the strings.

"Chaplain," he said, opening his eyes, "I don't need much praying. Just someone to hear my tunes, see my pictures. Maybe remember me a bit when I'm gone."

I nodded, understanding my role was not to preach or to console with words, but to witness—to honor the life of a man who had lived fiercely and was now facing the end with a blend of humor and resignation.

We spent the afternoon in the glow of nostalgia, Ralph playing his guitar and me listening, both of us transported to a time when music could change the world, even if it couldn't change the inevitability of time's passage. As I left, Ralph's laughter followed me out the door, a soft echo of a life that had been anything but silent.

Christian Themes and Values

The story of Ralph, an aging artist and musician reflecting on his life as he nears its end, interweaves several profound Biblical themes. These themes enrich the narrative and provide a deeper resonance with age-old spiritual concepts:

The Vanity of Earthly Pursuits: Ralph's reflection on his life as a pursuit of fame and art, which ultimately did not fulfill his deeper needs, mirrors the Biblical theme of the vanity of earthly pursuits. This is echoed in Ecclesiastes, where King Solomon reflects on the futility of chasing after worldly achievements and pleasures without finding lasting satisfaction or purpose.

Redemption and Reflection in Old Age: As Ralph reflects on his life, acknowledging his failures as a family man and his missed opportunities, there's a theme of redemption through self-awareness and reflection that aligns with Biblical teachings. Luke 15:11-32 (the Parable of the Prodigal Son) similarly talks about reflection leading to a return to what is meaningful—family and forgiveness.

The Importance of Witness and Memory: Ralph's desire not for prayers but for someone to remember his music and art underscores the Biblical importance of witness and remembrance. In the Bible, acts of witness and remembrance are crucial; for example, the Israelites are often reminded to remember the deeds of God and to tell those stories to future generations (Psalm 78:4).

The Transitory Nature of Life: Ralph's story is a reminder of the transitory nature of life and the inevitability of death, themes frequently addressed in the Bible. James 4:14, for example, compares life to a mist that appears for a little while and then vanishes, highlighting the brevity and fragile nature of human existence.

Finding Peace in the Midst of Turmoil: Despite the chaos and the unresolved aspects of his life, Ralph finds a moment of peace through music, reminiscent of Biblical passages that speak about finding peace through faith and expression, such as Philippians 4:7 which speaks about the peace of God that transcends all understanding.

Community and Connection: The chaplain's role in Ralph's life emphasizes the Biblical theme of community support and the strength found in companionship. Galatians 6:2 encourages believers to bear one another's burdens, and in this story, the chaplain helps bear Ralph's emotional and spiritual burdens simply by being present and listening.

End-of-Life Reflection and Legacy: Ralph's end-of-life reflections bring to the forefront the Biblical theme of considering one's legacy and the impact of one's life. In Psalm 90:12, the plea to "teach us to number our days, that we may gain a heart of wisdom" resonates with Ralph's contemplation of his past and the legacy he wishes to leave through his art and music.

Through Ralph's story, these themes are woven into a narrative that explores the complexity of life, the regrets that come with age, and the desire for remembrance and meaning, showing how even in our final days, our stories can echo the timeless questions and reflections found in the Bible.

Prayer

Heavenly Father, We thank You for the gift of memory and the call to bear witness to Your goodness and faithfulness in our lives. Help us, Lord, to remember Your works and Your words, that we may testify to Your power and love. Grant us the grace to be faithful witnesses, sharing the story of Your salvation with boldness and clarity. May our lives be living testimonies to Your grace, pointing others to the hope found in Jesus Christ. Teach us to cultivate a culture of remembrance within our families, our communities, and our churches. May we pass on the stories of Your faithfulness from generation to generation, so that Your mighty deeds are never forgotten. Lord, may our witness and memory bring glory to Your name and draw others into relationship with You. May we never forget the great things You have done, and may we always be ready to share Your love with those who need it most. In Jesus' name we pray, Amen.

72

Acceptance and Contentment

The air was thick in Rhonda's apartment, heavy with the scent of incense and the persistent hum of a nearby air purifier. She had propped the windows open slightly, letting in a measure of city air that seemed as tired as she was. Despite her frailty, her presence filled the room, a juxtaposition of weakened body and indomitable spirit.

Pudge, her little dog, circled around, sniffing suspiciously as I set my bag down. His growl was soft, more a greeting than a warning. Rhonda chuckled, a sound that was both bright and brittle.

"You made it up, okay?" she asked, her eyes twinkling mischievously.

"Yes, the elevator was a fine ride," I replied, watching her shuffle to the couch with careful steps that belied the cheer in her voice.

"I can't even think about stairs now," she sighed as she settled into the cushions. "Just getting from one room to another can be like climbing a mountain."

The change was quick; the light in her eyes dimmed as the reality of her condition intruded into the conversation. She fingered a string of rosary beads, her movements reflective.

"COPD," she murmured, "who knew breath could be such a luxury?"

She glanced up suddenly, her gaze sharp. "Are you Catholic?" she asked, holding the beads out slightly towards me.

I shook my head, settling into a chair opposite her. "No, Protestant. But like you said, we all pray to the same loving God."

Rhonda nodded, seemingly satisfied. "Some think you might look like a rabbi with that beard," she said with a faint smile.

I laughed, rubbing my chin. "Maybe I do. But we're all just trying to make sense of the time we're given, aren't we?"

"Yes, we are," she agreed, her voice a whisper of acceptance.

Rhonda leaned over to a small, round table and picked up a plate of cookies and a jug of milk. "Here you go, chaplain, priest, rabbi, or whatever you are," she said, offering a weak smile. "Let's have communion."

We broke the cookies as if they were sacramental bread, dipping them into the milk and sharing them in a quiet celebration of life in all its fleeting beauty. Each bite was a moment of connection, a simple act that bridged the gaps between faiths, beliefs, and the harsh realities of human frailty.

As we ate, Rhonda spoke of small joys and daily challenges, her words painting a picture of a life fiercely lived despite its constraints. The room seemed to hold its breath with her, each of us caught in the gravity of shared human experience.

When it was time to leave, I stood and watched her for a moment, the rosary beads still clutched in her hand, her eyes closed in a silent prayer. In that small, cluttered apartment, fourteen floors above the ceaseless city, there was a sanctuary made not of grand gestures but of milk and cookies, of shared silences and laughter.

"Take care, Rhonda," I said softly.

"Thank you for the communion," she replied, her voice steadied by something unseen and powerful.

As I closed the door behind me, the sounds of the city rushed back in, a stark reminder of the world outside. But in my heart, the quiet strength of Rhonda's spirit lingered, a testament to the enduring power of faith and fellowship in the face of life's relentless challenges.

Christian Themes and Values

Rhonda's story, with its intimate portrayal of a woman grappling with chronic illness and finding solace in shared human connections, touches on several profound Biblical themes:

The Sanctity of Life: Rhonda's condition highlights the Biblical theme that every life is sacred and valuable, regardless of physical frailty. Scriptures such as Psalm 139:13-16, where God is described as intimately involved in the creation of each life, underscore this idea, reflecting the inherent worth of every individual.

Fellowship and Communion: The simple act of sharing cookies and milk, likened to a communion, resonates deeply with the Biblical practice of communion in Christianity, which commemorates Christ's Last Supper and emphasizes unity and fellowship among believers (1 Corinthians 10:16-17). This moment symbolizes the breaking down of barriers between different faith traditions and underscores the universal need for connection.

The Presence of God in Suffering: Rhonda's ongoing battle with COPD and her reflective attitude towards her condition suggest the Biblical theme of finding God's presence in the midst of suffering. This theme is evident in passages like Psalm 23, where God is a comforting presence even in the "valley of the shadow of death."

The Power of Prayer and Spiritual Support: Rhonda's use of rosary beads and the chaplain's acknowledgment of a common God across different faiths highlight the importance of prayer and spiritual support. This reflects Biblical teachings on the power of prayer to provide peace and strength in times of hardship (Philippians 4:6-7).

Resilience and Hope: Despite her physical limitations, Rhonda's indomitable spirit exemplifies the Biblical virtues of resilience and hope. Scriptures such as Romans 5:3-5 speak to the idea that suffering produces perseverance, character, and hope—a hope that does not disappoint because of God's love poured out through the Holy Spirit.

Acceptance and Contentment: Rhonda's acceptance of her life's limitations mirrors the Biblical principle of contentment in all circumstances. Apostle Paul discusses this in Philippians 4:11-13, explaining that he has learned to be content whatever the circumstances through Him who gives strength.

Interfaith Dialogue and Respect: The chaplain and Rhonda's interactions, crossing religious boundaries with mutual respect and humor, align with the Biblical call for peace and understanding among different peoples. Ephesians 2:14-18, for instance, talks about Christ as the one who breaks down the dividing wall of hostility between us, promoting peace and unity.

The Spiritual Significance of Everyday Acts: The story elevates simple acts of sharing food and conversation to sacramental significance, illustrating the Biblical theme that God can be encountered in everyday moments. Jesus' ministry often involved sharing meals and profound truths with others, as seen in stories like the feeding of the 5000 (Mark 6:30-44) and the post-resurrection meal at Emmaus (Luke 24:30-31).

These themes weave through Rhonda's narrative, presenting a rich tapestry of spiritual insight and human connection, framed within the context of facing life's challenges with grace and faith.

Prayer

Heavenly Father, We come before You with hearts filled with gratitude for all the blessings You have bestowed upon us. Help us, Lord, to cultivate a spirit of acceptance and contentment in every circumstance, knowing that You are our provider and sustainer. Grant us the grace to accept the things we cannot change, trusting in Your sovereign plan for our lives. Help us to surrender our will to Yours, knowing that Your ways are higher than our ways, and Your thoughts are higher than our thoughts. Teach us to find contentment in You alone, regardless of our circumstances. May we learn the secret of being content in every situation, whether we have plenty or whether we are in want, knowing that our true riches are found in You. May we rest in the assurance of Your love and provision, knowing that You will never leave us nor forsake us. In Jesus' name we pray, Amen.

73

The Value of Companionship and Presence

The days following were a repetition of the mundane marked with moments of sharp, stinging clarity. Harold's condition worsened, as the ravages of disease claimed more of his vigor. His voice became a husky whisper, his movements slow and deliberate. Still, he bore his suffering with a quiet dignity that seemed to strengthen as his body weakened.

Tim, Harold's grandson, visited often, sitting by the bed, sometimes reading aloud, other times just sitting, the silence between them filled with all the things that could not be voiced. They watched the seasons change through the window, the leaves turning golden and then giving way to the bare bones of winter trees.

It was on one such day, with snow gently falling outside, that I dropped by unannounced. The room was dim, lit only by the soft glow of a bedside lamp. Tim was there, holding his grandfather's hand, a book of Hemingway's short stories lying forgotten on the bed.

As I entered, Tim looked up, his face a mask of weariness and worry. Harold's eyes were closed, his breath shallow but steady. There was a peace about him that had not been there before—a surrender not just to the disease but to the relentless tide of life and death itself.

We spoke little, sitting in a companionable silence that seemed to wrap itself around us like a warm blanket. At times, Tim would adjust the pillow behind Harold's head or check if he needed water, small acts of care that spoke volumes.

As the afternoon wore on, Harold opened his eyes and looked at each of us in turn. There was a clarity there, a lucidity that had been absent in previous weeks.

"Tim," he said softly, the effort evident in each syllable. "Don't look for answers in all this. Just... be here, with me."

Tim nodded, tears welling up in his eyes, but he held them back, a strength borne of love and resolve steadying his voice as he responded, "I am here, Grandpa. I'm not going anywhere."

I watched them, a grandfather and his grandson, finding their own peace in silence, a silent communion that needed no words, no divine interventions. It was then I realized that perhaps my role was not to provide answers or solace through doctrine and bible verses. Maybe, like Tim, my purpose was simply to be present, to bear witness to these profoundly personal journeys and, in doing so, honor the very essence of our shared humanity.

When I left that evening, the snow had stopped, and the stars were out, sharp pinpoints of light in the dark sky. The world felt vast, and I felt small within it—yet there was comfort in that smallness, in the knowledge that we all share in this human experience, each of us finding our own way through the trials and the quiet triumphs of our lives.

Christian Themes and Values

The story of Harold's final days, marked by his grandson Tim's companionship and quiet moments of reflection, conveys several powerful Biblical themes.

The Presence of God in Suffering: While not explicitly mentioned, the theme of God's presence in moments of suffering is illustrated through the quiet, comforting atmosphere in Harold's room. The themes, seen in Psalm 23, speaks of God walking with us through the "valley of the shadow of death," offering comfort and solace even when explicit religious symbols or prayers are absent.

The Dignity of the Dying Process: Harold's dignified bearing as his condition worsens reflects the Biblical understanding of each human's inherent worth and dignity, created in the image of God (Genesis 1:27). His quiet acceptance and grace in suffering resonate with the Biblical portrayal of suffering endured with dignity, as exemplified by Christ himself.

The Value of Companionship and Presence: The simple, profound acts of companionship and presence that Tim offers Harold echo the Biblical theme of "bearing one another's burdens" (Galatians 6:2). This reflects the Christian call to love one another through action, often more through presence than words, emphasizing the importance of being there for others in their time of need.

Ecclesiastes and the Seasons of Life: The observation of seasons changing through the window alongside Harold's progression in illness reminds us of the reflections in Ecclesiastes 3, which speaks about there being a time for every purpose under heaven, including a time to be born and a time to die. This theme underlines the natural cycle of life and death, and the acceptance of each season as it comes.

The Quiet Triumphs of the Human Spirit: Harold's moments of lucidity and the profound connection in silence between him and Tim highlight the quiet triumphs of the human spirit. These moments reflect the Biblical notion found in 2 Corinthians 12:9, where strength is perfected in weakness, and profound spiritual truths are often realized in silence and suffering, not in grand revelations.

Solace in Shared Human Experience: The narrative closes with the chaplain's realization of the vastness of the human experience and his small part in it, resonating with the Biblical theme of humility and the comfort found in communal human experiences. This echoes the sentiments of Ecclesiastes 4:9-12 about the strength found in companionship and shared experiences, and how two are better than one because they have a good return for their labor.

These themes, woven through the fabric of the story, offer a rich tapestry of spiritual insight into the universal human experiences of aging, loss, and companionship. They suggest that, often, the greatest spiritual comfort comes not from doctrinal teachings or miraculous interventions but from simple, profound human connections and the presence of love in quiet, everyday actions.

Prayer

Heavenly Father, We thank You for the gift of companionship and the blessing of Your presence in our lives. You have created us for community, to walk alongside one another in love and fellowship. Help us, Lord, to cherish the relationships You have given us and to appreciate the richness of Your presence among us. Grant us the grace to be present with one another, to listen with empathy, to speak with kindness, and to offer support and encouragement in times of need. May our friendships be a reflection of Your love, drawing us closer to You and to each other. Teach us to value the gift of Your presence, knowing that You are with us always, even to the end of the age. Help us to cultivate a deeper intimacy with You through prayer, worship, and the study of Your Word. Thank You, Lord, for the precious gift of companionship and Your abiding presence. May we never take these blessings for granted, but always be grateful for the love and fellowship You have provided us. In Jesus' name we pray, Amen.

74

The Presence of God in Suffering

I entered the house with the weight of my thoughts, heavy like a winter coat soaked through with rain. The air inside was thick with the scent of medicinal ointment and something sweet, like overripe fruit. The walls, once probably a bright cheerful color, now seemed to absorb the dim light, casting everything in a muted, sorrowful hue.

The cries had subsided into low, incoherent mutterings by the time I reached the living room. There, in a well-worn recliner, sat an elderly man, Trevor, his body a testament to the ravages of time and a rare neurological disease called Lewey Body dementia. His eyes, once perhaps sharp and commanding, now flickered with the confusion and fear that this terrible malady bestows mercilessly upon its sufferers.

His wife, Anna, a small, but very focused woman with hands gnarled by arthritis, hovered by his side. Her eyes, red-rimmed and weary, met mine with a mix of desperation and gratitude. "He's having a bad day," she whispered, as if afraid to disturb the fragile peace that had momentarily settled over the room.

I nodded, setting down my prayer book and pulling up a chair. Trevor glanced at me, a flicker of recognition passing over his features before being lost to the fog again. I reached out, taking his hand in mine. It was cold, the skin papery and thin, but his grip tightened ever so slightly.

I am in a silent reverie with God. "You ask why?" I started, my voice low, speaking to the Divine Spirit more to fill the silence than to impart any wisdom. "I ask the same question, every day. And I've come to realize that maybe it's not about finding an answer, but about finding what we can give in response to the question."

Trevor stared at me, and for a moment, his grip tightened. "It's cruel," I continued to the Divine Spirit, "this suffering. But it's not all there is. There's also this—" I gestured to the room, to Anna, to myself. "Us, being here together, bearing witness to each other's lives. Maybe that's where we find You, God, not in the why, but in the here, in the now, in the midst of the suffering."

Anna laid her hand over ours, her presence a silent echo of my words. We sat together like that for a long while, the room filled only with the sound of breathing and the occasional murmur from the suffering man.

As the afternoon shadows grew long and the room dimmed, I stood to leave. Anna followed me to the door, her steps slow and tired. "Thank you," she murmured, her voice thick with emotion. "For coming, for sitting, for not having all the answers."

Outside, the world seemed momentarily brighter, the sharp clarity of the setting sun casting long shadows across the lawn. I looked back at the house, a small island of light in the growing dusk.

No, I didn't have all the answers. Maybe I never would. But perhaps that wasn't the point. Perhaps the point was to wrestle with the questions, to engage in the struggle, and to be there, fully present, in the midst of it all. And maybe, just maybe, that was enough.

Christian Themes and Values

The story of the chaplain's visit to Trevor and Anna's home, set against the backdrop of Trevor's battle with Lewy Body dementia, is imbued with deep biblical themes that offer profound reflections on human suffering, divine presence, and the nature of spiritual care. Here are several prominent themes explored in this narrative.

The Mystery of Suffering: Trevor's affliction with a debilitating neurological disease raises the age-old question of why suffering exists, a theme deeply explored throughout the Bible, especially in the Book of Job. The story does not attempt to provide easy answers but rather echoes the biblical understanding that suffering is often a mystery beyond human comprehension but within the realm of divine sovereignty.

The Presence of God in Suffering: The chaplain's reflections suggest that God's presence is most profoundly experienced not in removing suffering but in sharing it. This theme resonates with Psalm 23, which speaks of God's comforting presence even as one walks through the darkest valley. The chaplain emphasizes finding God "in the here, in the now, in the midst of the suffering," reflecting the incarnational aspect of Christ who entered into human suffering.

The Ministry of Presence: The chaplain's ministry to Trevor and Anna is characterized by presence rather than preaching, listening rather than solving. This approach is reflective of the ministry of Jesus, who often provided comfort simply by being with people in their pain. This theme is supported by passages like Romans 12:15, which urges believers to "mourn with those who mourn," validating the ministry of presence as a profound form of spiritual care.

Community and Support: The scene where Anna places her hand over the hands of Trevor and the chaplain symbolizes the power of community and mutual support. It exemplifies the biblical injunction to bear one another's burdens (Galatians 6:2) and underscores the importance of communal resilience and empathy in facing life's trials.

Faith and Doubt: The chaplain's internal dialogue and his admission of not having all the answers highlight the coexistence of faith and doubt within spiritual life. This theme is explored in the Bible through figures like Thomas (John 20:24-29) and reflects the reality that faith often involves wrestling with uncertainty and seeking understanding through questioning.

Endurance and Perseverance: The quiet endurance of Anna and the silent struggle of Trevor mirror the biblical themes of perseverance and steadfastness in the face of trials, as mentioned in James 1:12, which promises blessing to those who persevere under trial. The chaplain's commitment to be present and engaged despite the difficulty of the situation reflects the call to endurance.

Sanctity and Dignity of Life: Despite Trevor's diminished physical and mental state, the story portrays his inherent dignity, which aligns with the biblical view that all life is valuable and created in the image of God (Genesis 1:27). The tender care he receives speaks to the sanctity of life at all stages.

The chaplain's narrative, with its rich theological and existential musings, invites us to consider that perhaps the most authentic response to the enigma of human suffering is not the quest for answers, but the offering of our presence, compassion, and shared humanity. In this, we find a reflection of God's own response to human pain.

Prayer

Heavenly Father, In times of suffering and pain, You are our ever-present help and comfort. We come before You, acknowledging the reality of our pain and the assurance of Your presence with us in the midst of it. Lord, when we face trials and tribulations, help us to lean on Your strength and find solace in Your love. May Your presence be a source of comfort and peace, even when the storms rage around us. Teach us to trust in Your sovereignty, knowing that You are working all things together for our good, even in the midst of our suffering. Help us to see beyond our present circumstances and to find hope in the promise of Your eternal love and redemption. Lord, in our moments of weakness, may Your Spirit intercede for us with groanings too deep for words. Give us the strength to persevere, knowing that You are with us, holding us close and carrying us through. Help us to find purpose in our suffering, knowing that it can produce perseverance, character, and hope. May our struggles draw us closer to You and deepen our faith in Your goodness and grace. In Jesus' name we pray, Amen.

75

The Mystery of Suffering and the Quest for Meaning

The day was gray, the sort of gray that seemed to press down from the sky and squeeze the color out of everything. Inside the hospital, the fluorescent lights hummed with a persistent, unnerving energy, casting sterile white light over the linoleum floors and pale walls. I walked down the corridor, my footsteps echoing slightly, a sound out of sync with the muffled cries and beeps that drifted out from the half-open doors.

In my pocket, my hand fiddled with a small, wooden cross to be given to one of my Catholic patients in the intensive care unit. I kept turning it over and over, feeling the smooth grain against my fingers. I knew it was a small comfort, a tactile reminder of why I was here, in this place of sickness and pain, a place that often felt like a jigsaw puzzle dumped out on the floor, pieces scattered and impossible to fit together.

I stopped at ICU room 30. Inside a young woman lay in the bed, her face pale and drawn, her eyes closed. Machines beside her clicked and whirred, each beep, a tiny heartbeat of artificial life. Her mother sat beside the bed, her face haggard, eyes red from crying. She looked up as I entered, a flicker of hope crossing her features.

"Chaplain," she murmured, standing up. "Thank God you're here."

I nodded, pulling up a chair beside her. "I'm here," I said simply.

"Why?" she asked, her voice breaking. "Why does it have to be so confusing, so hard?"

I looked at her, then at the young woman in the bed. I thought about the puzzle pieces, about the chaos and the mess that I so deeply despised. "I ask myself that same question," I admitted with some dismay. "I don't have all the answers. But I'm not here to solve the puzzle, just to help hold the pieces while we figure it out together."

Her hand reached out, gripping mine, her hold tight and desperate. "Can you pray with us?" she asked.

"Of course," I replied. And so, I prayed, not just for miracles or cures, but for true healing, peace, for strength, and for the presence of a love far greater than any chaos.

As I left the room, I felt the weight of her gratitude and the heavy burden of her sorrow. I walked back down the corridor, the echo of my footsteps a steady reminder of my purpose. Each room, each bed, each suffering face was a piece of the puzzle I couldn't solve. But that wasn't my role.

My role was to be present, to offer what comfort I could, to remind them of a presence greater than my own. As I passed back through the doors of the hospital, out into the drizzling rain, I felt not relief but a reaffirmation of my calling.

In a world full of puzzles, chaos, and confusion, I didn't need to have the answers. I just needed to be there, again and again, each day a new piece, a new challenge, a new chance to offer a moment of peace amidst the storm.

Christian Themes and Values

The story of the chaplain's visit to the hospital, providing spiritual support to a grieving mother and her critically ill daughter, encapsulates several deep Biblical themes that resonate with the core messages of Christianity.

The Ministry of Presence: The chaplain's role in the hospital is primarily one of being present. This echoes the Biblical theme found in Matthew 18:20, "For where two or three gather in my name, there am I with them." The chaplain embodies Christ's presence by simply being there with those who suffer, offering comfort and a listening ear rather than solutions, akin to Job's friends who initially sat with him in silence to offer support through their presence (Job 2:13).

Comfort in Times of Suffering: The chaplain's interactions with the mother, who is in deep anguish over her daughter's condition, illustrate the Biblical call to comfort those who mourn, as referenced in 2 Corinthians 1:3-4, where God is described as the "Father of compassion and the God of all comfort, who comforts us in all our troubles." The chaplain, through his actions, aims to be a vessel of God's comfort.

Faith Amidst Suffering: The mother's plea for prayer and the chaplain's response highlights the Biblical theme of turning to God in times of despair. This mirrors numerous Psalms where the Psalmist cries out to God in times of distress (e.g., Psalm 102:1). The chaplain's prayer is not just for physical healing but for peace and strength, acknowledging that while not all prayers for healing are answered in the way we hope, God's presence can bring inner peace and strength in the midst of suffering.

The Mystery of Suffering and the Quest for Meaning: The chaplain admits to not understanding why suffering is so pervasive and confusing, which aligns with Ecclesiastes' exploration of life's enigmas and injustices. This acknowledgment validates the themes that not all earthly occurrences have explanations or resolutions (Ecclesiastes 8:17).

The Role of Faith in Healing: The act of praying for true healing underscores the Biblical view that ultimate healing—whether physical, emotional, or spiritual—comes from God. This is seen in the numerous healing miracles of Jesus, such as the healing of the paralytic, where Jesus not only healed the man's physical ailments but also forgave his sins, addressing holistic healing (Mark 2:1-12).

Endurance and Perseverance: The chaplain's reflections on his role and calling demonstrate the Biblical principles of endurance and perseverance in ministry, akin to Paul's encouragement to the Galatians to not grow weary in doing good (Galatians 6:9). The chaplain's commitment to his pastoral duties, despite the emotional toll, reflects the perseverance encouraged in Hebrews 12:1-3.

Service and Sacrifice: Finally, the chaplain's selfless service in a setting of pain and confusion reflects Christ's model of servant leadership. Jesus taught that true leadership means serving others, illustrated by washing His disciples' feet and his ultimate sacrifice on the cross (John 13:1-17).

In summary, the chaplain's narrative within the hospital setting brings to life the Biblical themes of presence, comfort, enduring faith, and the quest for understanding in the midst of life's hardships, offering a reminder of the profound spiritual dimensions that can inform and transform pastoral care.

Prayer

Heavenly Father, In the midst of the mystery of suffering, we come before You seeking understanding and meaning. Help us, Lord, to trust in Your wisdom and to find purpose in the midst of our pain. Lord, we confess that we do not always understand why we must endure suffering, but we trust that You are a God who brings beauty from ashes and joy from mourning. Give us the faith to believe that even in our darkest moments, You are at work for our good and Your glory. Grant us the courage to wrestle with the questions and doubts that arise in the face of suffering, knowing that You are not afraid of our honest inquiries. Help us to seek You earnestly, knowing that You are the source of all wisdom and understanding. Teach us to find meaning in our suffering by following the example of Jesus Christ, who endured the cross. May we unite our sufferings with His and find purpose in sharing in His sufferings, knowing that through them, we may also share in His glory. In Jesus' name we pray, Amen.

76

The Power of Prayer and Spiritual Support

The hospital corridors were always too bright and too clean, and they echoed with the hollow sounds of medical efficiency. As I walked towards the burn intensive care unit, the smell of special antiseptics grew stronger, almost overpowering, but never quite masking the underlying scent of human suffering that no amount of cleanliness could erase.

Wells was my first patient in such a severe condition. I had met many faces, each carrying their own story of pain, but Wells's situation was something else. The accident had left him barely recognizable, and the machines around him beeped incessantly, like a grim orchestra playing a tune of life hanging by a thread.

I met Hillary outside the burn unit. She was a veteran chaplain in these corridors, her face marked with the calmness born of countless crises weathered. "It's tough in there," she said, nodding towards the door, "but remember, Wells's recovery isn't just about his physical wounds."

Inside, under the bright sterile lights, Wells lay motionless, a figure swathed in bandages, each layer a testament to the battle being waged between life and death. I was told he was under sedation, in a medically induced coma, somewhere deep within himself, perhaps not alone, perhaps wrestling with shadows we could barely comprehend. We prayed that he would not fall victim to sepsis or multiple-organ failure.

His family was there too, a small group of weary souls gathered around his bed. His wife, her eyes red-rimmed and puffy, whispering words of love and encouragement, believing he could hear her even in his induced slumber.

Over the months, my visits became a routine. I learned from Hillary how to approach such delicate situations—how to offer comfort without false hope, how to be present without being intrusive. We would often discuss the philosophical underpinnings of our work; the thin line we walked between life's brutal realities and the human need for peace and understanding.

Sometimes, I read aloud to Wells from a collection of verses his wife had given me, passages that spoke of strength, perseverance, and the profound hope of renewal. In those moments, the beeping machines seemed to recede, and a different kind of silence filled the room—a quiet that was thick with meaning and unspoken prayers.

As the weeks turned into months, Wells's condition slowly stabilized. The doctors spoke cautiously of progress, but we all knew that each increment of healing was bought with immense struggle. His physical recovery was mirrored by a subtle transformation within him, glimpsed in brief moments of lucidity, in the slight squeeze of a hand, or a fleeting smile.

When my clinical pastoral education internship ended, I visited Wells one last time. He was awake, his eyes clearer than I had ever seen them. He couldn't speak much, but his gratitude was palpable, a silent communication that filled the room with an unspeakable depth.

Leaving the hospital on my last day, I realized that Wells had taught me more about the resilience of the human spirit than any textbook ever could. Each scar, physical or otherwise, was a testament to a battle fought and survived, a stark reminder of both the fragility and the indomitable strength of life.

In chaplaincy, I had found my purpose not in solving the puzzles of why bad things happen to good people, but in bearing witness to the human capacity to endure and transform through suffering. This was the ministry I was called to—a ministry not of answers, but of presence.

Christian Themes and Values

The story of Wells's traumatic experience and recovery, accompanied by the chaplain's spiritual care, touches on several profound Biblical themes that underscore the nature of human suffering, healing, and divine presence:

The Presence of God in Suffering: The chaplain's role is emblematic of God's presence in places of pain and despair, reflecting the promise of Psalm 34:18, "The Lord is close to the brokenhearted and saves those who are crushed in spirit." This theme is vital as it underpins the chaplain's mission to bring spiritual comfort and a sense of divine nearness to those in dire circumstances.

The Power of Prayer and Spiritual Support: As the chaplain prays and reads scripture to Wells, the story emphasizes the Biblical belief in the power of prayer and God's Word to provide strength and hope in the darkest times, much like Paul and Silas praying and singing hymns in prison in Acts 16:25.

Healing and Renewal: The narrative of Wells's gradual physical recovery paralleled by inner transformation touches on the Biblical themes of renewal and restoration found in scriptures like Isaiah 40:31, "But those who hope in the Lord will renew their strength. They will soar on wings like eagles; they will run and not grow weary, they will walk and not be faint." This emphasizes that healing is not only physical but also spiritual and emotional.

The Ministry of Presence: The chaplain learns that their role is not to provide answers to the problem of suffering but to be present and bear witness to the pain and resilience of others. This reflects Jesus' ministry, where He often provided comfort simply by being with people in their suffering, such as when He visited Mary and Martha after the death of their brother Lazarus (John 11).

Resilience of the Human Spirit: Wells's recovery and the visible signs of his fighting spirit resonate with the theme of human resilience as celebrated in scriptures like James 1:12, "Blessed is the one who perseveres under trial because, having stood the test, that person will receive the crown of life that the Lord has promised to those who love him." This passage speaks to the courage and perseverance that individuals manifest in the face of trials.

Community and Support: The presence of Wells's family and their active participation in his healing process highlight the Biblical principle of community support and love, as outlined in Romans 12:15, "Rejoice with those who rejoice; mourn with those who mourn." The chaplaincy supports this through a ministry that fosters a communal approach to healing and enduring hardship.

Transformation Through Suffering: Wells's slight improvements, the moments of lucidity, and his palpable gratitude as he recovers indicate a transformation not just of the body but of the spirit. This mirrors the Biblical narrative of suffering leading to a deeper faith and understanding of life, as depicted in 1 Peter 1:6-7, where trials test faith, refine it, and lead to praise and glory.

In sum, the chaplaincy experience in the burn unit, as described, encapsulates these themes, providing a vivid illustration of the theological depths of the roles of those called to minister to the suffering and bear witness to the enduring power of faith and resilience in the human spirit.

Prayer

Heavenly Father, We come before You with grateful hearts, acknowledging the power of prayer and the importance of spiritual support in our lives. You have promised to hear our prayers and to be near to those who call upon You in faith. Help us, Lord, to lean on You and to seek Your guidance and strength through prayer. Thank You, Lord, for the privilege of bringing our requests to You in prayer. May we never underestimate the power of prayer to bring about Your will and Your kingdom on earth. Teach us to pray with faith and persistence, trusting that You are at work even when we cannot see the results. Lord, we are grateful for the spiritual support of our brothers and sisters in Christ. Help us to lift one another up in prayer, to encourage and strengthen one another in faith, and to bear one another's burdens in love. May our prayers be a source of comfort and healing to those who are hurting, a source of hope and encouragement to those who are struggling, and a source of guidance and wisdom to those who are seeking Your will. Thank You, Lord, for the power of prayer and the gift of spiritual support. May we always rely on You and draw strength from our unity in Christ. In Jesus' name we pray, Amen.

77

The Sanctity of Life

In the famous large city hospital where I was doing my chaplain internship, the neonatal intensive care unit was a quiet place despite the presence of so many tiny, fighting spirits. The first time I stepped into the NICU, I felt like I was entering the "Holy of Holies", a sacred space and a world far removed from the rest of the hospital's constant buzz and urgency. Here, life was at its most fragile, each breath a precious achievement.

The nurse who met me had eyes that reflected years of watching over the smallest and most delicate of creations. She introduced me to the dedicated NICU chaplain, a woman whose calm demeanor belied the depth of strength needed in her role. They both moved with quiet efficiency and a profound respect for the lives in their care.

I was shown how to properly gown up, the sterile gloves snapping against my wrists, a mask pressing against my face, every precaution taken to protect the unit's vulnerable occupants. Each step was a meditation, preparing to enter a space that was as sacred as any cathedral.

In one of the incubators lay a baby girl, her body dwarfed by the technology surrounding her but her presence as significant as any. Today was special for her; despite her precarious beginnings, she was about to receive a blessing—a baptism—that connected her to a community and a faith that awaited her growth and recovery.

The nurse carefully lifted the tiny infant just enough for the chaplain to perform the baptism. A small clam shell, filled with water, was used—a symbol of life's simplicity and nature's embrace. The chaplain's words were soft but carried the weight of a heartfelt prayer, asking for strength, health, and a blessed life for this child.

I was there to witness and support, my own prayer a silent addition to the spoken words, a request to whatever powers watched over these small beings for protection and grace. The ritual was brief, the baby barely stirring as the warm water touched her forehead, but the moment was profound.

The NICU, with its beeps and whispers, felt like holy ground. As I stood there, it became clear that hospital chaplaincy was not just about the somber moments of life's end but also about these beginnings, these quiet victories against the odds.

The baby girl did thrive, each day gaining strength until she was ready to leave the hospital. The news of her going home was a joy shared not just by her family but by all of us who had touched her life in those early weeks.

Leaving the NICU that day, I felt a renewal of my own faith in life's resilience. The hospital was a place where every aspect of human existence was played out—from the most heartbreaking to the most uplifting. In the sacred space of the NICU, I had been reminded of the profound beauty and celebration inherent in my work, standing as a witness to both the vulnerability and the incredible strength of human life.

Christian Themes and Values

The story of the chaplain intern's experience in the neonatal intensive care unit (NICU) at a hospital is filled with biblical themes that intersect with the spiritual significance of their work. Here are the key biblical themes explored in this narrative.

Sanctity of Life: The delicate care and attention given to the infants in the NICU underscore the biblical view that all life is sacred and created by God. This is aligned with Psalm 139:13-16, where the psalmist acknowledges that God formed him in his mother's womb and knew him even before he was born. The story reflects this deep reverence for life at its most fragile stage.

Baptism and Spiritual New Birth: The baptism of the baby girl in the NICU symbolizes the Christian sacrament of initiation and inclusion into the faith community. In the biblical context, baptism represents a spiritual cleansing and new birth, as discussed in John 3:5, where Jesus speaks of being born of water and the Spirit as essential for entering the kingdom of God.

Ministry of Presence and Healing: The chaplains and nurses' gentle, careful movements around the infants symbolize a ministry of presence, which echoes the healing and comforting presence of Christ, who often ministered to those who were sick and vulnerable. This theme is evident throughout the Gospels, where Jesus' healing is not just about physical recovery but providing a compassionate presence (e.g., Mark 5:21-43).

Community and Interconnection: The baptism connects the baby to a wider community of faith, emphasizing the Christian belief in the universal Church as a family. This theme is supported by passages like 1 Corinthians 12:12-27, which speak of the Church as one body with many parts, highlighting the interconnectedness and mutual dependence of all members.

Protection and Providence: The prayers for the baby's health and well-being reflect the biblical promises of God's protection and providence, such as in Matthew 19:14 where Jesus said, "Let the little children come to me, and do not hinder them, for the kingdom of heaven belongs to such as these." This highlights the belief in God's special attention to the innocent and helpless.

Resilience and Hope: The narrative of the baby's recovery and eventual discharge from the hospital embodies themes of resilience and hope, central to many biblical stories and teachings. This mirrors the scriptural assurances found in Jeremiah 29:11, where God speaks of giving us hope and a future.

Sacredness of Every Moment: The chaplain intern's realization of the sacredness inherent in both life's beginnings and endings aligns with Ecclesiastes 3:1-8, which speaks of there being a time for every purpose under heaven. The NICU is presented as a place where the sacredness of every moment, no matter how small, is acknowledged and celebrated.

This story illustrates how biblical themes are woven into everyday experiences, showing that the presence of the divine can be recognized in all aspects of life, from the joyous to the challenging. The NICU, a place of both vulnerability and profound strength, serves as a reminder of the spiritual dimensions of caregiving and the chaplaincy's role in witnessing and nurturing life's sacred moments.

Prayer

Heavenly Father, We come before You with reverence and awe, recognizing the sanctity of life that You have bestowed upon us. You are the author of life, and every person is fearfully and wonderfully made in Your image. Help us, Lord, to cherish and uphold the sanctity of every human life. Forgive us, Lord, for the times when we have failed to recognize the value of life, whether through our words, actions, or inactions. Renew in us a deep respect for the dignity and worth of every individual, from conception to natural death. Grant us the compassion to defend and protect the most vulnerable among us – the unborn, the elderly, the sick, and the marginalized. Help us to be voices for the voiceless, advocates for the defenseless, and champions of justice for all. Lord, may our hearts be moved with love and compassion for those who are facing difficult circumstances, and may we offer them support and assistance in their time of need. May Your grace and mercy abound in every situation, leading to healing, restoration, and reconciliation. Thank You, Lord, for the precious gift of life. May we honor You by honoring the sanctity of life in all its forms. In Jesus' name we pray, Amen.

78

The Presence of God in Life's Transitions

Selina's room at the hospice was small but filled with the sort of light that made you think of late spring mornings. The kind of light that seemed too earnest for the sobering reality of an in-patient hospice unit. Yet, there it was, illuminating the frail figure of a woman whose spirit refused to acknowledge the confines of her aging body.

When I first met Selina, she greeted me not with frailty, but with a historian's command of her own life narrative. Her stories unfurled like the pages of a well-thumbed book, eager to reveal the chapters of a century. "I've seen things you wouldn't believe, young man," she told me with a wink, settling more comfortably into her pillows.

Her laughter was light, almost musical, despite the oxygen tube that looped under her nose. "They tell me I don't have much time left," she said, taking a spoonful of apple sauce with a steady hand, "but I've been dying since the day I was born. We all are, aren't we?" Her chuckle softened the edges of her words.

Selina spoke often of the bright light she had seen decades ago, a beacon in the chaos of a near-death experience. "It was Jesus, or maybe an angel, but definitely some sort of emissary of God," she mused, her eyes distant yet vivid with the memory. "It was like being bathed in pure love, nothing else mattered. It was a promise that there's something more than just this," she gestured around her at the hospice room.

I listened, often in silence, as she recounted that moment. As a chaplain, my role was to affirm, not to discount; to listen, not to lead. Selina wasn't looking for validation—her faith was unshakable—but she relished the sharing, the connection that came from a shared understanding of something beyond our mortal reach.

Each visit, I found her surrounded by fading photographs and letters, the ephemera of a long life. But it was the intangible she cherished most, the memories, the spiritual encounters that seemed as real to her now as they were fifty years ago.

"You know, I'm not afraid," she confided during one of my visits, her voice steadier than her breathing. "I've been there already, to that edge where life and something else blur into one. It's peaceful and calm. I was sent back once, but next time, I think I'll stay."

Our conversations often turned to theology, to philosophy, to the myriad interpretations of life's final transition. But they were never morose. Selina approached her own mortality with the curiosity of a scholar and the acceptance of a sage.

When her time came, it was peaceful—a gentle sigh into that bright light she had described so vividly. Her passing was like a whispered benediction, a serene end to a storied life.

In the aftermath, I thought often of the lessons she imparted, of the grace with which she faced the end. Selina taught me more about living than dying, about embracing each day not as a step toward the inevitable but as a moment complete unto itself, suffused with the possibility of light, of love, and of peace. Her stories, like echoes of that profound light she so cherished, lingered long after she was gone, reminding us of all to look beyond the horizon with wonder and hope.

Christian Themes and Values

Eternal Life and the Hope of Resurrection: Selina's reflections on her near-death experience and her anticipation of something beyond mortal existence touch on the Christian belief in eternal life, as promised in John 11:25-26, where Jesus states, "I am the resurrection and the life. The one who believes in me will live, even though they die." Selina's serene approach to her impending death reflects a deep faith in this promise.

The Presence of God in Life's Transitions: Selina's recounting of her encounter with a bright light, interpreted as Jesus or an angel, resonates with Biblical descriptions of divine encounters that bring comfort and assurance, such as Paul's conversion experience on the road to Damascus (Acts 9:3-6). Her experience reinforces the theme of God's comforting presence during critical life moments.

The Peace of God: Selina's description of her near-death experience as being "bathed in pure love" echoes the Biblical theme of the peace that comes from God, which surpasses all understanding (Philippians 4:7). This peace seems to sustain her as she faces the end of her life, showing a profound spiritual calmness that transcends human fear.

Wisdom and Reflection on Life: Selina's life stories and the way she shares them reflect the Biblical value placed on wisdom and the recounting of one's life experiences as a form of legacy and teaching. This is similar to the wisdom literature in the Bible, such as the book of Proverbs, which values the sharing of knowledge and life lessons.

Acceptance of Mortality: Her acknowledgment that "we've been dying since the day we were born" touches on the Biblical understanding of human mortality outlined in Hebrews 9:27, "Just as people are destined to die once, and after that to face judgment." Selina's acceptance is portrayed not as resignation but as a profound understanding of life's cycle.

Faith as a Personal Journey: The narrative shows that faith is a deeply personal journey, illustrated by Selina's individual experiences and convictions rather than institutional doctrines. This aligns with the Biblical theme of a personal relationship with God, emphasized throughout the New Testament as central to Christian faith.

Comfort and Support in Community: The chaplain's role as a listener and a supportive presence reflects the Christian call to bear one another's burdens (Galatians 6:2) and to comfort others in their troubles with the comfort we ourselves receive from God (2 Corinthians 1:4).

Theological Reflections on Death: The discussions about theology and philosophy regarding life's final transition highlight the importance of grappling with existential questions, a theme found throughout the wisdom books in the Bible.

Selina's story, as told through the chaplain's perspective, encapsulates these themes, presenting a narrative rich in spiritual insight, peace in the face of death, and the promise of something greater beyond this life. This serves as a powerful reminder of the Christian hope in eternal life and the presence of divine love and peace throughout the journey of life and beyond.

Prayer

Heavenly Father, As we journey through life's transitions, we are grateful for Your constant presence with us. You are the Alpha and the Omega, the beginning and the end, and You are with us in every step of our journey. Help us, Lord, to trust in Your guidance and provision as we navigate the changes and uncertainties of life. Lord, as we face new beginnings, grant us the courage to step out in faith, knowing that You are leading us into Your perfect plan for our lives. May Your presence be our confidence and assurance as we embark on new paths and embrace new opportunities. Lord, in the midst of transitions, may we find our stability and security in You. Help us to anchor our souls in Your unchanging love and faithfulness, knowing that You are our rock and our refuge in every season of life. As we journey through life's transitions, may we draw closer to You, growing in faith and dependence on Your grace. May Your presence guide us, strengthen us, and fill us with hope, knowing that You are with us always, to the very end of the age. In Jesus' name we pray, Amen.

79

Community and Collective Responsibility

The hallways of the nursing home carried the weight of abandonment, with each echo a reminder of lives retreating into silence. It was late afternoon, and the filtered light seemed too gentle for the starkness of these lives pressed between aging walls. I walked through the hallway as residents called out, their voices blending into a choir of need and loneliness. They knew why I was there. Death was no stranger to this place.

"Pray for me, chaplain," some shouted. "The dead guy is in that room," another said with shrill indifference.

In room 204, Terry lay still. The room smelled faintly of antiseptic and something dirty and musty, artificially masking the stench of decay. He was covered by a thin, white sheet, his face untouched by the passage of hours, staring at nothing. I had never met Terry while he lived, yet here I was to shepherd him in death.

The social worker's notes had been brief: "Terry, mid-thirties, cerebral palsy, estranged family, no visitors in months. Patient seems to have had a stroke and died alone. Medical Examiner to be notified." The sadness of these lines, so starkly laid out, was a weight I felt deeply.

I turned to the nursing assistants who lingered at the door, their expressions a mix of relief and duty. "Would you join me, please?" I asked. They nodded, and together with a custodian who had known Terry only by room number and care needs, approached the bedside with heads bowed.

As I prepared to give the last rites, I considered the anonymity of Terry's suffering, the solitude of his final moments. There was a profound injustice in dying unmoored from the bonds of love and community, yet here, in this neglected room, Terry's humanity demanded recognition.

"Though no family comes to claim him, Terry is not alone," I began, my voice steady in the fetid air. "We are here as witnesses to his life, which was more than its end. In the eyes of the divine, no one is truly forgotten."

The prayers I offered were simple but fervent, a plea for peace and a testament to a life that mattered, if only because every life matters. We stood around Terry in silence, the room filled with a sacred presence that transcended the everyday neglect it usually housed.

After the prayers, as I prepared to leave, one of the assistants, a young woman with sorrowful eyes, touched my arm. "Thank you," she said, her voice a whisper. "It feels like he was someone, for a moment."

"He was always someone," I replied. "We all are. It's just that sometimes the world forgets to notice."

Leaving the nursing home, the dusk settling like a soft blanket over the city, I carried Terry with me. He, like so many others, had slipped through the cracks of a world too busy, too harsh, too indifferent. But in that room, for those moments, he had been seen. In the end, perhaps that was all we could offer to witness, to remember, and to affirm the dignity inherent in each passing soul.

Christian Themes and Values

The Sanctity of Human Life: The chaplain's actions underscore the Biblical principle that every life is sacred, irrespective of one's social status, health, or the circumstances of their death. This theme aligns with Genesis 1:27, which states that humans are created in the image of God, and thus, every life possesses inherent dignity and worth.

The Ministry of Presence and Comfort: The chaplain's decision to perform the last rites and the communal prayer highlights the Christian call to comfort those who mourn and to be present in the lives of the suffering and marginalized, as reflected in Matthew 25:36, where Jesus commends those who visit the sick and imprisoned, saying, "I was sick and you looked after me."

The Reality of Human Mortality and Neglect: Terry's solitary death points to the Biblical lament over human mortality and societal neglect. Ecclesiastes 9:5 reminds us that "For the living know that they will die, but the dead know nothing," emphasizing the stark reality of death and the often-uncomfortable acknowledgment of our own mortality.

Community and Collective Responsibility: The story highlights the Biblical imperative for community responsibility towards the vulnerable and isolated. In the parable of the Good Samaritan (Luke 10:25-37), Jesus teaches the importance of caring for those in need, regardless of their background or circumstances, illustrating the call to act as neighbors to all.

The Role of Memory and Witness: The chaplain's reflections on Terry being "seen" in his final moments, and his assertion that "We all are [someone]," reflect the Biblical theme of God's omniscient presence and the idea that no one is forgotten by God. Psalms 139:15-16 speaks of God's intimate knowledge of us, even from the womb, suggesting a divine witness to every human life.

Justice and Injustice: The recognition of the "profound injustice" in Terry's lonely death resonates with the Biblical concern for justice, as seen in Proverbs 31:8-9, which urges us to "Speak up for those who cannot speak for themselves, for the rights of all who are destitute." This passage calls for advocacy on behalf of those who are overlooked or neglected by society.

Hope and Redemption: Although Terry's life ended in obscurity and neglect, the chaplain's prayers and the sacred nature of the last rites session inject a note of hope and redemption, affirming that in the eyes of God, every life is significant. This aligns with the Christian hope of eternal life and redemption through Christ, as articulated in Romans 8:38-39, which assures us that nothing "in all creation, will be able to separate us from the love of God that is in Christ Jesus our Lord."

This story illustrates how the principles and teachings of Christianity call believers to acknowledge the dignity of every person, provide comfort and presence in moments of need, and remember those society has forgotten.

Prayer

Heavenly Father, We thank You for the gift of community and the call to collective responsibility. You have created us to live in relationship with one another, to support and uplift one another in love. Help us, Lord, to embrace our role in building up the community and to fulfill our collective responsibility to care for one another. Grant us the wisdom to recognize the needs of those around us and the courage to respond with compassion and generosity. May we be willing to share our resources, time, and talents for the well-being of the community, knowing that as we give, so we shall receive. Teach us to bear one another's burdens, to rejoice with those who rejoice, and to weep with those who weep. May our actions be a reflection of Your love, bringing healing, hope, and reconciliation to our communities. In Jesus' name we pray, Amen.

80

The Ministry of Presence

The inpatient hospice unit was quiet as I walked through its halls, a sanctified quiet that only those who work around dying folks understand. The day was just like any other, marked by a sobering reminder of the inevitability that all life must end, punctuated today by the soon-to- depart Jacob.

I had been visiting Jacob for months, watching the steady decline, supporting his family, navigating the tumultuous waters of grief with them, and working as part of an intensive hospice team. It had become a routine of sorts, this integration into their lives, a piece of their world as they faced the unthinkable. Yet, when the moment came, and Jacob passed, the family gathered, closed in around their grief which was intimate and sacred and suddenly, there was no space left for me.

"Thanks for your good work," Jacob's wife had said, her voice steady, eyes dry. It was the end of the line for me, not in terms of my work—there were always more patients, more families—but for this particular journey with this particular family.

The call came later, official and impersonal. "Death visit completed. Family grieving naturally and appropriately. Funeral home called. Not a medical examiner case." As if those sterile words in the email could encapsulate the depth of a family's pain, or the finality of a life ended. As if my role, now unnecessary, could be switched off like a light.

I drove home in the dim light of evening, the weight of the incomplete lingering like a stubborn fog. It wasn't uncommon, this feeling. The life of a hospice chaplain is often one of unfinished symphonies and abrupt goodbyes.

You step into the river of someone's life at its most turbulent and leave before the waters still.

Perhaps I'd stop by the funeral, I thought. It wasn't expected or required, but it was something. A final gesture, a silent nod to the shared humanity that did not end with death. A confirmation that my role, however briefly it intersected with their lives, was more than procedural.

At the funeral, I stood at the back, watching the family I had come to know in such a profound and peculiar way. They didn't see me, absorbed in their farewell, the finality of a casket, the stark reality of a grave. But I was there, paying my respects not just to the deceased, but to the journey we had shared.

As I left, the words "Well, at least I know that I've done my job and God thanks me anyway" echoed quietly in my mind. It wasn't about being remembered or thanked; it was about being there, in those crucial, closing moments of a person's life story, even if the last page turned without me.

And so, with a silent prayer for the departed and a nod to the enduring struggle of the living, I walked back to my car, ready for the next call, the next family, the next opportunity to serve. This was the life I had chosen, or perhaps that had chosen me—a ministry at the edge of mortal existence, where every goodbye was both an ending and a reminder of why I started.

Christian Themes and Values

The Transience of Life: The inevitability of death that pervades the hospice setting underscores the biblical teaching on the transience of life, reminiscent of passages like James 4:14, which states, "What is your life? You are a mist that appears for a little while and then vanishes." This theme highlights the temporal nature of human existence compared to the eternity that follows.

The Ministry of Presence: The chaplain's role is primarily one of presence—being with families in their moments of profound grief and transition, which echoes the Biblical theme of "comforting those who mourn" (Matthew 5:4) and "bearing one another's burdens" (Galatians 6:2). This ministry of presence is reflective of Christ's example of compassion and empathy towards those suffering or in pain.

Sacredness of Death: The description of death as intimate and sacred aligns with the Biblical view that every moment of life, including its end, holds spiritual significance. This can be linked to Ecclesiastes 3:1-2, which speaks of a time for everything, including "a time to be born and a time to die." The chaplain's experience shows reverence for these divinely appointed times.

Service and Calling: The chaplain's reflection on their role and the impact of their work—even when it feels incomplete—mirrors the Biblical notion of service as a calling that is often fulfilled in ways that go beyond visible results. This is similar to the parable of the sower (Matthew 13:3-9), where the seeds are sown without certainty of which will grow, reflecting the unpredictable yet faithful nature of spiritual and pastoral work.

Isolation and Community in Grief: The family's turning inward in their grief, and the chaplain feeling momentarily excluded, touches on the dual Biblical themes of community and individual mourning. While Christianity emphasizes communal support (Romans 12:15, "Rejoice with those who rejoice; mourn with those who mourn"), it also recognizes the deeply personal nature of grief, as seen in the solitude of figures like Job.

Continuation of Ministry: The chaplain's decision to attend the funeral unobtrusively, and their ongoing commitment to serve other families, illustrates the perseverance and dedication advocated in the Bible. 2 Timothy 4:2 instructs, "Preach the word; be prepared in season and out of season; correct, rebuke, and encourage—with great patience and careful instruction."

Eternal Perspective: The chaplain's internal acknowledgment of their service being ultimately recognized by God, regardless of human acknowledgment, reflects an eternal perspective encouraged in Colossians 3:23-24, "Whatever you do, work at it with all your heart, as working for the Lord, not for human masters... It is the Lord Christ you are serving."

This story illustrates the chaplain's role as both a spiritual guide and a compassionate presence, navigating the sacred journey of life's end with humility and deep faith, and highlighting the profound Biblical truths about life, death, and the calling to serve others in their most critical moments.

Prayer

Heavenly Father, We thank You for the ministry of presence, for the gift of being able to be with one another in times of joy and sorrow, in times of celebration and grief. You are the God who is always present with us, and You call us to be present with one another, sharing in each other's joys and sorrows. Lord, help us to be fully present with those around us, listening with empathy, comforting with compassion, and sharing in their joys and struggles. May we offer the gift of our presence as a reflection of Your love and care for each of Your children. Teach us to be attentive to the needs of others, to offer a shoulder to lean on, a listening ear, and a caring heart. Help us to be present with those who are lonely, hurting, or in need, offering them Your comfort and peace. In Jesus' name we pray, Amen.

81

Skepticism and Faith

In the dim light of Irv's bedroom, where the sun filtered through half-drawn blinds, casting long shadows across the floor, we sat discussing life's deeper questions. The air was thick with the scent of cigar smoke mixed with the old books that lined his small room—remnants of his professorial past.

Irv, despite the tubes and oxygen that now partially defined his existence, managed to keep his humor sharp and his inquiry even sharper. "Have you read Kierkegaard, chaplain?" he'd ask, chuckling softly as he struggled to adjust his pillows. "Not Spinoza's dry texts, I hope. They might cure insomnia, but they don't stir the soul. Einstein loved Spinoza's God."

He was a cynic about religion, yet endlessly fascinated by it. To Irv, life was a grand debate stage, and he was perpetually in the middle of a rebuttal. "The church, it's a sham, a scam, and a bad plan," he'd declare with a theatrical wave of his hand, the sparkle in his eyes belying the harshness of his words. "I've had a lot of Catholic friends, and they've told me a lot of stories."

"I mean, think about it," Irv continued, "Jesus was just a good rabbi, perhaps a bit naïve and neurotic. Could you imagine him preaching to the Pharisees while balancing on one foot?" His laugh, though weakened by illness, still filled the room with its resonance.

We often find ourselves tangled in metaphysical musings. "We're all caterpillars, eh, chaplain? Hoping to turn into butterflies." His tone softened. "But who wants to get stuck in the pupa stage? Just a bag of mucous hanging in the sunlight."

One afternoon, Irv looked at me with a peculiar earnestness. "Do you think I'll become a butterfly when I die, chaplain?" he asked, his voice carrying a hint of jest, yet edged with genuine curiosity.

"Is this some sort of Zen koan?" I asked, half-smiling.

"Yea, sure, but don't think too hard," he quipped back. "In fact, don't think at all. You know, the best thing you can do at times like this is to simply take a crap and enjoy it."

We laughed together, the sound mingling with the soft beeps of his monitors. It was moments like these, stripped of any pretense or solemnity, which revealed the essence of human connection. Amid the philosophical debates and the playful banter, there was a profound understanding between us. A recognition of life's fleeting nature and the importance of every shared laugh and exchanged idea.

As his days dwindled, our conversations grew more reflective, less about the contrivances of religious dogma and more about the essence of the human spirit and the connections we forge. Even as his body weakened, Irv's mind remained a bastion of inquiry and humor, his spirit undeterred by the encroaching finality of his journey.

When Irv finally passed, it was as if a library had burnt down, you know, like the great Roman library in Alexandria, so vast was the repository of knowledge and insight that left with him. At his memorial, not held in any church but in the very room where we had spent countless hours discussing life and death, I shared stories of our debates and the laughter that ensued.

"He was a caterpillar who indeed became a butterfly," I concluded, glancing around at the faces of those he had touched, each of us transformed in some way by his questioning, his humor, and his unrelenting humanity. As I spoke, I could almost hear his laughter echoing, a reminder that even in our darkest moments, there can be light, and in every end, a transformation awaits.

Christian Themes and Values

The Value of Wisdom and Inquiry: Irv's persistent questioning and intellectual curiosity reflect the Biblical value placed on seeking wisdom. This is reminiscent of the book of Ecclesiastes, where the Teacher pursues wisdom and understanding as a way to grasp the meaning of life. Like Ecclesiastes, Irv engages deeply with life's existential questions, seeking to understand rather than merely to accept.

The Human Condition and Mortality: Irv's acknowledgment of his condition and the philosophical discussions about life and death echo the Biblical understanding of human mortality and the fleeting nature of life (Psalm 103:15-16). His analogy of caterpillars transforming into butterflies parallels the Christian concept of resurrection and transformation beyond death.

Skepticism and Faith: Irv's skepticism about organized religion and his characterization of Jesus as "just a good rabbi" highlight the theme of doubt and faith wrestling within an individual. This theme is present throughout the Bible, notably in the story of Doubting Thomas (John 20:24-29), where doubt leads to a deeper understanding and affirmation of faith.

Community and Companionship: The chaplain's presence and engagement with Irv underscore the Biblical theme of community and bearing one another's burdens (Galatians 6:2). Their conversations and shared laughter provide comfort and companionship, illustrating how relational connections can transcend doctrinal differences.

Humor and Joy in Suffering: The use of humor, even in the face of death, resonates with the Biblical notion that joy can be found in all circumstances (Philippians 4:4). Irv's ability to laugh and find humor in his situation reflects a profound spiritual resilience, a coping mechanism that brings light to dark times.

The Search for Authenticity and Meaning: Irv's discussions about the essence of human spirit and the connections we forge are aligned with the Biblical quest for authentic living and meaningful relationships, highlighted in Jesus' commandment to love one another (John 13:34-35). This theme is central to Irv's interactions and his legacy.

Transformation and Hope: The metaphor of Irv as a caterpillar transforming into a butterfly captures the Christian hope in eternal life and transformation through Christ. This metaphor is tied to the Biblical promise of new life and hope beyond the physical existence (1 Corinthians 15:51-54).

Legacy and Memory: Irv's passing likened to the loss of a great library, and the celebration of his life in the space where he shared his thoughts, emphasizes the Biblical theme of legacy and the lasting impact of one's life and teachings (2 Timothy 4:7). Irv's intellectual and spiritual legacy continues to resonate, much like the philosophical and theological discussions preserved in Scripture.

The story of Irv, a fiercely inquisitive and cynical former professor in his final days, presents a rich tableau of biblical themes explored through the lens of philosophical inquiry and human connection. These themes weave together to form a narrative that not only challenges the conventional understanding of faith and skepticism but also celebrates the depth and complexity of human connection, the relentless pursuit of truth, and the transformative power of companionship and dialogue in the face of life's ultimate transition.

Prayer

Heavenly Father, We come before You acknowledging the tension between skepticism and faith that often resides within us. Help us, Lord, to navigate this tension with humility and trust in Your wisdom and guidance. When doubts arise and questions linger, grant us the courage to bring them before You, knowing that You are not afraid of our doubts and uncertainties. Strengthen our faith, Lord, that we may trust in Your promises even when we cannot see the answers. Lord, help us to remember that faith is not the absence of doubt but the decision to trust You despite our doubts. Teach us to lean not on our own understanding, but to acknowledge You in all our ways, trusting that You will make our paths straight. Grant us discernment, Lord, to recognize the difference between healthy skepticism that leads us to seek truth and faith that anchors us in Your promises. May our doubts lead us closer to You, rather than driving us away. Lord, we lift up to You all who are struggling with doubt and skepticism today – those who are wrestling with questions of faith, searching for meaning and truth. May Your Spirit speak peace to their hearts and lead them into a deeper understanding of Your love and grace. Thank You, Lord, for Your patience and faithfulness, even when we falter in our faith. Strengthen us, Lord, and help us to trust in You more deeply, knowing that You are the author and perfecter of our faith. In Jesus' name we pray, Amen.

82

The Challenges of Caregiving

When I told my mother about the assisted living facility up north, she hurled a bowl of sugar at me, and the white grains scattered like snow across the kitchen floor. "You're not going to put me in some goddam nursing home up north," she yelled, her voice sharp enough to slice through the humid Florida air.

"Well, not right now, but . . ." I started, but she cut me off with a wave of her hand and a command to "take a hike and go back to Maryland."

So, I left her there in her sun-drenched bungalow in Boca, surrounded by palm trees and her relentless independence. She gave up driving not long after, relinquishing her car keys like a captain abandoning his ship. In their place, she adopted a diet of ice cream—breakfast, lunch, and dinner, each serving paired with a glass of her favored Cabernet Franc. It was an odd sort of freedom, punctuated by her fiery spirit.

Over the next four years, I flew down every few months. Each visit was a check on her fortress of solitude—how she managed to survive, and how many home aides had fled her service. It seemed she was a general as much as a mother, leading a one-woman rebellion against the advance of age.

When she reached ninety-five, the fortress finally surrendered. It wasn't an enemy that breached her walls but time itself, eroding them slowly until they could no longer stand. I put her in an ambulance, her kingdom shrinking to the size of a gurney as she was driven north to Maryland, to an assisted living facility that looked more like a resort than the nursing homes she feared.

I tried to serve as her chaplain, her spiritual guide through the twilight of her years, but I was a disaster. To her, everything I said about God, Jesus, Buddha, or the Tibetan Book of the Dead was as substantial as smoke. "All nonsense," she'd declare with a scoff, dismissing my attempts to weave spirituality into her days.

Then came Rod, a chaplain from another hospice, with a voice like silk and a gentle demeanor that somehow breached her defenses. She liked him, really liked him, and listened to what he had to say. One day, as we stood watching her nap, the sun casting peaceful patterns over her face, Rod gave me advice I'd carry like a talisman. "You can't minister to your own family. They know all of your failings and faults, and they'll only see you through those cloudy, cataract-filled lenses."

He was right. My efforts to be her spiritual guide were colored by years of history, by every argument and every tender moment we had shared. I couldn't be her chaplain, not in the way she needed.

So, I took Rod's words to heart and stepped back. I got a new pair of glasses, metaphorically speaking—rose-colored, to see her not as a project to be managed or a soul to be saved, but as my mother, vibrant and stubborn to the end. And in that shifting view, I found a new way to be with her, simply as her son, sharing in her final days with laughter, ice cream, and yes, even a glass or two of Cabernet Franc.

Christian Themes and Values

Honor and Respect for Parents: The commandment to "honor your father and your mother" (Exodus 20:12) is a foundational theme in this narrative. Despite the initial conflicts and the mother's resistance to assisted living, the son's continued efforts to ensure her well-being reflect his deep respect and honor for her as his parent.

The Challenges of Caregiving: The Biblical call to care for the vulnerable and elderly is evident in the son's persistent visits and eventual decision to move his mother to an assisted living facility. This mirrors the Christian responsibility to care for those who once cared for us, as suggested in 1 Timothy 5:4, which urges believers to "show piety at home and to repay their parents; for this is good and acceptable before God."

The Limits of Family in Spiritual Guidance: The son's struggle to be his mother's spiritual guide and the wisdom shared by Rod, the hospice chaplain, reflect the Biblical wisdom that sometimes our roles within our family need discernment and humility. This is reminiscent of Jesus' teachings in Matthew 10:36, where familial relationships can sometimes complicate the reception of spiritual guidance: "a man's enemies will be the members of his own household."

Acceptance and Adaptation: The son's acceptance of his mother's fiercely independent nature and his adaptation to simply being her son, rather than her spiritual guide, aligns with the Biblical theme of unconditional love and acceptance, as described in 1 Corinthians 13:4-7, where love "bears all things, believes all things, hopes all things, endures all things."

The Role of External Counselors: Rod's effective ministry to the mother underscores the importance of external spiritual counsel, as sometimes those not within the immediate family can provide a clearer, unbiased perspective. This can be linked to the role of prophets and wise counselors in the Bible who guide and provide wisdom to those in need.

End-of-Life Care and Dignity: The story respects the mother's dignity in her final years, highlighting the importance of providing care that honors the individual's character and preferences. This aligns with the Biblical principle found in Proverbs 16:31, "Gray hair is a crown of glory; it is gained in a righteous life."

The Journey Toward Death: The narrative delicately handles the spiritual and emotional dimensions of approaching death, emphasizing the need for peace, comfort, and acceptance in one's final days, resonant with Psalms 23, which speaks of God's comforting presence even in the "valley of the shadow of death."

This story portrays the complexities of familial relationships, caregiving, and spiritual guidance, offering rich insights into the emotional and spiritual journeys that accompany the aging and dying process within a biblical context.

Prayer

Heavenly Father, We come before You with hearts burdened by the challenges of caregiving. We acknowledge the immense responsibility and the deep sacrifices that caregivers make each day. Strengthen us, Lord, and grant us Your grace to face these challenges with love, patience, and perseverance. Lord, as caregivers, we often feel overwhelmed and exhausted by the demands placed upon us. Give us the strength to carry on, even when we feel weary, knowing that You are our source of strength and our ever-present help in times of need. Help us to find moments of rest and renewal in Your presence, Lord, and to cast all our cares upon You, for You care for us. Grant us wisdom and compassion as we care for our loved ones. Help us to see them through Your eyes, with love and dignity, and to meet their physical, emotional, and spiritual needs with grace and tenderness. Give us the courage to ask for help when we need it and to lean on the support of others. May we find strength and encouragement in the community of believers, who walk alongside us in our caregiving journey. Thank You, Lord, for the privilege of caring for others. May our caregiving be a reflection of Your love and compassion to those in need. In Jesus' name we pray, Amen.

83

Identity and Unity in Christ

At the historically black university where I attended seminary, I was often reminded to "preach the word as if your life depended on it, because it does." My professors were some of the greatest preachers to ever grace the pulpits of America, men and women whose voices could stir the soul and awaken the dormant spirit of any congregant who had the privilege to listen.

I was the only white man in my class, a minority in a sea of powerful voices and even stronger convictions. This detail, though trivial to some, was profound for me; it highlighted unity and division, all at once. Every day was an education not just in theology but in the human spirit, in the struggles and triumphs that echoed through the halls of that great institution.

The nine years it took to earn my master's and doctorate felt like both an eternity and a fleeting moment. Each lecture, each discussion, each sermon sharpened my understanding of the Divine God, and of my place not just in the church, but in the world.

One lesson stood out more than any other, a sort of culmination of all the teachings when my professor, a revered man in the community whose age seemed immeasurable, spoke of Jesus in the desert. He told us that our faith, like Jesus', would drive us into deserts of our own, would test us at the edges of our endurance and in the depths of our despair.

"Remember Moses at the burning bush," he said, his voice a calm command that filled the room. "He found his calling in a place of solitude and desolation. You might find yours in the same way."

Inspired by these words, I took a sabbatical after my graduation and traveled to a quiet desert town, where the red sands stretched like the surface of some distant, barren planet. I spent days in contemplation and nights under the vast, unpolluted skies, where stars seemed to speak in whispers of the infinite.

It was there, alone with the wind and the whispers, that I felt closest to the burning bush of Moses, to the solitude that transformed him. I understood that my education had equipped me not just to preach the word but to live it—to find the divine in desolation of the desert, to carry the message back from the wilderness to those who needed to hear it.

As I returned from the desert, feeling every grain of sand still clinging to my boots as a testament to my journey, I knew that my path was forever altered. My preaching, my ministry, and my life had taken on a new depth, a richness born of solitude and reflection. Something that led me to serving God through chaplaincy.

And so, in every prayer, in every comforting thought and word as a chaplain, I carried that desert with me. I brought the heat of the sun and the clarity of the night sky into the lives of those I ministered, preaching in action with the fervor and passion that had been ignited in me, trusting that every word, every gesture, was a step on the sacred path I had been called to walk.

Christian Themes and Values

The Power and Necessity of the Word: The admonition to "preach the word as if your life depended on it" highlights the Biblical theme of the power and essentiality of Scripture. This resonates with 2 Timothy 3:16-17, which emphasizes that all Scripture is God-breathed and useful for teaching, rebuking, correcting, and training in righteousness.

Education and Spiritual Growth: The seminary experience, filled with rigorous academic and spiritual instruction, reflects the Biblical importance of growth and maturation in faith, as noted in Ephesians 4:11-1This passage speaks to the role of church leaders in equipping the saints for the work of ministry and building up the body of Christ.

Identity and Unity in Christ: Being the only white man in a historically black institution underscores themes of unity and diversity within the body of Christ, echoing Galatians 3:28, where there is neither Jew nor Greek, slave nor free, male nor female, for all are one in Christ Jesus. This setting highlights the importance of transcending cultural and racial barriers within Christian communities.

Trials and Testing of Faith: The professor's reference to Jesus in the desert and the personal sabbatical in a desert town link to the Biblical theme of trials and divine testing, which are meant to refine and strengthen one's faith. Jesus' temptation in the desert (Matthew 4:1-11) serves as a model for enduring hardship and emerging stronger in faith.

Solitude and Revelation: The story draws on the theme of solitude as a space for divine encounter and revelation, akin to Moses' experience at the burning bush (Exodus 3:1-10). Solitude is portrayed as a transformative environment where significant spiritual revelations occur, shaping one's calling and ministry.

Divine Calling and Response: The narrative illustrates the theme of responding to God's call, as the student realizes his vocation not just in preaching but in living out the theological principles he has learned. This reflects Isaiah's response to God's call in Isaiah 6:8, where he says, "Here am I. Send me!"

Ministry of Presence and Service: Returning from the desert with a new understanding, the protagonist engages in a ministry of chaplaincy that emphasizes presence, comfort, and practical application of Biblical principles. This aligns with the Biblical mandate to comfort those in distress (2 Corinthians 1:3-4) and to act justly and love mercy (Micah 6:8).

Transformation and Witness: The lasting impact of the desert experience on the student's life and ministry embodies the theme of personal transformation leading to effective witness and service, illustrating Romans 12:1-2's call to be transformed by the renewing of the mind, enabling one to live out God's will.

The integration of these themes provides a tapestry that portrays the spiritual journey of a believer shaped by education, personal reflection, and a profound encounter with God. This journey underscores the holistic development of faith that informs, challenges, and equips individuals for lifelong ministry and service.

Prayer

Heavenly Father, We come before You with grateful hearts for the identity and unity we have in Christ. You have called us by name and made us Your children through the saving work of Your Son, Jesus Christ. Help us, Lord, to live out our identity as Your beloved children and to walk in unity with one another as members of Your body, the Church. Lord, in a world that often seeks to divide us based on our differences, help us to remember that our true identity is found in Christ alone. May we find our worth and value in being Your redeemed children, rather than in the things that divide us. Grant us the humility to recognize that we are all members of one body, with different gifts and callings, yet united in our common faith in Jesus Christ. Help us to celebrate and embrace the diversity within Your Church, knowing that it reflects Your beauty and creativity. Guide us, Lord, in living out our identity as Your children in every aspect of our lives – in our families, our communities, and our workplaces. May we reflect Your love, mercy, and grace to those around us, drawing others into relationship with You. In Jesus' name we pray, Amen.

84

The Transformative
Power of Love

Matthew had lived many years under the shadow of his family's expectations, a respectable Jewish family with deep roots and traditions stretching back generations. The Hanukkah candles, the Passover Seder, the prayers in Hebrew — these were the rituals of his youth, the framework upon which his identity had been built.

Yet, within him, there had always stirred a different kind of spirit, an inquisitiveness that led him beyond the familiar teachings and into the arms of a figure both deeply revered and controversial — Jesus Christ. Matthew's transformation was not a rejection of his Jewish heritage but an expansion of it. He saw it as a bridge extending towards a broader understanding of love and divinity, a fulfillment of ancient prophecies in a personal and transformative way.

His family didn't understand at first; such transitions were fraught with the specter of betrayal. It was like he had walked on the moon, as he often told his close friends — venturing into unknown realms from which return was uncertain. "I'm still Matthew," he would assure his dad, over cups of steaming coffee, his father's eyes welling up with a mixture of anger, fear and frustration. "Think of it as discovering a new room in the house we've always lived in."

To the broader world, Matthew referred to himself using various terms: Christian universalist, Christian humanist, transformationalist. Each label attempted to capture the essence of his faith, yet each fell short, tangled in theological implications and historical baggage. Over time, he realized that these labels served more to confound than to clarify.

Instead, he chose to embody his beliefs through actions. He volunteered at hospices, joined interfaith dialogues, provided counsel to those struggling with their own spiritual identities. His approach was simple: to live as a testament to the transformative power of love, a love he saw personified in Jesus Christ, yet universal in its reach.

"It's not about leaving behind who you are," Matthew would explain, his voice steady and assured as he addressed gatherings or intimate conversations. "It's about letting your understanding of love grow so vast that it encompasses even the most foreign and frightening things."

His life was a continuous act of walking that moon-like landscape, where each step was an act of faith, a demonstration of his belief in a God of transformation — a God who could turn the ordinary into the extraordinary, the human into the divine.

At community gatherings, instead of engaging in debates over doctrine or tradition, Matthew shared stories of kindness, acts of courage and moments of deep, human connection. His words were not sermons but testimonies to the power of living a life dedicated to love and service.

Over time, people began to see beyond the labels, to see Matthew — a man who loved deeply, served faithfully, and lived his truth with quiet dignity. In his journey, they recognized not a departure from faith but a deepening of it. They saw not a forsaking of heritage but an embracing of a universal call to love, a path marked by footsteps that, though solitary at first, were joined by others drawn by the light of his conviction.

Matthew's story, in its simplicity and complexity, echoed the truth he held dear: that we are all, regardless of the paths we walk, in search of light and love. And perhaps, in walking our diverse paths with integrity and compassion, we could all find that we are not so different after all.

Christian Themes and Values

Matthew's story illustrates several Biblical themes interwoven with his personal spiritual journey from a traditional Jewish background to embracing Christian beliefs, all while maintaining a respect for his heritage. Here are some of the key Biblical themes explored:

Fulfillment of Prophecy: Matthew's embrace of Jesus Christ as a continuation of his Jewish faith reflects the New Testament theme of Jesus as the fulfillment of Old Testament prophecies. This is often highlighted in the Gospel of Matthew, which frequently cites Old Testament prophecies to show how Jesus' life and mission complete these ancient predictions (e.g., Matthew 1:22-23).

Identity and Unity in Christ: Matthew's transformation highlights the themes of being spiritually reborn or transformed through Christ. This theme is central in passages like 2 Corinthians 5:17, where Paul writes, "Therefore, if anyone is in Christ, he is a new creation. The old has passed away; behold, the new has come." Matthew's journey symbolizes this new identity in Christ while maintaining his roots.

Interfaith Dialogue and Universal Love: Matthew's participation in interfaith dialogues and his description as a Christian universalist reflect the Biblical mandate to love universally. This theme resonates with Jesus' teaching in John 13:34-35, "A new command I give you: Love one another. As I have loved you, so you must love one another."

Living Faith Through Action: Matthew's commitment to volunteering and providing counsel is an embodiment of the Biblical instruction to live out one's faith through works, as emphasized in James 2:17, "In the same way, faith by itself, if it is not accompanied by action, is dead." His life becomes a testament to his faith through his actions of love and service.

Identity and Heritage: The story also touches on the theme of navigating one's spiritual identity without losing connection to one's heritage, similar to the experience of early Jewish Christians who struggled to retain their Jewish identity while embracing the teachings of Jesus. This reflects the broader scriptural narrative of continuity and change within the context of divine revelation.

Facing Opposition and Misunderstanding: Matthew's experiences with his family's initial perception of betrayal echo Jesus' experiences of misunderstanding and rejection by His own community and even His family, as described in Mark 6:4, "Jesus said to them, 'A prophet is not without honor except in his own town, among his relatives and in his own home.'"

The Power of Personal Testimony: Matthew's choice to share stories of kindness and human connection rather than engaging in doctrinal debates underscores the power of personal testimony in faith, a crucial theme found throughout the Acts of the Apostles. Testimonies serve as powerful tools for spiritual connection and understanding.

Universal Call to Love: Ultimately, Matthew's life reflects the universal call to love, which transcends religious boundaries and is a central message of the Christian Gospel. This is epitomized in passages like 1 John 4:8, "Whoever does not love does not know God, because God is love."

Matthew's narrative is a compelling portrayal of a spiritual journey marked by complexity, faithfulness, and a profound commitment to living out the principles of love and service that are central to both his Jewish upbringing and his Christian faith.

Prayer

Lord, our Creator and Sustainer, in the vast tapestry of existence, you have woven each of us with unique threads, crafting us in your image, and breathing life into our souls. Yet, in our diversity, we find our unity in Christ, our cornerstone and foundation. Grant us the wisdom to embrace our individual identities, celebrating the gifts and talents you have bestowed upon us. May we walk confidently in the knowledge of who we are in you, knowing that our worth is found not in the world's standards, but in your boundless love. At the same time, help us to recognize the unity we share as members of your body, the

Church. Bind us together with cords of love and understanding, regardless of our differences. Teach us to see one another through your eyes, as brothers and sisters in Christ, united by our faith and love for you. In times of doubt and uncertainty, remind us that our true identity is found in you alone. Let us find our strength and purpose in being your beloved children, called to live out your will on earth. Guide us, O Lord, to live out our identities as unique individuals while embracing the unity we have in Christ. May our lives reflect your grace, love, and truth to a world in desperate need of your healing touch. In the name of Jesus Christ, who unites us all, we pray. Amen.

85

Compassion and Care for the Suffering

Rebecca had seen more of life and death in her years as a hospice nurse than most would in several lifetimes. Her hands, though steady when administering care, were maps of veins like the roads she traveled on her countless house calls. Each wrinkle on her face told a story of a night spent by a dying patient's side, each gray strand of hair a reminder of the lives she'd touched.

We sat in the corner of a conference room, a weekly ritual. The morning light streamed through the window, casting a glow on her spectacles as she dissected her bacon with methodical precision. Between bites, the conversation shifted seamlessly from her grandchildren's latest antics to the gritty details of her work—feces, vomit, the worrisome color of a patient's urine.

"What was the color of the urine?" she asked, not skipping a beat, "Sort of brown with a sour smell. Very loose stools, and nothing in the rectal vault."

She visited Maebel twice a week, checking for any signs of improvement that might disqualify her from continued hospice care. "She's been eating only two small meals a day and pocketing most of it," Rebecca reported with clinical detachment. "I think she's still eligible. I don't advise a discharge at this time."

Her patients varied as widely as the Maryland weather. There was the man whose home was overrun with roaches, where she had to dress as if stepping onto another planet just to administer basic care. "How can I serve this guy? It's so disgusting," she exclaimed during one staff meeting, the frustration palpable in her voice.

Yet, despite the daily confrontations with decay and neglect, Rebecca's compassion never waned. I saw the tears she couldn't quite hide when talking about a long-time patient nearing the end. "Oh my God, I wish she would die already. She's suffering so."

The resilience of hospice workers like Rebecca often went unnoticed, their emotional labor unmeasured. They absorbed the stories of those they cared for, carrying the weight of lives ending and the dignity of death. And every week, they reappeared at the interdisciplinary team meetings, laden with stories and complaints about the incessant changes in rules and Medicare regulations. The technology that was supposed to ease their burden was often added to it.

"But they do their jobs, and they are a blessing," I found myself thinking, watching Rebecca gather her things, preparing for another visit, another life at its twilight. Praise God for their service, indeed.

As she left the meeting, the morning hustle began to swell around us. Rebecca disappeared into the thrum of the day, another figure in the crowd, yet carrying with her a sacred purpose that few could shoulder. In the quiet aftermath, the empty seat across from me spoke of the countless untold stories of those who give themselves daily to the care of the dying, a reminder of the profound humanity at the heart of hospice work.

Christian Themes and Values

Rebecca's experiences as a hospice nurse are rich with biblical themes that reflect deep spiritual truths about human life, suffering, and service.

Compassion and Care for the Suffering: Rebecca's daily work with the terminally ill reflects Jesus' teachings on compassion and care for the weakest and most vulnerable in society. This mirrors the parable of the Good Samaritan (Luke 10:25-37), where Jesus highlights the importance of caring for those in need, regardless of their situation or background.

The Sanctity of Life: Rebecca's dedication to her patients, even in their final moments, underscores the sanctity of life—a core principle in many biblical passages. In Psalm 139:13-16, the scripture speaks about God's knowledge and care for us from the womb, suggesting a divine regard for life at all stages.

Bearing One Another's Burdens: Rebecca's role involves not only physical care but also emotional support, embodying the biblical exhortation found in Galatians 6:2, "Bear one another's burdens, and so fulfill the law of Christ." Her work goes beyond mere duty; it is a form of bearing the emotional and physical burdens of those nearing the end of life.

The Dignity of Death: The dignified care Rebecca provides to those in their last days resonates with the Christian understanding of death not just as an end but as a transition to something beyond this life. This care ensures that patients maintain their dignity in death, reflecting the belief that each person is valuable and loved by God until their final breath.

Resilience and Perseverance: The challenges and emotional weight that Rebecca carries showcase the biblical themes of perseverance and resilience, similar to Paul's reflections on his hardships in 2 Corinthians 12:9-10, where he discusses how God's grace is sufficient, and power is made perfect in weakness.

Servanthood: Rebecca's service can be likened to the themes of servanthood, emphasized in Mark 10:45, where Jesus describes his mission: "For even the Son of Man came not to be served but to serve, and to give his life as a ransom for many." Her work in hospice care exemplifies this servant leadership.

Witness to Suffering: Rebecca's emotional response to her patients' suffering reflects the theme of being a witness to human pain and suffering, a motif seen in the actions of Jesus Himself, who was often moved by compassion upon seeing the crowds and their afflictions (Matthew 9:36).

The Role of Faith in Professional Life: Although not explicitly religious in her professional interactions, Rebecca's vocation as a hospice nurse can be seen as a form of living out one's faith through action—demonstrating love, compassion, and respect for all life, which are central tenets of Christianity.

Rebecca's story provides a powerful illustration of how biblical themes of compassion, servanthood, and the sanctity of life are enacted in the everyday lives of those who work in challenging and emotionally demanding fields like hospice care. Her story is a testament to the profound humanity and sacredness embedded in the care for those at the twilight of their lives.

Prayer

Gracious God, In your infinite compassion, you see the suffering of your children and hear their cries for help. You are the source of all comfort and healing, and we come before you with hearts burdened by the pain of those who are hurting. Grant us, O Lord, the eyes to see and the hearts to feel the suffering of others. Help us to cultivate compassion in our lives, to reach out with love and kindness to those who are in need. May we be your hands and feet, bringing relief to the afflicted and solace to the troubled. Guide us to care for the sick, the lonely, and the marginalized with tenderness and empathy. Give us the strength to bear their burdens, the patience to listen to their stories, and the courage to stand with them in their darkest moments. Help us to create communities of compassion, where no one is overlooked or forgotten, and where the needs of the vulnerable are met with love and dignity. May we be instruments of your peace, spreading your light and hope to all who are suffering. Teach us, O Lord, to see you in the faces of those who are in pain, knowing that whatever we do for the least of your children, we do for you. May our acts of compassion be a reflection of your boundless love and mercy. We lift up to you all who are suffering, asking for your healing touch and your comforting presence to surround them. May they find strength and hope in you, knowing that they are never alone. In the name of Jesus Christ, our compassionate Savior, we pray. Amen.

86

In the Image of God

In the calm expanse of early morning, when the sun's first rays cut sharp lines against the horizon, a man named Elijah sat by the ocean's edge, his eyes tracing the ceaseless roll of waves. He was a solitary figure, marked more by the passage of many years and the quiet contemplation of them than by any particular desire to be understood by others. Elijah had spent much of his life in pursuit of something he called the Divine Truth—a concept as vast and enigmatic as the sea before him.

As he watched the sunrise, illuminating the water with bursts of gold and crimson, Elijah reflected on the core essence of his long journey. "Love," he whispered to himself, the word mingling with the salty breeze. "In the image of God, we are woven from the fabric of Love itself."

The realization had come to him not as a thunderclap, but as the slow, steady unveiling of a universal truth, hidden yet omnipresent. To Elijah, acknowledging that he was made in the image of God meant recognizing Love as his own essence, an eternal flame that flickered within, guiding him through the shadowed parts of life.

His years had taught him that Love was not merely a sentiment, but the foundation of his being. It was a force that transcended the ego's incessant demands and the petty clutches of desire. Through countless acts of selflessness, moments of pure giving without thought of return, Elijah had chipped away at the veneer of selfishness that once encased him.

Now, sitting by the water's edge, he saw his life as a path marked by compassion, kindness, and an unshakeable commitment to understanding others. Each step was a thread in a greater tapestry, each action a note in a sacred melody that resonated through the chambers of his heart and echoed across the universe.

Elijah knew his name, his true name, was Love. It was a sacred vibration that the winds carried across oceans, that the stars hummed in the quiet of space, etched into the fabric of existence itself. In this profound understanding, he found liberation. For him, Love knew no boundaries—it was boundless, transcending all limits, encompassing all things.

As the sun climbed higher, casting a brilliant path across the water, Elijah felt a profound peace settle over him. He was no longer just a man by the sea; he was a part of the sea and the sky and the earth, a small but essential part of a cosmos held together by the thread of Divine Love. In that moment, he was truly free, his soul aglow with the radiant light of an eternal flame.

Christian Themes and Values

Elijah's reflective journey by the ocean encapsulates several profound Biblical themes centered around the nature of God, the essence of human life, and the transformative power of love.

Imago Dei (Image of God): Elijah's meditation on being made in the image of God resonates with the theological concept of "Imago Dei" found in Genesis 1:27, "So God created mankind in his own image, in the image of God he created them; male and female he created them." This doctrine emphasizes that human beings are reflections of God's character, endowed with dignity and worth.

Love as the Essence of Being: The story reflects the Biblical assertion that love is fundamental to the nature of God and, consequently, to human nature as beings created by God. This is echoed in 1 John 4:8, "Whoever does not love does not know God, because God is love." Elijah's realization that love is the core essence of his being aligns with this scriptural truth that to live in love is to live in God and God in us.

The Transformative Power of Love: Elijah's transformation through acts of selflessness and compassion illustrates the Biblical theme of sanctification through love. This transformation is akin to the teachings of Jesus on the greatest commandment in Matthew 22:37-39, which emphasizes loving God and loving one's neighbor as oneself as the fulfillment of the law.

Spiritual Liberation and Peace: The narrative culminates in Elijah experiencing a profound sense of peace and liberation, which parallels the peace that Christ promises to His followers in John 14:27, "Peace I leave with you; my peace I give you. I do not give to you as the world gives. Do not let your hearts be troubled and do not be afraid." Elijah's peace is a direct result of his deep connection with the divine love that permeates all creation.

Unity with Creation: Elijah's feeling of unity with the sea, sky, and earth embodies the Biblical theme of the harmony between creation and humanity when aligned under God's love. This reflects Romans 8:21, which speaks of creation itself being liberated from its bondage to decay and brought into the freedom and glory of the children of God.

Eternal and Boundless Nature of Divine Love: The depiction of love as boundless and transcending all limits aligns with the descriptions of God's eternal and infinite nature as described in Psalms and prophetic books. Psalm 103:11, for example, states, "For as high as the heavens are above the earth, so great is his steadfast love toward those who fear him."

Elijah's story, by capturing these themes, offers a reflection on the spiritual journey toward understanding and living out the truths of divine love, reflecting the deep and abiding biblical principles of creation, human identity, and the redemptive power of love.

Prayer

Heavenly Father, We come before You with hearts filled with gratitude for the privilege of being created in Your image. You have formed us with love and care, each one unique and precious in Your sight. Help us, Lord, to recognize the inherent value and dignity that You have bestowed upon us as image-bearers of God. Lord, in a world that often seeks to diminish the worth of individuals, help us to remember that every person is created in Your image and has inherent value and dignity. May we treat others with respect, kindness, and love, knowing that they are beloved by You. Grant us the wisdom to see beyond outward appearances and recognize the beauty of Your image reflected in each person we encounter. Help us to honor and affirm the uniqueness and diversity of Your creation, celebrating the rich tapestry of humanity. Lord, may our lives reflect Your image more fully each day, as we grow in love, holiness, and compassion. Help us to bear witness to Your love and grace through our words and actions, bringing hope and healing to a broken world. Thank You, Lord, for creating us in Your image and for the privilege of bearing Your likeness in the world. May we always strive to reflect Your image in all that we do, bringing glory to Your name. In Jesus' name we pray, Amen.

87

Spiritual Growth
Through Trials

Thomas had always felt his life to be a relentless ebb and flow, much like the tides of the sea he loved so much. A sailor by trade and a philosopher by nature, he'd spent years navigating both the literal and metaphorical storms of existence. His ship, a sturdy sloop with peeling paint and a well-worn deck, was as much a part of him as his own sinewy arms and weather-beaten face.

In his solitary journeys across the vast, indifferent ocean, Thomas wrestled with the existential struggles that defined his being. The ocean was unforgiving, a constant reminder of his frailty and the ultimate power of nature. Yet, it was in this confrontation with the wild sea that Thomas found a profound sense of connection with the Divine Creator, a force as omnipresent as the salt in the air and as mysterious as the depths below.

Each wave that crashed against the bow of his boat, each squall that threatened to topple him, echoed the inner tumult of his soul—ever-changing, ever-fluid. Life's trials—loss, betrayal, the death of comrades at sea—were his relentless tide, pulling at the moorings of his spirit, testing his resolve.

Yet, it was in these depths of despair that Thomas discovered the essence of his growth. The harsh winds that filled his sails also toughened his character, carving out virtues of resilience and strength. With every storm weathered, every danger navigated, he unearthed a bit more of his humanity, his capacity to endure and to hope.

Amidst the chaos of a tempest, when the horizon was obscured by a fury of wind and rain, Thomas found his solace in knowing that this, too, was part of a larger dance—a dance of light and shadow, of struggle and ease. The solitude of the sea provided him with space to reflect, to wrestle with his doubts, and to emerge with a clearer sense of purpose.

In facing the unknown, with only the stars to guide him by night and the sun by day, Thomas found his courage. The solitude was not a burden but a gift; it allowed him to hear the whispers of the wind, the ancient rhythms of the earth and sky that spoke of a greater journey.

As he stood at the helm, watching another dawn break over the boundless water, Thomas felt a deep, unshakable peace. Here, in the struggle of his finite journey, he had discovered his meaning and purpose. It was not about conquering the sea or mapping uncharted territories, but about mastering the inner currents, understanding his place in the cosmos, and embracing the divine struggle that shaped his soul.

Christian Themes and Values

Thomas's story, set against the backdrop of his solitary seafaring life, is rich with Biblical themes that resonate with the spiritual journey of many biblical figures.

The Sovereignty of God Over Creation: Thomas's acknowledgment of the ocean's vast and unforgiving nature parallels biblical themes of God's sovereignty over creation, as seen in Job 38, where God questions Job about the creation of the earth and commands the waters, highlighting His ultimate control over the natural world.

Human Frailty and Divine Strength: Thomas's experiences of vulnerability in the face of nature's might reflect the themes of human frailty contrasted with divine strength. This theme is prevalent throughout the Psalms, such as Psalm 46:1-3, which portrays God as a refuge and strength, an ever-present help in trouble, despite the earth giving way and mountains falling into the sea.

Spiritual Growth Through Trials: The trials Thomas faces, such as storms and solitude, echo the biblical principle that suffering and challenges refine and strengthen one's character and faith. This is similar to the message in James 1:2-4, which encourages believers to consider it pure joy when facing trials because the testing of faith develops perseverance.

Solitude as a Space for Divine Encounter: Thomas's solitude at sea, providing space for deep reflection and encounter with the divine, mirrors the biblical motif of seeking solitude for spiritual clarity and communion with God. Examples include Jesus' frequent withdrawals to lonely places to pray, as noted in Luke 5:16.

The Quest for Meaning and Purpose: Thomas's journey towards understanding his place in the cosmos and mastering the inner currents of his soul is reminiscent of the existential quest found in Ecclesiastes. Here, the Preacher searches for meaning in various earthly pursuits only to find fulfillment in fearing God and keeping His commandments (Ecclesiastes 12:13-14).

Resilience and Endurance: The resilience Thomas develops through confronting physical and existential storms parallels the biblical exhortation to endure hardship as discipline. Hebrews 12:7-11 discusses enduring hardship as discipline from God, which produces a harvest of righteousness and peace for those trained by it.

Peace That Transcends Understanding: Finally, the peace Thomas experiences despite his circumstances aligns with Philippians 4:7, which speaks of the peace of God, which transcends all understanding and guards the hearts and minds in Christ Jesus. Thomas's sense of peace amidst the chaos of the sea reflects this supernatural calm.

Thomas's reflective and challenging journey on the sea serves as a metaphor for the spiritual voyage that many undertake, using the Biblical framework of creation's grandeur, life's trials, and the quest for deeper understanding and peace. Each element of his story highlights the transformative power of embracing one's vulnerabilities and the spiritual lessons learned through perseverance and solitude.

Prayer

Divine Creator, We come before You with hearts open to Your refining work in our lives through trials and challenges. We acknowledge that in the midst of difficulties, You are at work shaping us, molding us, and drawing us closer to You. Grant us the grace to grow spiritually through the trials we face. Lord, when we are faced with trials, help us to count it all joy, knowing that the testing of our faith produces steadfastness. Give us the perseverance to endure, trusting in Your promise that You will never leave us nor forsake us. Teach us to see trials as opportunities for growth and refinement, rather than obstacles to our faith. May we lean on You in times of trouble, finding strength and comfort in Your presence. Lord, may our trials deepen our dependence on You and increase our intimacy with You. Help us to surrender our will to Yours, knowing that Your plans for us are good and that You work all things together for our good. Grant us the wisdom to discern Your purposes in the midst of trials, and the faith to trust You even when we cannot see the way forward. May our faith be strengthened, our character refined, and our hope renewed as we walk through the valleys of life. Divine Creator, we lift up to You all who are facing trials and challenges today. May Your presence be their comfort and strength, and may You bring beauty from the ashes of their struggles. Thank You, Lord, for the opportunity to grow spiritually through trials. May we emerge from them stronger, wiser, and more deeply rooted in Your love. In Jesus' name we pray, Amen.

88

Solitude and Spiritual Insight

In the mountains of the north, where the wind speaks more of the world than the bustling cities below, John had built his cabin. It was a solitary place, made of rough logs that had seen more winters than the old man could count on his weathered fingers. Here, he sought the Divine Spirit, not through the clamor of words or the doctrines of men, but in the silence and grandeur of nature.

John had lived other lives before this one—lives filled with noise, argument, and the endless clamor of human discourse. He had been a scholar, a preacher, and a seeker of truths written in books and spoken in the halls of debate. But the more he spoke and the more he read, the more he realized that the truth, the essence he sought, was slipping through his fingers like fine sand.

One autumn, as the leaves turned from green to a thousand shades of fire and gold, John decided that the words were too many, the doctrines too confining. He left his books and his pulpit behind and retreated to the mountains, where the voice of the Divine could be heard in the rustling leaves and the whisper of the streams.

His days were spent in simple tasks—chopping wood, mending his tools, walking the paths carpeted with pine needles. He spoke little, for there were few to listen, and realized that in the absence of words, he felt closer to the essence he had sought so fervently throughout his life.

In the stillness of the mountain nights, under the vast dome of starlit sky, John found a communion that no sermon or scripture had ever afforded him. The Divine Spirit, he realized, was not in the thunderous declarations of faith, nor in the intricate expositions of theologians. It was in the quiet heart of the world, in the unspoken understanding that connected him to every rustling leaf, every cloud, and every star overhead.

His heart no longer sought to capture the essence in the net of language. The ineffable truth of the Divine Spirit was a landscape that he lived in, breathed in, and loved in silence. His soul, stripped of the need to explain or define, found its voice in the unspoken communion with all existence.

As the years wore on, the lines on John's face deepened, carved by wind and weather like the rocks around his home. But his eyes held a light that was serene and full of depth. In that sacred silence, in the solitude of his mountain retreat, John embraced the Truth he had always sought—a truth beyond words, a presence in the stillness, the Love and Unity and Eternal Grace that was the heartbeat of the universe.

And when people came to visit, drawn by tales of a wise man in the mountains, they found a man of few words, whose peaceful gaze and gentle smiles spoke of mysteries too profound for words. In the presence of his quiet understanding, they too learned to listen to the silence, finding there the echoes of the Divine Spirit they had come too loudly to seek.

Christian Themes and Values

John's story, set against the serene backdrop of his mountain retreat, encapsulates several profound Biblical themes that underscore a spiritual journey deeply embedded in solitude, nature, and a quest for direct communion with the Divine.

The Divine in Creation: John's retreat into the mountains reflects the Biblical theme of finding God in the grandeur of creation. This is reminiscent of Psalms 19:1, "The heavens declare the glory of God; the skies proclaim the work of his hands." His experience suggests that the natural world is a testament to the presence and power of the Creator.

Solitude and Spiritual Insight: The solitude John embraces is a biblical motif often associated with deep spiritual insight and encounter. Moses on Mount Sinai (Exodus 24:15-18) and Jesus' 40 days in the wilderness (Matthew 4:1-2) are pivotal Biblical events that take place in solitude, illustrating how physical isolation can enhance spiritual clarity and closeness to God.

The Limitations of Human Language: John's realization that words and doctrines were inadequate to fully grasp the divine reflects the Biblical understanding of the ineffability of God's nature, as seen in Job 26:14, "And these are but the outer fringe of his works; how faint the whisper we hear of him! Who then can understand the thunder of his power?" This suggests that divine essence often transcends human articulation.

Inner Transformation and Renewal: John's transformation from a scholar and preacher to someone who finds truth in the silence of nature aligns with Romans 12:2, "Do not conform to the pattern of this world but be transformed by the renewing of your mind. Then you will be able to test and approve what God's will is—his good, pleasing and perfect will." His change reflects a shift from external religious expressions to internal spiritual understanding.

The Pursuit of True Wisdom: The narrative echoes the quest for wisdom that is valued highly in the Bible, particularly in books like Proverbs and Ecclesiastes. John's journey underscores a shift from conventional wisdom to a deeper, experiential knowledge that is aligned with Proverbs 3:13-18, which extols the virtues of true wisdom and understanding.

Communion with God: The communion John experiences in his isolation, where he feels a profound connection with every part of creation, mirrors the mystical union with God discussed in mystical Jewish texts and the Christian mystical tradition. This communion indicates an intimate, personal relationship with God that transcends traditional religious practices.

The Influence of a Spiritual Life: Finally, the impact John has on visitors, who find spiritual inspiration in his presence and learn to appreciate silence, underscores the Biblical theme of the transformative power of a life lived in accordance with divine principles. This reflects Matthew 5:16, "In the same way, let your light shine before others, that they may see your good deeds and glorify your Father in heaven."

John's story illustrates a spiritual odyssey that, while uniquely personal, encompasses universal themes of seeking and finding God beyond the conventional confines of religious structures and expressions, resonating with a deep biblical understanding of the relationship between creation, solitude, and the divine presence.

Prayer

Eternal Holy Spirit, In the solitude of our hearts, we seek Your presence and Your guidance. You have promised to meet us in the quiet places, to speak to us in the depths of our souls. Grant us the grace to find spiritual insight and renewal in times of solitude. Lord, in the busyness of life, help us to carve out moments of stillness and solitude, where we can be alone with You. May these times of quiet reflection be opportunities for us to listen to Your voice and to receive Your wisdom and direction. Teach us, Lord, to embrace solitude as a gift rather than a burden, knowing that it is in these moments of quietness that we can draw near to You and experience Your presence in a deeper way. Lord, as we seek You in solitude, open our hearts and minds to receive Your truth and revelation. Help us to gain spiritual insight and understanding, illuminating Your Word and Your ways for us. Grant us the courage to face ourselves honestly in silence, to confront our fears, doubts, and weaknesses, and to surrender them to You. May Your Spirit work in us, transforming us into vessels of Your love, grace, and truth. In Jesus' name we pray, Amen.

89

The Quest for Authenticity

Luke leaned against the railing of his porch, watching the slow dance of autumn leaves as they spiraled to the ground. He had lived long enough to know that the masks we wear often become our reality, obscuring the truth of who we really are. Now in the quiet twilight of his years, he sought a simpler, more honest existence. He whispered a prayer into the cooling air, "Lord Jesus, grant me the wisdom to see beyond the masks I wear."

His life had been a series of roles—father, husband, executive—all performed with the precision of a well-rehearsed actor. Yet now, with his children grown up and his career a matter of the past, Luke found these identities slipping away, like the leaves from the trees, revealing the bare branches of his true self.

In the silence that filled his days, the kind of profound quiet that only a remote mountain cabin could offer, Luke felt the stirrings of something genuine. It was as if the light of Christ, so often obscured by the busyness of his former life, now found the space to shine through. The illusions of importance, the pretense of necessity, began to peel away under the gentle scrutiny of his introspection.

He spent his mornings in contemplation, not of scriptures or doctrines, but of the life he had led and the man he wished to become. The crisp mountain air seemed to clear not just his lungs but his thoughts as well, stripping away the layers of ego that had defined him for so long.

As the season wore on, Luke felt a change within himself, akin to the transformation of the landscape around him. What had been hidden by the lush foliage of his ambitions and achievements was now laid bare—an essence of spirit, unadorned and unblemished. It was not a new discovery, but a long-forgotten acquaintance, rekindled into life by his willingness to confront his own soul.

With each passing day, Luke embraced this essence more fully. He learned to live without masks, to speak without pretense, and to love without conditions. In the simplicity of his new life, he found a freedom that the complexities of his old life had never afforded. It was a liberation not just from the illusions he had harbored but from the very need to harbor anything at all.

One chilly evening, as the first snowflakes of the season began to fall, Luke stood outside, his face turned upward, feeling the soft kisses of the snow against his skin. He smiled, realizing that this, here and now, was the foundation of his being—the simple, profound essence of his existence, illuminated by the light of Christ, burning like an eternal flame within him.

"Thank you," he said softly, into the silence around him, a simple expression of his heart's newfound truth.

Christian Themes and Values

The Quest for Authenticity: Luke's desire to see beyond the masks he wears aligns with the biblical exhortation for truthfulness in one's identity and actions, as expressed in Ephesians 4:25, "Therefore, having put away falsehood, let each one of you speak the truth with his neighbor, for we are members one of another." His prayer for wisdom to discern and shed these masks echoes the pursuit of genuine selfhood in Christ.

The Process of Sanctification: The story captures the essence of sanctification, where Luke's movement away from his former life and identities mirrors the spiritual process of becoming more like Christ. This theme is vivid in 2 Corinthians 5:17, "Therefore, if anyone is in Christ, he is a new creation. The old has passed away; behold, the new has come." Luke's transformation reflects this shedding of the old self and embracing a new, spiritually enriched life.

Simplicity and Spiritual Freedom: Luke's embrace of a simpler life reflects Jesus' teachings on the value of simplicity and the dangers of material encumbrances, as noted in Matthew 6:19-21, "Do not store up for yourselves treasures on earth... but store up for yourselves treasures in heaven... For where your treasure is, there your heart will be also." His newfound appreciation for an unadorned existence underlines the spiritual freedom that comes from detaching from worldly pretenses and complications.

Inner Reflection and Prayer: The serene environment of the mountain cabin and the quiet introspection it fosters illustrates the Biblical theme of seeking God through solitude and prayer, similar to Jesus' own withdrawals for prayer in places away from the crowds, as seen in Luke 5:16, "But Jesus often withdrew to lonely places and prayed."

Transformation Through Christ: The light of Christ illuminating Luke's life represents the transformative power of faith. This is reminiscent of Biblical passages such as Psalm 119:105, "Your word is a lamp to my feet and a light to my path," indicating the guiding and transformative presence of God's truth in one's life.

Renewal of Spirit: Luke's experience of spiritual renewal and the shedding of superficial identities can be linked to Romans 12:2, which urges believers not to conform to the pattern of this world but be transformed by the renewing of their minds. This renewal is fundamental to understanding and embracing God's will "his good, pleasing and perfect will."

Unconditional Love and Liberation: Finally, Luke's learning to live without conditions and live without the masks reflects the liberating and unconditional love of Christ, which frees individuals from the bonds of pretense and fear, as portrayed in 1 John 4:18, "There is no fear in love. But perfect love drives out fear, because fear has to do with punishment. The one who fears is not made perfect in love."

Luke's story of seeking and finding a deeper, truer existence encapsulates a profound journey of spiritual awakening and the embrace of an authentic life grounded in Christian principles and the liberating truth of Christ's teachings.

Prayer

Holy Divine Mother, In a world filled with pretense and falsehood, we come before You seeking authenticity and truth. You have called us to live lives of integrity and honesty, reflecting Your character to the world around us. Grant us the courage and strength to pursue authenticity in all areas of our lives. Help us to strip away the masks and facades that we often hide behind, and to be transparent before You and others. May our words and actions be genuine reflections of Your love, grace, and truth. Teach us to embrace our true selves – the unique individuals You created us to be – and to live authentically in Your presence and in the world. May we find our identity and worth in You alone, rather than in the opinions or expectations of others. In our quest for authenticity, help us to be honest about our struggles, doubts, and failures. May we bring them to You in humility and repentance, trusting in Your grace and forgiveness. Grant us discernment to recognize authenticity in others and to surround ourselves with those who are genuine and sincere in their faith and relationships. Thank You, Dear God, for Your example of authenticity in the person of Jesus Christ. May we follow His lead, living lives of integrity and truth for Your glory. In Jesus' name we pray, Amen.

90

God as Transcendent and Immanent

Brett sat alone on the worn wooden bench overlooking the ocean, the crashing waves a constant roar beneath the silence of his contemplation. The gulls wheeled and cried overhead, indifferent to the man grappling with the mysteries of the Divine.

He had come to the sea seeking solitude, needing the vast, unending horizon to quiet his restless spirit. Brett was a man caught between worlds—the tangible and the ineffable, the known and the unknowable. He sought God in the waves, in the cold spray of the sea, and in the deep blue that stretched to eternity.

To Brett, God was both a profound enigma and an intimate presence. He felt the Divine as a transcendent force, dark and unknowable, yet also immanent, pulsing through the very essence of life. It was a paradox that both troubled and comforted him.

As the sun dipped below the horizon, painting the sky in strokes of orange and pink, Brett reflected on the interconnectedness of all beings. Each soul, he believed, mirrored the Divine Essence, linked in a fabric of sacred connection that stretched across the expanse of creation. This web of spiritual kinship was woven through acts of love, compassion, and empathy—forces as real and potent as the tide pulling at the shore.

In his solitude, Brett found communion not only through prayer but through his deep bond with nature. Here, amid the raw beauty of the coast, he felt closest to the Divine Creator, sensing the eternal truth that throbbed in the heart of the ocean and within himself.

With each wave that broke upon the shore, Brett felt a call to embrace the Divine Light that shone within and around him. He knew he was a part of something immense, a grand tapestry of existence where every thread was vital, every connection sacred.

As darkness settled over the water, Brett rose from the bench. He felt renewed, as if each crashing wave had washed away a layer of uncertainty, leaving him closer to the eternal, closer to understanding the sacred connections that bound him to all of creation. He walked back towards the path that led home, carrying with him the peace of knowing that in the vast, mysterious sea of life, he was intimately connected to the Divine, a part of the eternal dance of light and shadow, substance and spirit.

Christian Themes and Values

God as Transcendent and Immanent: Brett's perception of God as both unknowable and intimately present reflects Biblical descriptions of God's nature. Psalm 139:7-10 captures this dual aspect of God, noting, "Where can I go from your Spirit? Where can I flee from your presence? If I go up to the heavens, you are there; if I make my bed in the depths, you are there." This illustrates the theological concept that God is both beyond our understanding (transcendent) and present in our everyday lives (immanent).

Creation as a Reflection of the Divine: Brett's connection to God through the natural beauty of the ocean aligns with Romans 1:20, which states, "For since the creation of the world God's invisible qualities—his eternal power and divine nature—have been clearly seen, being understood from what has been made, so that people are without excuse." The natural world is often depicted in the Bible as a testament to God's power and presence.

The Search for Spiritual Truth: Brett's contemplative search for understanding mirrors the journey of many Biblical figures who sought deeper truths about God and existence. This theme is akin to the journey of Job, who wrestled with understanding the nature of God and human suffering, ultimately encountering God in a profound and transformative way (Job 38-42).

Inner Transformation: The sense of renewal Brett feels by the sea recalls 2 Corinthians 4:16, where Paul writes, "Therefore we do not lose heart. Though outwardly we are wasting away, yet inwardly we are being renewed day by day." This verse speaks to the ongoing process of spiritual renewal and growth that believers experience.

Interconnectedness and Unity: Brett's reflection on the interconnectedness of all life and the spiritual kinship that binds every soul suggests themes found in 1 Corinthians 12:12-27, which discusses the Body of Christ. In this passage, Paul explains that just as a body, though one, has many parts, so it is with Christ—every individual is interconnected and plays an integral role in the whole.

Solitude and Communion with God: Brett's solitary communion with the Divine through nature is reminiscent of Jesus' own practices of withdrawing to solitary places to pray, as seen in Mark 1:3These moments of solitude are vital for spiritual clarity and communion with God.

The Eternal Dance of Creation: Finally, Brett's realization of being part of an eternal dance of creation touches on the theme of Ecclesiastes 3:11, "He has made everything beautiful in its time. He has also set eternity in the human heart; yet no one can fathom what God has done from beginning to end." This acknowledges the mysterious, timeless order of God's creation and our place within it.

Brett's experience underscores a deeply spiritual understanding of life and existence, framed by the magnificent backdrop of creation, which is both a reflection of and pathway to the Divine. His story invites readers to consider their own spiritual journeys and the ways in which they connect with the transcendent truths of their faith.

Prayer

Divine Light, You are both transcendent and immanent – beyond our understanding yet intimately present with us. We stand in awe of Your majesty and glory, and we are humbled by Your nearness and love. Help us to embrace the mystery of Your nature and to worship You with reverence and gratitude. As we contemplate Your transcendence, we marvel at Your greatness and Your power. You are the Creator of the universe, the Alpha and Omega, the beginning and the end. Your ways are higher than our ways, and Your thoughts are higher than our thoughts. Yet, even in Your transcendent majesty, You choose to be near to us, to dwell among us, and to walk with us in our journey of faith. You are Immanuel, God with us, ever-present and compassionate, guiding us with Your wisdom and grace. You are the Messiah, the Christ. Help us to experience Your presence in our daily lives, to recognize Your hand at work in the world around us. May we be attentive to Your voice speaking to us through Your Word, Your Spirit, and Your creation. Thank You, God, for Your transcendence and Your immanence, for Your power and Your love. May our lives be a reflection of Your glory and Your grace, as we seek to honor You in all that we do. In Jesus' name we pray, Amen.

91

Spiritual Rebirth

Mary knelt by the riverside, her hands clutching the rough fabric of her jeans, her eyes fixed on the slow-moving water reflecting the fading light of dusk. The river, like her life, had seen much pass through—some floating on the surface, some submerged and lost to the deeper currents.

The concept of rebirth had never been clear to Mary. Raised in the shadows of strict religious doctrine, she had always equated spiritual awakening with rites and rituals, the kinds of which often left her feeling more isolated than inspired. But as she sat there on the banks of the river, the words of her grandmother echoed in her mind, transformed into a meaning she could finally grasp.

"Through Jesus Christ, you're called to a rebirth, not of conformity but of transformation," her grandmother had said. It wasn't about the external compliance to doctrines, but a metamorphosis of the inner being, a shedding of the ego and its illusions.

As the water flowed, Mary felt a stirring within, akin to the gentle pull of the river's undercurrents. To be Born Again was to allow her flow, her divine rhythm, to take hold of the soul and mold it anew. It was a departure from the self she knew—a self-constructed from years of fear and compliance—to emerge as a true child of God, radiant with the light of truth.

The river whispered of old ways dying like the fallen leaves that drifted past, making room for new growth, for green shoots of potential. To be reborn was to embrace her natural cycle of death and renewal, to become a vessel of love and grace.

Mary stood up, feeling a lightness as if the heavy garments of her past were finally unraveled and washed away by the river. She looked up to the sky, now painted with the hues of twilight, and felt a communion with something greater, a voice beyond the water and the wind.

To be born again was not just a promise of a new beginning; it was the unfolding of the entire journey—each step, each stumble, embraced as part of the sacred dance of transformation. It was a path that led not just through the chapel's doors but into the vast, echoing cathedral of the world.

With a renewed sense of purpose, Mary stepped away from the riverbank, ready to walk the path of her true spiritual awakening, as a beloved child of God, reborn not through the waters of the river, but through the transformative current flowing deep within.

Christian Themes and Values

Spiritual Rebirth: Central to the story is the theme of being "born again," which is directly drawn from John 3:3-7 where Jesus explains to Nicodemus that one must be born again to see the kingdom of God. This rebirth is not a physical one but a spiritual transformation that fundamentally changes a person from within.

Transformation and Renewal: Mary's internal change aligns with Romans 12:2, which urges believers not to conform to the pattern of this world but be transformed by the renewing of their mind. This transformation allows believers to test and approve what God's will is—His good, pleasing, and perfect will.

The Flow of Divine Grace: The river metaphor in Mary's story symbolizes the continuous and cleansing flow of God's grace which is essential for spiritual renewal and growth. This imagery echoes the living water Jesus speaks of in John 4:10-14, offered to the Samaritan woman at the well, representing the sustenance and renewal only Christ can provide.

Death and Resurrection: The reference to old ways dying and new growth emerging is a reflection of the Biblical theme of death leading to resurrection, symbolizing the Christian's death to sin and new life in Christ. This is seen in Colossians 2:12, through faith in the working of God, who raised Jesus from the dead.

Natural Creation Reflecting Spiritual Truths: The setting by the river and the references to natural cycles highlight how physical creation reflects spiritual truths, a theme echoed in Romans 1:20. Nature itself teaches about God's invisible qualities—His eternal power and divine nature.

Inner vs. Outer Transformation: Mary's realization that true rebirth is an inner transformation rather than adherence to external rites and rituals reflects Jesus' criticisms of the Pharisees in Matthew 23:25-28 for their focus on outward appearance rather than inner purity.

Freedom from Past Constraints: Mary's feeling of liberation from her past fears and compliance illustrates Galatians 5:1, which emphasizes that Christ has set us free, and we should stand firm, not letting ourselves be burdened again by a yoke of slavery.

Personal Communion with God: The moment Mary feels communion with something greater than herself reflects the personal relationship with God that Christianity advocates, akin to the personal calls and encounters with God experienced by biblical figures such as Moses, Abraham, and David.

Mary's journey from a ritualistic understanding of faith to a profound personal spiritual awakening underscores the transformative power of personal encounter with God, emphasizing the continuous nature of spiritual growth and the deepening of one's relationship with the Divine.

Prayer

Heavenly Divine Mother, We come before You in awe of Your transforming power and the gift of spiritual rebirth that You offer us through Jesus Christ. You have called us out of darkness into Your marvelous light, and we praise You for the new life we have in Him. We thank You for the opportunity to be born again, to experience a spiritual renewal that comes from Your Holy Spirit. We confess our need for Your grace and forgiveness, and we surrender our lives to You anew. Grant us, Lord, the courage to let go of our old ways and to embrace the new life You offer us in Christ. May we be transformed by the renewing of our minds, becoming more like Jesus in our thoughts, words, and actions. Divine Mother, we lift up to You those who have not yet experienced spiritual rebirth. May Your Spirit work in their hearts, opening their eyes to the truth of Your love and leading them to faith in Jesus Christ. Thank You for the gift of new life in Christ. May we walk in the freedom and joy of Your salvation, living each day in the power of Your Spirit and for Your glory. In Jesus' name we pray, Amen.

92

Hope and Assurance in God's Love

Lenny sat on the edge of the dock, his legs dangling over the water as the first cool breeze of evening teased the surface into ripples. The sun had set half an hour ago, but its afterglow still painted the sky in strokes of orange and purple. Lenny watched, his mind turning over the events of the day—a day like many others, filled with small failures and smaller victories, yet each seeming monumental at the moment of their unfolding.

In his hand, he held a small, well-worn book, its pages dog-eared from frequent reading. It was a collection of meditations and verses that his mother had given him when he first moved away from home, a tether to keep him grounded when the distance felt too vast.

"Know this," he read aloud to the quiet lapping of the water, "for it is a truth as immutable as the stars in the sky: you are a beloved child of God." The words were familiar, almost memorized, but each reading brought a new layer of understanding, a new comfort.

Today had been tough. A project at work had gone awry, his car had broken down, and in the chaos, he had forgotten his sister's birthday. But as he read, his burdens seemed to lighten, slipping into the vast, indigo lake, becoming part of something larger, more enduring than his temporary woes.

He looked up at the sky, now studded with the first bright stars of the night and thought about the vastness of it all—the universe, his life, the presence of God in both. "When you stumble and fall," he continued, "remember that God feels your pain as acutely as you do." It was a strange comfort, knowing that his pain was shared, that his joys were celebrated.

There was laughter today, too, he remembered. Jokes shared over the lunch table, a funny text from his sister thanking him for the 'surprise' choice to not call on her birthday, teasing him. "In each smile that graces your lips, each moment of contentment that fills your soul, God rejoices alongside you," he read on, the words blending into the night around him.

Lenny closed the book and let the silence envelop him. The gentle sounds of the night, the rustle of leaves in the gentle wind, the distant call of a night bird, felt like whispers from beyond, reminders that he was not alone, never had been, never would be.

So, take heart, the book seemed to say, a silent companion as sure as any friend. In every trial and triumph, through the ups and downs of this vast, beautiful journey, God walks with you, guiding you with love and grace.

The realization filled Lenny with a warmth that matched the lingering heat of the departed sun. He stood, stretched, and took a deep breath of the cool night air. He was ready to face tomorrow, with all its unknown challenges and unexpected joys, because he was cherished, cherished, loved beyond measure.

Christian Themes and Values

Identity as a Child of God: Lenny's reflection on the truth that he is a beloved child of God echoes the Christian understanding of identity rooted in God's love and acceptance. This theme reflects passages like John 1:12 and Romans 8:16-17.

God's Presence in Trials and Triumphs: Lenny finds solace in the idea that God shares in his pain and rejoices in his moments of contentment. This mirrors biblical promises of God's presence in both times of trouble and joy (Psalm 23:4, Romans 12:15).

Divine Comfort in Scripture: Lenny draws comfort from the verses in the well-worn book his mother gave him, which serve as a tether to his faith and a source of solace in difficult times. This theme emphasizes the role of scripture in providing guidance and comfort (Psalm 119:105, 2 Timothy 3:16-17).

God's Guidance and Grace: The story emphasizes God's role as a guide and source of grace, walking alongside Lenny through life's ups and downs. This reflects biblical teachings on God's guidance and provision (Psalm 32:8, Ephesians 2:8-10).

Hope and Assurance in God's Love: Lenny's realization that he is never alone, that God walks with him through every challenge and joy, fills him with warmth and assurance. This theme echoes the biblical promise of God's steadfast love and faithfulness (Psalm 23:6, Romans 8:38-39).

Overall, the story intertwines these themes to convey a message of hope, comfort, and assurance in the midst of life's uncertainties, rooted deeply in Christian faith and understanding.

Prayer

Dear Creator God, We come before You with hearts filled with hope and assurance in Your unfailing love. Your love is our anchor in the storms of life, our source of strength in times of weakness, and our assurance of salvation. Help us to cling to Your love with unwavering faith and confidence. Lord, in a world filled with uncertainty and fear, remind us of the hope we have in You. Your love never fails, and Your promises are steadfast. May we find comfort and peace in knowing that nothing can separate us from Your love. Grant us the assurance of Your presence with us at all times. Help us to trust in Your faithfulness, even when circumstances may seem bleak. May Your love be a constant reminder that You are always near, guiding us, protecting us, and sustaining us. Lord, may Your love transform us from the inside out, filling us with joy, peace, and a deep sense of belonging. Help us to live as Your beloved children, confident in Your love and eager to share it with others. Thank You, Lord, for Your boundless love that never gives up on us. May we rest securely, living each day with hope and assurance in Your unchanging faithfulness. In Jesus' name we pray, Amen.

93

Divine Comfort in Times of Trouble

Gordon sat alone on a bench under the sprawling arms of an old elm, its leaves whispering secrets in the late afternoon breeze. He was a sturdy man, face lined with the years and the fields he had worked, eyes reflecting the depth of many unseen battles. His hands, rough and calloused, rested on his knees, bearing the evidence of a lifetime of labor.

The park was quiet, a small oasis in the middle of a bustling city that didn't stop for anyone. Here, Gordon found his respite, his moment of peace. Today, more than others, he needed quiet—the kind that spoke louder than the cacophony of his own troubled thoughts.

Gordon's heart was heavy. His wife, Mary, had been ill, the kind of sickness that whispered dire promises of inevitable parting. Every day he watched her fade a little more, like the sunset before him, beautiful yet slipping into the dark. Each night, as he held her hand, feeling the delicate tremble of her fingers, he felt as if God were somewhere far away, a spectator uninterested in the plight of an old farmer.

But then he remembered the words of the chaplain, words meant to comfort but so hard to hold onto: "You are a beloved child of God. In every moment, from pain to joy, you are cradled in the embrace of Divine Love." Gordon shifted on the bench, wrestling with doubt and faith intertwined tightly within his soul.

As he pondered, a young couple walked by, their laughter breaking through his reverie. They were oblivious to Gordon, lost in their own bubble of joy. It was then he recalled more words, "In each smile that graces your lips, each moment of contentment that fills your soul, God rejoices with you."

Gordon looked around, noticing for the first time the vibrant colors of the flowers bordering the path, the way the sunlight dappled through the leaves above, casting patterns of light and shadow that danced quietly on the ground. It struck him then, how present God was in all these pieces of creation, in the beauty and the simplicity.

A gentle breeze stirred, carrying with it the faint scent of jasmine. It was Mary's favorite. Closing his eyes, Gordon let the warmth of the sun caress his face, the way he imagined God's love might feel—a silent companion in his journey through life.

"Know that you are never alone," he whispered to himself, the words a balm to his weary heart. In the challenges and in the celebrations, in the daily struggles and the moments of peace, God walked with him. This realization didn't erase the pain or the fear of what was coming, but it anchored him, a steadfast promise of companionship and eternal love.

Opening his eyes, Gordon felt a strength he hadn't felt in days. He stood up, ready to return to Mary, to sit by her side and hold her hand through the night. He would tell her about the elm, the sun, and the breeze, and together, they would remember that in every trial and triumph, they were cherished, loved beyond measure.

Christian Themes and Values

Divine Comfort in Times of Trouble: Gordon grapples with his wife Mary's illness, feeling as if God is distant and uninterested. However, he remembers the words of the chaplain, reminding him that he is a beloved child of God. This theme reflects biblical passages that speak of God's comfort in times of trouble (Psalm 23:4, Isaiah 41:10).

God Rejoices with Us in Moments of Joy: Gordon is reminded that God rejoices with us in moments of happiness and contentment. This reflects the biblical idea that God delights in his creation and shares in our joy (Zephaniah 3:17, Psalm 16:11).

Awareness of God's Presence in Creation: Gordon finds solace in the beauty of the park, recognizing God's presence in the vibrant colors of the flowers, the sunlight filtering through the trees, and the gentle breeze. This theme echoes biblical passages that speak of God's presence in creation (Psalm 19:1-4, Romans 1:20).

Assurance of God's Companionship: Gordon realizes that he is never alone, even in his struggles. He understands that God walks with him through every trial and triumph, providing strength and companionship. This reflects the biblical promise of God's presence and faithfulness (Isaiah 43:2, Matthew 28:20).

Hope in Eternal Love: Despite the challenges Gordon faces, he finds strength and hope in the assurance of God's eternal love. This theme reflects the Christian belief in God's unwavering love for his children (Romans 8:38-39, 1 John 4:16).

Overall, the story intertwines these themes to convey a message of hope, comfort, and assurance in the midst of life's uncertainties, rooted deeply in Christian faith and understanding.

Prayer

Heavenly Light, In times of trouble and distress, we turn to You, our refuge and strength. You are the God of all comfort, who comforts us in our affliction. We bring our burdens to You, knowing that You are able to bring peace and solace to our troubled hearts. Lord, we thank You for Your promise to never leave us nor forsake us. In the midst of our trials, may we feel Your presence surrounding us like a comforting embrace. Help us to find rest in Your loving arms and to trust in Your perfect peace that surpasses all understanding. Grant us the strength to endure the challenges we face, knowing that Your grace is sufficient for us. May Your Spirit nourish our souls, bringing healing, hope, and restoration.

We lift up to You all who are facing trials and difficulties today. Comfort them, Lord, with Your presence and surround them with Your love. Bring them the assurance of Your faithfulness and the hope of Your salvation. In Jesus' name we pray, Amen.

94

Divine Creation and Identity in God

Fiona sat at the edge of the pier, her legs dangling over the cool, dark water below. The sun was setting, casting a golden glow that shimmered across the surface of the lake. It was quiet here, away from the city, away from the roles she played—a wife, a mother, an executive—all mantles that weighed heavily upon her.

She often thought of herself as an actor in a perpetual play, donning various masks for different scenes, each one crafted with precision to meet the expectations of the other. Yet, in the dying light of the day, with no one around but the call of the distant loons, Fiona felt the urge to drop her performances and face the essence of her being.

"Lord God," she whispered, the words mingling with the cool breeze, "bless me with the courage to be vulnerable, to stand in the radiance of your unwavering authenticity."

She remembered her mother's words, spoken softly on her deathbed, reminders that she was a divine creation, meant to be more than the sum of her earthly roles. "You are unbound by these earthly constraints," she had said, her voice steady despite the pain.

As the sun dipped lower, Fiona closed her eyes, letting the warmth seep into her skin. She imagined peeling off the layers of her carefully constructed façade, the layers that shielded her from the truth of who she was beneath it all.

For in the vulnerability of her being, she found the essence of her humanity—the raw, unadorned beauty of her soul that she often hid under a cloak of perceived competence and stoic leadership.

With each breath, she released the need for approval, the thirst for validation that had driven her for so long. Instead, she embraced the purity of her authentic self as seen through the lens of divine love. In the presence of such love, she found freedom—a liberating, profound freedom to be fully and completely himself.

"And so," she continued, her voice now just a murmur against the backdrop of a now starlit sky, "I surrender to Your will, trusting that in my vulnerability, I find the greatest strength."

She stayed there until the stars blanketed the sky, feeling a deeper connection to the universe and to herself than she had in years. It was in her surrender, that Fiona realized, that she found the deepest connection to God and to all that is. The pier, the lake, the fading light—all bore witness to her transformation, a woman shedding the weight of pretense to reveal the truth of her divine nature beneath.

Christian Themes and Values

Authenticity and Vulnerability: Fiona's desire to shed her various societal masks and embrace her true self reflects the Biblical exhortation for authenticity found in Ephesians 4:22-24, which encourages believers to "put off your old self...and to put on the new self, created to be like God in true righteousness and holiness." Her prayer for the courage to be vulnerable resonates with the value placed on vulnerability as a strength in the Bible, not a weakness.

Divine Creation and Identity in God: Fiona's remembrance of her mother's words about being a divine creation taps into the Biblical affirmation of human beings created in the image of God (Genesis 1:27). The theme underscores that each person is crafted with intrinsic worth and purpose beyond earthly roles and expectations.

The Burden of Earthly Roles: The pressures of Fiona's roles as a wife, mother, and executive mirror the burdens discussed in Matthew 11:28-30, where Jesus invites those who are weary and burdened to come to Him for rest. Fiona's experience by the lake represents her moment of coming to Jesus in a metaphorical sense, seeking relief and authenticity away from life's pressures.

Surrender to God's Will: Fiona's surrender to God's will, trusting in divine guidance even in vulnerability, aligns with Proverbs 3:5-6, which teaches trust in the Lord with all your heart and lean not on your own understanding. Her surrender is depicted as a path to true strength and freedom, illustrating the paradox often noted in Christianity that true freedom is found in submission to God.

Finding Peace in God's Presence: The peace Fiona experiences as he connects more deeply with himself and the universe reflects the peace that Philippians 4:7 describes, which transcends all understanding and guards the hearts and minds in Christ Jesus. Ther peace is often portrayed as coming from a deeper connection with God and understanding one's place in Her creation.

Transformation through God's Love: Fiona's transformation by the lake, where she feels unburdened and authentically herself, is a depiction of 2 Corinthians 5:17, where anyone in Christ is a new creation; the old has gone, the new is here. This theme emphasizes the transformative power of God's love and presence.

Fiona's story illustrates a journey of spiritual and personal rediscovery, where solitude and nature serve as catalysts for deepening his relationship with God and understanding his true identity. This narrative is a reflection of the importance of stripping away life's constructed identities to embrace the essence of our being as created by and loved by God.

Prayer

Divine Creator, We come before You in awe of Your divine creation and the identity You have given us as Your beloved children. You formed us in Your image, with purpose and intentionality, and You have called us by name. Help us, Lord, to understand and embrace our identity in You. Lord, as we marvel at the wonders of Your creation, may we recognize the beauty and intricacy of Your handiwork in every living thing. From the vastness of the galaxies to the smallest of creatures, You have displayed Your power and majesty. Help us to steward Your creation with reverence and care. Grant us, Lord, the wisdom to see ourselves as You see us – as beloved children, wonderfully made. May we find our worth and value in You alone, rather than in the opinions or standards of the world. Help us, Lord, to live out our identity in Christ, reflecting His love, grace, and truth to the world around us. May our lives be a testimony to Your transforming power and the hope we have in You. Thank You, Lord, for the gift of creation and for the privilege of being called Your children. May we honor You with our lives and bring glory to Your name. In Jesus' name we pray, Amen.

95

The Incarnate Presence of Jesus

Mark walked through the orchard in early spring, the air crisp and the branches bare against the still-grey sky. He had spent his life chasing dreams that danced just out of reach—perfect love, unending success, the idyllic peace that comes from a life without fault. Now, with the ground firm beneath his boots and the smell of earth in the air, he understood the futility of his pursuits.

"We don't seek solace in fleeting fantasies or distant ideals," he mused to himself, watching a solitary apple bud preparing to bloom. It was a revelation that had crept upon him not in moments of joy or triumph, but through the quieter, harsher winters of his soul.

Mark stopped by the old, gnarled tree at the heart of the orchard, its branches twisted by years of bearing fruit. Here, he had learned to embrace the full spectrum of his humanity, in all its complexity and imperfection. He touched the rough bark, feeling the pulse of life still strong within the old wood.

"It's about accepting what is, Tim," Mark said to his friend who had joined him in the orchard, "not chasing after what could be."

Tim nodded, his eyes thoughtful. "But isn't it hard to let go of those dreams? To accept that they might never come true?"

Mark shook his head. "It's not about giving up on dreams, Tim. It's about understanding that true fulfillment doesn't come from chasing after illusions. It's found in embracing reality, with all its imperfections."

"It sounds like you've found some peace," Tim remarked.

355

"It's more than that," Mark replied. "It's like I've discovered a truth that's been there all along, hidden beneath my own desires and expectations."

As they continued walking through the rows of trees that would soon burst into life, Mark felt a deeper connection to this truth. Jesus, the incarnate God who comes in person, is not a distant notion to be worshipped in abstract, but a reality to be lived and experienced through the mundane, the sorrowful, and the joyous moments of everyday life.

As he returned to the path leading back to his house, the sky began to lighten, the dawn breaking with a subtle promise. Mark knew that each day brought its own challenges, its own moments of imperfection, but now he approached them with a calm heart, fortified by the understanding that true solace was found not in escaping reality, but in embracing it fully, with all its shadows and light.

Christian Themes and Values

Futility of Earthly Pursuits: Mark's realization of the futility of chasing after fleeting fantasies and distant ideals reflects biblical teachings on the emptiness of worldly pursuits. This concept echoes passages such as Ecclesiastes 1:2-3, which speaks of the vanity of chasing after "vanity of vanities."

Embracing Imperfection and Reality: Mark's understanding that true fulfillment comes from embracing reality, with all its imperfections, resonates with biblical teachings on accepting human frailty and relying on God's grace. This concept is reminiscent of passages like 2 Corinthians 12:9, where Paul acknowledges his weakness and finds strength in God's power.

Discovering Truth and Peace: Mark's discovery of truth hidden beneath his own desires and expectations reflects the biblical theme of finding peace and wisdom through seeking God's truth. This aligns with verses such as Proverbs 3:5-6, which encourages trusting in the Lord and seeking His guidance.

Incarnate Presence of Jesus: The idea that Jesus is not a distant notion but a reality to be lived and experienced through everyday life echoes the Christian belief in the Incarnation—the embodiment of God in human form. This concept is central to Christian theology, emphasizing the tangible presence of Jesus in the lives of believers (John 1:14, Mark 1:23).

The Indwelling Christ: Mark's understanding of Christ not as a distant savior but as a living presence within reflects the theme of the indwelling Christ in Colossians 1:27: "To them God has chosen to make known among the Gentiles the glorious riches of this mystery, which is Christ in you, the hope of glory." This encapsulates the Christian doctrine that Christ lives within believers, guiding and transforming them from the inside.

Finding Solace in Embracing Reality: Mark's final realization that true solace is found in embracing reality, with all its imperfections, reflects the Christian understanding of finding peace and contentment in God's presence, even amidst life's challenges. This echoes biblical teachings on finding rest and comfort in God (Mark 11:28-30, Philippians 4:7).

Overall, the story weaves together these Christian and biblical concepts to convey a message of finding fulfillment and peace by embracing reality and experiencing the presence of Jesus in everyday life.

Prayer

Heavenly Father, We thank You for coming to us in person, for the gift of Jesus Christ, whose incarnation brings us hope, renewal, and transformation. Help us, Lord, to recognize and embrace the reality of His presence among us, both in our lives today. Grant us, Lord, the eyes to see Your presence in our midst – in the faces of those we meet, in the beauty of creation, and in the moments of grace and mercy that we experience each day. May we encounter You in the Word, in our sacred rituals, and in the fellowship of believers. Help us, Lord, to follow Your example of humility, compassion, and self-sacrifice. May Your presence

Richard Gordon Zyne

in our lives transform us from the inside out, shaping us into Your likeness and empowering us to live lives that reflect Your love to the world. Thank You, Lord Jesus, for Your incarnate presence among us, in personal dialogue with You. May we never take for granted the gift of Your presence in our lives, but may we always rejoice in Your love and grace. In Your holy name we pray, Amen.

96

Grief, Loss, and the Continuity of Life

The river, swollen by recent rains, moved with a powerful, inexorable pull, drawing leaves, branches, and debris into its current. It flowed to somewhere, to a place that had nothing to do with her.

Frieda had come to the river every day since Juan had died, standing by the water as though it could give her back some fragment of his essence. Each visit was marked by the same ritual; she would arrive at dawn, when the world was a study of shadows and half-lights and would leave when the sun climbed high enough to turn the river a glaring silver.

Frieda's grief was silent, profound, a thick veil that seemed to separate her from the world. She watched the river and thought about the ephemerality of life, the suddenness with which things could be swept away. Juan had been alive, and then he wasn't, and nothing had prepared her for the finality of that transition.

The river, she thought, must know something about loss—carrying away everything in its path, unflinchingly, never looking back. Maybe that's why she kept returning; it seemed the only thing vast enough to mirror the depth of her grief.

Today, as she stood watching the water, a man with a dog came to the river. The dog, a young, sprightly Labrador, bounded ahead and splashed into the water, chasing sticks that the man threw. Frieda watched the dog swim, its enthusiasm a stark contrast to her stillness.

"Good morning," the man called out to Frieda, retrieving his soaking, happy dog. "Beautiful day, isn't it?"

"Yes," she replied, the word hollow as she turned to look at him. His presence was a gentle intrusion, a reminder of life continuing around her.

"My wife loved this river," he said unexpectedly, as if he had read her thoughts. "After she passed, I didn't think I'd come back here. But here I am."

Frieda looked at the man, recognizing the shared territory of loss. "It's hard," she managed to say, her voice a mere whisper against the rush of the river.

"It is," he agreed, nodding. "But I think they'd want us to keep coming back. To remember, but also to see it keeps flowing. And so must we, in whatever way we can."

The man threw another stick, and the dog darted after it with undiminished joy. Frieda watched the dog and then the river—both relentless in their movement.

"Maybe you're right," she said, more to herself than to him.

As the man and his dog continued down the path, leaving Frieda alone with the river, something shifted within her. The river was the same, as were the rocks and the trees and the path, but she stood there a little differently. It was not a relinquishing of grief, but an acceptance of the relentless flow of life, of the need to keep moving with it.

Frieda didn't know if she'd ever find certainty again, or if the waves of doubt would ever stop crashing against her. But standing there, she felt a stir of something like surrender, an openness to the mystery of all that was unknown. It was not an answer, but it was, perhaps, a beginning.

Christian Themes and Values

Grief and Loss: Frieda's profound grief over the death of Juan reflects the biblical theme of mourning and loss. The Bible acknowledges the reality of grief and offers comfort to those who mourn (Matthew 5:4, Psalm 34:18).

Ephemerality of Life: Frieda contemplates the suddenness with which life can be swept away, mirroring the biblical concept of the brevity and fragility of human life (James 4:14, Psalm 90:12).

Hope Amidst Loss: The encounter with the man and his dog at the river illustrates the shared experience of loss and the hope that can be found in continuing to move forward despite grief. This reflects the biblical theme of finding hope in the midst of suffering (Romans 5:3-5, Psalm 30:5).

Acceptance and Surrender: Frieda's realization of the need to accept the relentless flow of life and to surrender to the unknown echoes the biblical idea of surrendering to God's will and trusting in His plan, even amidst uncertainty (Proverbs 3:5-6, Romans 8:28).

Continuity of Life: The river's unending flow symbolizes the continuity of life, even in the face of loss and change. This reflects the biblical theme of God's faithfulness and the assurance that life continues, despite the trials and tribulations we face (Psalm 46:4, Lamentations 3:22-23).

Overall, the story captures the complexities of grief and loss while offering glimpses of hope, acceptance, and the enduring nature of life. It resonates with Christian themes of finding comfort in the midst of sorrow and trusting in God's presence and guidance through life's challenges.

Prayer

Eternal Healing Spirit, In the midst of grief and loss, we come before You, our Comforter and Sustainer. You are the God who understands our sorrows and who walks with us through the valley of the shadow of death. Grant us, Lord, Your peace and strength as we navigate the pain of loss and the reality of death. Lord, we grieve the loss of loved ones who have gone before us. Their absence leaves a void in our lives, and our hearts ache with sorrow. Comfort us, Lord, with the assurance of Your presence and the hope of the resurrection. Help us to find solace in the continuity of life, knowing that our loved ones who have passed from this life are now in Your loving embrace. May the memories we cherish of them bring us comfort and joy, reminding us of the love that binds us together in You. Grant us the grace to surrender our grief to You, trusting in Your promise to turn our mourning into dancing and to bring beauty from the ashes of our sorrow. Help us to find healing and renewal in Your presence, even in the midst of our pain. Eternal Healing Spirit, in the face of loss, may we hold fast to the hope of eternal life in Christ. May the assurance of Your transformative power fill us with faith and confidence, knowing that death has been swallowed up in victory. In Jesus' name we pray, Amen.

97

Life's Transitory Nature

Zooey wasn't fishing for fish; she didn't really care if she caught anything. It was more about the waiting, the silence, and the chance to sit still. Zooey's father, a sturdy, quiet man with hands toughened by years of labor, sat beside her. They spoke little, for there was an understanding between them that transcended words.

Her father was the one who had taught her how to fish, how to sit quietly and watch the cork, how to be patient. These lessons on the lake were less about fishing and more about life. "Sometimes, it's about what you're not doing," her father had said once, his voice melding with the gentle lapping of water against the shore.

A small tug on the line jerked Zooey from her thoughts. She pulled, feeling the slight weight, but there was nothing there when she reeled in. She smiled slightly and recast. Her father watched her, his eyes soft, but he said nothing.

As the sun began to sink, casting long shadows across the water, Zooey felt the silence between them deepen, filling with unsaid thoughts and emotions. She looked over at her father, whose gaze was fixed on the horizon. The lines on his face, usually so hard and determined, seemed to soften in the fading light.

"You know," her father finally spoke, his voice a low rumble, "every moment like this is a moment of truth. We see things as they really are. Not as we want or pretend them to be."

Zooey nodded, understanding that he was not just talking about the lake or the fishing. It was about life—about seeing things clearly, without pretense.

The cork bobbed again, more insistently this time. Zooey held her breath, waiting, then gave the rod a firm tug. This time, there was a resistance, a weight that danced at the end of her line. She reeled slowly, methodically, feeling each movement of whatever was at the end.

When she finally lifted the line from the water, a small, gleaming trout hung from it. Its scales caught the last rays of the sun, flashing brightly before it was enveloped in shadow. Her father reached over, carefully removing the hook from the trout's mouth, and then, without a word, he released it back into the lake.

Zooey watched as the fish disappeared beneath the surface, leaving only ripples behind. Her father put his hand on her shoulder, a gesture filled with warmth.

"Life's a lot like that, isn't it?" he said. "You catch things, only to let them go. But it's the catching that matters. The trying. And the letting go when it's time."

Zooey leaned into her father's side, feeling the truth of his words settle around her like the evening's cool shadows. They gathered up their gear, leaving the lake behind, its surface once again smooth, untouched, as if they had never been there at all.

Christian Themes and Values

Patience and Waiting: The practice of fishing itself, which requires patience and stillness, mirrors Biblical principles such as those found in Psalms 37:7, "Be still before the Lord and wait patiently for him." This theme is a fundamental aspect of faith and trust in God's timing, not just in acquiring what one desires but also in appreciating the act of waiting as a form of spiritual discipline.

Teachings through Simplicity: The simple act of fishing serves as a conduit for life lessons between Zooey and her father. This method of teaching through everyday activities reflects Jesus' use of parables—simple stories used to convey deep spiritual truths, as seen throughout the Gospels. These stories make abstract truths tangible and relatable.

The Value of Presence and Silence: The silent communion between Zooey and her father highlights the Biblical theme of presence—being fully present in each moment and with each other, which can be more expressive than words. This idea is reflected in Biblical passages that emphasize the power of presence and silence before God (e.g., Job 2:13, where Job's friends sat with him in silence, recognizing the depth of his grief).

Seeing Things as They Are: Zooey's father's comment about seeing things as they really are touches on the Biblical theme of spiritual discernment and truth. In John 8:32, Jesus teaches, "Then you will know the truth, and the truth will set you free." This speaks to the clarity that comes from genuine spiritual insight, unclouded by the pretenses or illusions of the world.

Detachment and Letting Go: The act of catching the trout and then releasing it back into the lake embodies the Biblical principles of detachment and letting go as seen in Matthew 6:19-21, where believers are taught to store up treasures in heaven rather than on earth, emphasizing the impermanence of earthly possessions and the importance of spiritual richness.

Life's Transitory Nature: The release of the trout and the acknowledgment that "it's the catching that matters, the trying, and the letting go when it's time" reflect Ecclesiastes 3:1-6, which speaks to the seasonality of life and the importance of recognizing the appropriate times for holding on and letting go.

Reflection and Impact: The imagery of the lake's surface returning to calmness, as if untouched, after their departure, illustrates the transient yet impactful nature of human actions, much like the parable of the sower in Matthew 13, where different types of soils reflect different responses to the word of God.

Zooey's story, enriched with her father's wisdom, offers a meditation on life's deeper truths and the spiritual growth that can occur through ordinary, shared experiences. The narrative teaches that while life can often seem like a series of mundane activities, there is a deeper spiritual narrative playing out, which can teach us about the essence of our existence and our relationship with the Divine.

Prayer

Heavenly Father, We come before You acknowledging the transitory nature of life, like a vapor that appears for a little while and then vanishes away. Help us, Lord, to understand the brevity of our days and to live each moment with purpose and intentionality. Lord, in a world that is constantly changing, remind us of the eternal truths that anchor our souls. May we fix our eyes on You, the unchanging God, who is the same yesterday, today, and forever. Lord, as we reflect on the transitory nature of life, we are reminded of the importance of relationships and the value of every moment we have with our loved ones. May we cherish each day, expressing our love and gratitude to those around us, and seeking reconciliation where needed. Help us, Lord, to find comfort in Your promise of eternal life through Jesus Christ. May the hope of resurrection fill us with peace and assurance, knowing that death is not the end but the beginning of a new and glorious reality in Your presence. Thank You, Lord, for the gift of life, however fleeting it may be. May we live each day in light of eternity, seeking to glorify You in all that we do. In Jesus' name we pray, Amen.

98

Finding True Purpose in God

Carlos sat in the shadow of the old church bell tower, the stone cool and rough against his back. His hands were stained with paint; blue, yellow, red—the colors of the murals he painted on the walls of the city, trying to bring beauty to the grey, crumbling plaster. But tonight, he felt the weight of his years, and the colors seemed dull, like they were fading before the paint even dried.

He looked up at the stark white cross against the darkening sky. As a young man, he had left the church, left the teachings of his youth for the allure of the streets, where he thought he could make a name for himself. He wanted to be remembered, to be someone people talked about. And for a while, they did. His murals became known, and his name was whispered in corners and shouted in bars.

But now, those whispers felt empty. Carlos had seen young kids looking up to him, wanting to be like him, to follow in his footsteps, and it scared him. He hadn't been following a path; he'd been running from one. Running from the quiet, steadfast faith of his grandmother who had taken him to church every Sunday, her face serene as she lit candles and prayed.

"Forgive me, Jesus," Carlos murmured, his voice barely stirring the evening air. His words were sincere, a confession of the soul to the sky. He had strayed far and long, and he felt the pull to return—not to the church as a building, but to something deeper, the faith he saw in his grandmother's eyes.

That night, Carlos dreamed of painting not walls, but lives, coloring them with hope and light, not just with paint but with words and actions. When dawn broke, painting the clouds in hues of orange and pink, he rose with a new aspiration.

He started small, teaching kids to paint after school, showing them how to blend colors and telling them stories of saints and heroes who were brave and true. He spoke of forgiveness and redemption, weaving his own regrets and newfound hopes into the lessons, showing them that it was never too late to change the path you were on.

With every story, every lesson given, Carlos felt lighter, as though each word of hope painted over the doubts and fears he had carried for so long. He was not just teaching; he was learning—learning to walk a path lit by something greater than himself.

Years passed, and the city began to change. Murals still adorned the walls, but now they told stories of faith and transformation, scenes of light overcoming darkness. And at the center of this change was an old artist who had once thought he could light the world alone, only to find that the brightest light was the one he had walked away from.

Carlos never forgot the evening under the church tower, the prayer whispered into the wind. It had brought him back, not just to his roots, but to a deeper, truer path. And in this journey, he found that the greatest transformations were not the ones he painted on walls, but the ones painted on hearts, including his own.

Christian Themes and Values

Prodigal Son and Redemption: Carlos's journey echoes the parable of the Prodigal Son found in Luke 15:11-3Like the prodigal son, Carlos leaves behind his initial faith and family values for a life of personal ambition and recognition. His eventual realization of emptiness and his return to the roots of his faith highlight the theme of redemption and the forgiving, welcoming nature of divine love.

Transformation Through Faith: Carlos's transformation from a celebrated muralist whose work initially served his ego to an educator and mentor using his art to inspire and teach moral values aligns with 2

Corinthians 5:17: "Therefore, if anyone is in Christ, the new creation has come: The old has gone, the new is here!" His story illustrates how faith can profoundly alter one's life's purpose and actions.

Role of Art in Worship and Testimony: Carlos uses his gift of art to express spiritual themes and teach the young about values such as bravery, truth, forgiveness, and redemption. This reflects the use of art in the Bible to glorify God and tell His stories, as seen in the craftsmanship of Bezalel and Oholiab in the construction of the Tabernacle (Exodus 35:30-35).

Mentorship and Legacy: By mentoring the youth, Carlos shifts his legacy from one of personal fame to communal upliftment, which mirrors the biblical theme of discipleship and teaching found in Matthew 28:19-20, "Go therefore and make disciples of all nations..." Through his actions, Carlos invests in the spiritual and moral development of the next generation.

Impact of Genuine Faith on Community: The transformation of Carlos and, subsequently, his community underscores the impact of genuine faith and repentance. The murals, once symbols of his personal glory, become beacons of faith, hope, and transformation, illustrating the biblical principle that faith should actively influence and improve the community (James 2:14-26).

Forgiveness and New Beginnings: Carlos's plea for forgiveness and his subsequent new life direction emphasize the themes of confession, repentance, and the renewing grace of God as found in 1 John 1:9, "If we confess our sins, he is faithful and just and will forgive us our sins and purify us from all unrighteousness."

Finding True Purpose in God: Finally, Carlos's return to faith and the deeper understanding of his purpose reflects the biblical theme of finding one's calling in God's plan. This mirrors the sentiment in Ecclesiastes 12:13, "Fear God and keep his commandments, for this is the whole duty of man."

Carlos's story illustrates that true fulfillment and joy are found not in earthly recognition but in a life lived in service to others and adherence to divine principles. His spiritual homecoming and the transformation of his life's work demonstrate the profound change that faith can bring both to an individual and to their community.

Prayer

Heavenly Father, We come before You seeking true purpose and meaning in our lives. You have created us with a purpose, and our hearts yearn to discover and fulfill it. Help us, Lord, to find our true purpose in You and to live each day according to Your will. Lord, in a world filled with distractions and competing desires, help us to discern Your calling on our lives. May we seek first Your kingdom and Your righteousness, trusting that as we do, all other things will fall into place. Grant us, Lord, the courage to surrender our own plans and ambitions to You, trusting that Your plans for us are good and perfect. Help us to follow where You lead, even when the path is uncertain or difficult. Lord, may our true purpose be found in loving and serving You and others. May we use our gifts, talents, and resources to build up Your kingdom and to bring glory to Your name. Thank You, Lord, for the privilege of being called according to Your purpose. May we walk in the fullness of that purpose each day, bringing honor and glory to Your name. In Jesus' name we pray, Amen.

99

Transformation through Trials

On the plains of Montana, under the vast expanse of the sky, lived a man named Cal. He was a rancher, a solitary figure in an unforgiving landscape where the wind told stories and the stars kept secrets. Cal's life was simple, tending to his cattle and the endless chores that bound his days like the pages of an unwritten book.

One winter night, as a sharp chill swept across the plains, Cal's oldest mare, Bella, fell ill. She was an old horse, wise in the ways of the fields and storms, her coat matted and her movements slow. In the cold barn, Cal sat with Bella, his lantern casting long shadows, listening to the wind outside. It seemed to whisper endings and beginnings, a cycle he had seen many times but never quite understood.

As he watched over Bella, Cal thought about the harshness of life on the plains and the moments of beauty that burst forth seemingly from nowhere—the way the sun set fire to the rims of the distant mountains, or how the snow lay quiet and undisturbed, a blanket of peace.

"Forgive me," he murmured to Bella, for the times he had been a hard man, driven by the need to survive, maybe forgetting the softer Bellas of life. The mare looked at him, her eyes deep pools reflecting years of trust and companionship.

That night, as Cal waited for the dawn, fearing it might be Bella's last, he thought of the stories his grandmother had told him about Jesus, the shepherd of souls, who walked the earth with the weight of infinite love and the light of boundless grace. He had spoken of hope, not as a fragile thing, but as a force as powerful as the spring rivers that broke through the winter's ice.

As the first light of dawn crept across the barn, something shifted in Cal. Bella stirred, her breath coming easier, and though she was still weak, there was a strength returning to her eyes. Cal watched the sunrise, the sky blooming with light, and he felt a surge of something he had not known in a long time—hope.

In the weeks that followed, Cal tended to Bella with a gentler touch, his heart softer, his words kinder. The mare recovered slowly, each day a small testament to the resilience of life. And Cal found himself changed too. He began to mend fences not just around his fields but within himself, reconnecting with neighbors, visiting the old church his grandmother had loved, listening more deeply to the whispers of the wind.

It was not a loud or dramatic transformation. Like the changing of seasons, it was gradual, the land and the man both awakening. In the care of an old mare, Cal discovered the grace he had long forgotten, the hope that did not just endure but flourished, even in the frozen ground of the harshest winters.

Bella, in her quiet way, had shown him that even in the depths of the coldest nights, there was a light that never truly faded, a warmth that lay in wait, ready to emerge with the dawn. And in this realization, Cal found not just the strength to carry on but the wisdom to do so with a heart full of grace.

Christian Themes and Values

Shepherd and Flock: The reference to Jesus as the "shepherd of souls" directly ties to John 10:11 where Jesus describes Himself as the good shepherd who lays down his life for the sheep. This imagery resonates with Cal's own role as a caretaker for his animals, particularly his attentive care for Bella during her illness, embodying the shepherd's dedication.

Forgiveness and Redemption: Cal's plea for forgiveness to Bella for perhaps having been too harsh at times mirrors the Biblical theme of seeking redemption and the transformative power of grace. This reflects themes from passages like Ephesians 4:32, which encourages believers to be kind and compassionate to one another, forgiving each other, just as in Christ God forgave them.

Resilience and Hope: The motif of hope as a powerful, enduring force is central to the Christian faith, akin to Romans 5:3-5, which speaks of suffering producing perseverance, character, and hope—a hope that does not disappoint. Cal's renewed sense of hope at dawn as Bella shows signs of recovery illustrates this Biblical principle that hope is rejuvenated through faith and love.

Transformation through Trials: Cal's transformation, prompted by his vigil and reflection during Bella's illness, underscores the themes that personal trials can lead to spiritual awakening and growth. James 1:2-4 discusses how trials test faith, produce perseverance, and mature the individual, a theme mirrored in Cal's gradual, introspective change.

Creation Speaking of God's Presence: The narrative setting where the natural environment—from the wind's whispers to the sunrise—plays a crucial role in conveying spiritual truths aligns with Romans 1:20. This verse explains that God's qualities can be clearly seen, being understood from what has been made. Cal's connection to the land and his responsiveness to its signals reflect this theme.

Community and Reconnection: Cal's reengagement with his community and the church represents the Biblical importance of fellowship and communal faith as seen in Hebrews 10:24-25, which urges believers to consider how to spur one another on toward love and good deeds, not giving up meeting together.

Endurance and Perseverance: The theme of enduring through hardships and emerging strengthened is central to the Christian narrative of perseverance and faith under trial, similar to Cal's experience through the winter with Bella and his personal spiritual revival.

Cal's journey is a beautiful metaphor for the Biblical path of redemption and renewal. His story reflects the profound transformation that can occur when one reconnects with faith, forgives oneself and others, and finds hope and grace in the trials of life. Through caring for Bella and reflecting on the teachings about Jesus, Cal rediscovered a life imbued with hope, community, and a deeper connection to the divine, illustrating the timeless nature of Biblical truths applied to everyday life.

Prayer

Divine Creator, In the midst of trials and tribulations, we come before You, trusting in Your promise to work all things together for good for those who love You. Help us, Lord, to see beyond the difficulties we face and to embrace the transformation that You are bringing about in our lives. Lord, we thank You for the refining fire of trials, which strengthens our faith and deepens our dependence on You. May we count it all joy when we face various trials, knowing that the testing of our faith produces perseverance. Grant us the wisdom to see Your hand at work in the midst of our struggles, shaping us into vessels of Your grace and love. Help us to surrender our will to Yours, trusting that Your plans for us are good and perfect. May our trials not be wasted but used by You to bring about growth, maturity, and spiritual transformation in our lives. Help us to learn the lessons You have for us in the midst of our difficulties and to emerge from them stronger and more resilient than before. Thank You, Lord, for Your faithfulness and love that never fails. May our trials be a testimony to Your power and grace at work in us, transforming us into the image of Jesus Christ. In His name we pray, Amen.

100

Humility Before God

Thomasina stood on the rugged shore, watching the relentless waves crash against the cliffs. Her hair was whipped about by the wind, and her eyes, fierce and unwavering, mirrored the turbulent sea. She had come here to escape, to think away from the chatter and demands of her university life where she was known as a brilliant mind, a future scientist, a beacon of intellect in the relentless pursuit of truth.

But here, against the vastness of the ocean and under the expanse of the sky, her achievements felt strangely hollow. Thomasina had built her life like a fortress of knowledge, each fact and theory a stone block in a towering wall meant to shield her from the mysteries of existence she could not control.

"Creator God," she cried, her voice carried away by the wind, "I have strayed." It was a confession meant for the waves, for the wind, for the sky that stretched above her like a canvas of infinite possibility.

Back home, her room was littered with books, papers, and the trappings of her scholarly pursuits. She had always believed that enough knowledge would eventually piece together the puzzle of existence, would quiet the questions that stirred in her at night. Yet, the more she learned, the less she felt she truly knew.

As she stood there, the wind seemed to shift, carrying with it words of affirmation that she hadn't realized she needed. It was as if the sea itself spoke, its voice merging with the deeper calling of her heart: "Thomasina, child of the Creator, beloved."

These words, simple and profound, reached her not through the intellect she so valued, but through a deeper, quieter channel within her. It was the work of God, not as a distant architect of a mechanistic universe, but as a present, living, loving force, the undercurrent of all life.

Forgive me, she thought, for my hubris and arrogance. Her heart ached with the recognition of her own limitations, the walls she had built not just against others, but against the very grace that sought to sustain her.

In the days that followed, Thomasina returned to her studies, but with a new perspective. She began to see her pursuit of knowledge not as a fortress to be built, but as a garden to be tended—something living, something that connected her to the world and to others in a way that walls never could.

She started to engage more with her peers, not just as competitors in the intellectual arena, but as fellow travelers on a journey too vast for any one person to journey alone. She joined discussions that spanned from science to philosophy to theology, finding joy in the shared exploration of questions that no one could answer fully.

Christian Themes and Values

Humility Before God: Thomasina's realization of her own limitations and the insufficiency of human knowledge alone mirrors the biblical theme of humility before God. In Proverbs 11:2, it is said, "When pride comes, then comes disgrace, but with humility comes wisdom." Her confession to the Creator acknowledges this humility, recognizing that human achievement cannot replace divine wisdom.

Seeking God's Presence: Her prayer, "Creator God, I have strayed," echoes the biblical call for returning to God, reminiscent of James 4:8, "Come near to God and he will come near to you." This theme of seeking to reconnect with God highlights a personal, introspective approach to faith that goes beyond intellectual understanding.

Divine Affirmation of Identity: The voice Thomasina hears, affirming her as a beloved child of the Creator, aligns with scriptures that speak of God's personal love and care for each individual, such as in 1 John 3:1,

"See what great love the Father has lavished on us, that we should be called children of God! And that is what we are!" This moment underscores the personal relationship between the divine and the individual, independent of human achievement.

The Integration of Faith and Knowledge: Thomasina's shift in perspective, from viewing knowledge as a fortress to seeing it as a garden, suggests a biblical understanding of wisdom as something that grows and connects us to others and to God, as seen in Colossians 2:2-3, "My goal is that they may be encouraged in heart and united in love, so that they may have the full riches of complete understanding, in order that they may know the mystery of God, namely, Christ, in whom are hidden all the treasures of wisdom and knowledge."

Community and Shared Exploration: Her new engagement with peers and broader discussions reflects the biblical theme of community and the body of Christ, where each member contributes to the growth of the whole, as described in 1 Corinthians 12:12-2This shift from competitive isolation to communal exploration embodies the Christian ideal of unity and mutual edification.

The Limitations of Human Reasoning: Thomasina's experience underscores Ecclesiastes' exploration of the limitations of human wisdom and the inscrutability of God's ways (Ecclesiastes 8:17). It reflects the biblical view that while human pursuit of knowledge is valuable, it must be tempered with the recognition of God's transcendence and mystery.

Spiritual Renewal: Ultimately, Thomasina's transformation reflects the theme of spiritual renewal and the ongoing nature of faith development, akin to the apostle Paul's description of spiritual growth in 2 Corinthians 4:16, "Therefore we do not lose heart. Though outwardly we are wasting away, yet inwardly we are being renewed day by day."

Thomasina's journey from intellectual isolation to a renewed sense of spiritual identity and community involvement illustrates a profound biblical narrative of transformation through humility, the search for divine presence, and the embrace of communal faith exploration.

Prayer

Creator God, We come before You with humble hearts, recognizing Your greatness and our own unworthiness. You are the Creator of the universe, the King of kings and Lord of lords, and yet You choose to draw near to us, Your humble servants. Help us, Lord, to approach You with reverence and humility, acknowledging Your sovereignty and our dependence on You. Lord, forgive us for the times when pride has crept into our hearts, when we have exalted ourselves above You or others. Teach us to walk in humility, following the example of Jesus Christ, who humbled Himself and became obedient to death. Grant us, Lord, the grace to recognize our need for You in every area of our lives. Help us to surrender our will to Yours, trusting in Your wisdom and goodness. May we submit to Your authority and seek Your guidance in all that we do. In a world that often values pride and self-promotion, help us to stand firm in our identity as Your children, finding our true worth and significance in You alone. May we boast only in You, knowing that apart from You we can do nothing. Thank You, Lord, for Your mercy and grace that cover our sins and shortcomings. May Your Spirit work in us, transforming us into humble servants who bring glory to Your name. In Jesus' name we pray, Amen.

101

Spiritual Transformation

Nate was an old man now, bones aching and eyes tired, but with a spirit that still yearned for the unknown. His life had been long, filled with many turns like the rivers he had fished and the trails he had walked. Now, in the quiet twilight of his years, he sought not conquests or discoveries, but understanding and peace.

Nate reached the top of the ridge as the sun peeked above the horizon, casting golden beams that cut through the chill of dawn. He looked out over the expanse, a vast wilderness that stretched beyond sight, mountains rolling under a waking sky, each peak and valley carved by time and the hand of an unseen force.

He remembered the words he had read once, written in the front of a worn Bible his mother had given him, about an infinite God whose essence permeated all existence. As a young man, he had grappled with those words, trying to fit them into his understanding of the world, measuring them against everything he knew of science and nature.

But here, on this ridge, the vastness before him felt like a direct reflection of those ancient, unfathomable ideas. Each tree, each blade of grass, even the air he breathed seemed to pulse with a deeper rhythm, a quiet whisper of the divine.

"Infinite God," Nate whispered to the wind, the words barely audible, "I see now how small my understanding has been."

He sat down on a cold rock, pulling his jacket tighter against the morning breeze. He watched the sky change colors, feeling a part of this grand tapestry yet distinctly apart. His thoughts wandered to the infinite—how every star in the sky, every wave in the ocean, every grain of sand was a testament to something far greater than himself.

For a long time, Nate sat there, thinking about beginnings and endings, about the atoms that made up his body and the stars that burned light years away. It was not a fearful contemplation but a peaceful acknowledgment of his place in a design far greater than he could comprehend.

As the sun climbed higher, warming the earth and deepening the hues of the landscape, Nate felt a sense of release. His quest for understanding had not ended, but its nature had changed. No longer did he seek to conquer the mysteries of existence; instead, he sought to appreciate the wonder of them, embracing his part in the infinite.

"May I always remember this moment," he said as he stood, ready to walk back to his cabin. "May I keep my heart open to the mystery and my eyes open to the beauty."

And with that, Nate descended the ridge, each step a humble act of faith in the vast, incomprehensible dance of the cosmos.

Christian Themes and Values

God's Infinite Nature: Nate's acknowledgment of the vastness of the universe and his recognition of God as infinite resonates with biblical descriptions of God's transcendence beyond human comprehension. Psalm 147:5 declares, "Great is our Lord, and abundant in power; his understanding is beyond measure."

Human Humility Before God: Nate's realization of the smallness of his own understanding compared to the infinite wisdom of God reflects the biblical theme of human humility before the divine. Proverbs 3:5-6 advises, "Trust in the Lord with all your heart and lean not on your own understanding; in all your ways submit to him, and he will make your paths straight."

Appreciation of Creation: Nate's awe and appreciation of the natural world as a manifestation of the divine echo biblical themes of creation's beauty and God's handiwork. Psalm 19:1 proclaims, "The heavens declare the glory of God; the skies proclaim the work of his hands."

Spiritual Transformation: Nate's shift from seeking to conquer the mysteries of existence to embracing the wonder of them reflects a spiritual transformation reminiscent of biblical themes of renewal and enlightenment. Romans 12:2 encourages believers to "be transformed by the renewing of your mind, that you may discern what is the will of God, what is good and pleasing and perfect."

Faith and Reverence: Nate's resolve to keep his heart open to mystery and his eyes open to beauty demonstrates a posture of faith and reverence toward God's creation. Hebrews 11:6 teaches, "And without faith it is impossible to please him, for whoever would draw near to God must believe that he exists and that he rewards those who seek him."

Overall, Nate's contemplation on the ridge reflects a journey of spiritual awakening, humility before the divine, and a deep appreciation for the beauty and mystery of God's creation, all of which resonate with biblical themes of faith, reverence, and awe in the presence of the infinite.

Prayer

Infinite Creator God, We come before You seeking spiritual transformation, knowing that You are the author and perfecter of our faith. You have called us to be conformed to the image of Jesus Christ, and to walk in newness of life by the power of Your Spirit. Grant us, Lord, the grace to embrace the process of transformation and to yield ourselves fully to Your work in our lives. Lord, we confess that we are often resistant to change, comfortable in our familiar ways and reluctant to let go of our old habits and attitudes. But You call us to be transformed by the renewing of our minds, to put off the old self and put

Richard Gordon Zyne

on the new self-created to be like You in true righteousness and holiness. Lord, may our transformation be evident in our thoughts, words, and actions. Help us to bear the fruit of Your Spirit – love, joy, peace, patience, kindness, goodness, faithfulness, gentleness, and self-control – so that others may see Your likeness in us and be drawn to You. In Jesus' name we pray, Amen.

102

Nature as Revelation

Alexander walked the long stretch between the village and the river, where the trees hung heavy with the late summer's bounty. The sun was high, its light filtered through leaves, dappling the path ahead. Each footstep was deliberate, the crunch of dry leaves beneath his boots a testament to the isolation he felt, not just from the village but from himself.

He had left early, with the quiet murmur of his mother's voice trailing behind him, a soft, anxious note that spoke of errands and expectations. But Alexander was not headed to the market, nor to see the old men who gathered to play dominoes under the awning of the general store. He was walking towards something undefined, a yearning in his chest that had grown too large for the confines of his small, rural life.

The river, when he reached it, was low, the stones at its edge exposed like the raw nerves of the earth. He found a spot under an elm, its bark rough against the small of his back. He sat, pulling his knees to his chest, and watched the water flow over pebbles and debris, a silent witness to the perpetual motion of the world.

In his pocket, his hand found a smooth stone he had picked up days ago—a habit from childhood, collecting rocks that caught his eye. It felt cool, solid, an anchor in the swirl of his thoughts. He thought about the village, about the murmurs of dissatisfaction he heard on every corner, about the church that stood at the center of it all, its doors wide but somehow unwelcoming. He thought about the teachings that never quite touched his soul the way the river did, or the way the wind rushed through fields of wheat like a promise.

Alexander was not alone for long. A small figure approached, a boy from the village whose name hovered on the edge of his memory. The boy sat beside him without a word, his presence a silent acceptance of shared solitude.

They watched the river together, the boy throwing small sticks and leaves into the water, Alexander turning the stone over in his hand. After a while, the boy spoke, his voice low and thoughtful.

"Do you ever feel like you're just waiting for something to happen?" he asked.

"Every day," Alexander replied, and something in his honest admission bridged the gap between them.

They talked then, not about the church or the dissatisfactions of village life, but about the trees, the river, and the creatures that called it home. They talked about the paths they had not taken, and the world beyond the fields that stretched out, vast and unexplored.

When it was time to leave, Alexander stood and offered his hand to the boy, helping him up. He handed him the stone, a small token of a shared moment.

"Keep this," he said. "And remember that sometimes what we're looking for isn't in the teachings or the buildings. It's in the connections we make, right here."

The boy nodded, clutching the stone.

Alexander walked back to the village, the weight in his chest lighter, his steps more certain. He had found no answers, but perhaps a better question, one that involved not just his own spirit but the spirit of the community around him. Compassion, he realized, was not just a feeling but an action, a reaching out. And community was not a place, but the bonds forged in understanding and shared moments of solitude under the elm by the river.

Christian Themes and Values

Spiritual Seeking and Inner Yearning: Alexander's walk towards the river symbolizes a spiritual journey, echoing the biblical theme of seeking God or understanding beyond conventional confines, as illustrated in Jeremiah

29:13, "You will seek me and find me when you seek me with all your heart." His physical journey mirrors an inner quest for meaning and truth outside the traditional paths laid before him.

Community and Fellowship: The spontaneous interaction between Alexander and the boy highlights the Biblical importance of fellowship and community. In Matthew 18:20, Jesus says, "For where two or three gather in my name, there am I with them." This theme underscores that spiritual connections and community can form in simple, shared human experiences and not just within institutional religious settings.

Nature as Revelation: The narrative places significant emphasis on the natural world as a source of spiritual revelation and peace. This reflects Romans 1:20, which suggests that the qualities of God can be seen in what He has created. Alexander finds more spiritual resonance with the flowing river and the rustling trees than he does in the church, suggesting that the divine can be encountered directly through creation.

Solitude and Reflection: Alexander's solitude by the river, where he contemplates his life and feels his isolation, touches on themes found in the Psalms, where solitude often leads to deeper self-reflection and an encounter with God (Psalm 46:10, "Be still, and know that I am God"). His experience shows that quiet reflection can lead to profound insights and emotional relief.

Disillusionment with Institutional Religion: Alexander's dissatisfaction with the church echoes themes in the Gospels where Jesus critiques the religious leaders of his time for their hypocrisy and the burdens they place on believers (Matthew 23:1-4). This theme is relevant as it explores the idea that spiritual authenticity might be found outside traditional religious practices.

Inter-generational Connection and Wisdom Sharing: The meaningful exchange between Alexander and the boy underscores the biblical value of wisdom sharing between generations, reminiscent of the relationship between Eli and Samuel or Paul and Timothy. These relationships are pivotal for spiritual growth and mutual enrichment.

Symbolism of the Stone: The stone that Alexander gives to the boy symbolizes solidity, permanence, and the tangible reminders of spiritual and personal connections, akin to biblical symbols like the stone tablets of the Ten Commandments or even Jesus being referred to as the cornerstone (Ephesians 2:20).

Alexander's story encapsulates the journey of a man seeking authenticity and understanding in his life, using Biblical themes of searching, community, nature, and disillusionment with institutional forms of religion to weave a narrative that celebrates the quieter, often overlooked moments of spiritual discovery and connection.

Prayer

Holy Immanent God, we come before You in awe of Your creation, which reveals Your glory and greatness. You have spoken to us through the beauty and majesty of the natural world, showing us Your power and wisdom. Help us, Lord, to see Your hand at work in the wonders of creation and to respond with hearts of gratitude and reverence. Lord, as we contemplate the mountains, the seas, the forests, and the skies, may we be reminded of Your sovereignty and care for all that You have made. Help us to be good stewards of Your creation, protecting and preserving it for future generations. Grant us, Lord, the wisdom to learn from the lessons of nature – the cycles of life, the seasons of change, and the interdependence of all living things. May we see Your faithfulness reflected in the rhythms of creation and trust in Your provision for our needs. Thank You for the gift of nature as revelation. May we be attentive to Your presence in the world around us. In Jesus' name we pray, Amen.

103

Jacob Wrestling
with the Angel

In the early light of a North Carolina morning, George walked along the edge of the college campus where the trimmed grass met wilder lands. He wore a suit too formal for such a wander, his tie loosened, and his sleeves rolled up against the Southern heat. It was here, among the whispers of pine and the calls of distant birds, that he felt the weight of his own pilgrimage most acutely.

George was a man torn between worlds. Born to the rhythms of New York and raised in the folds of Judaism, he found himself in the heart of Baptist country, tasked with guiding an institution through the shoals of advancement and tradition. But as the sun climbed and the dew lifted, his mind wasn't on budgets or enrollment figures. It was on the spiritual journey—his and that of those he encountered.

Months earlier, an article detailing his beliefs had stirred the local waters into a frenzy. It described his view that Christ manifested in all faiths, that salvation wasn't the monopoly of any one creed. To the fundamentalist church members, this was not just unorthodox; it was anathema. The fallout was swift. Letters flooded in, each a stone of condemnation and rejection.

Walking now, George recalled the face of an old man he'd once met along the Outer Banks, a face creased like worn leather, eyes bright with a mix of cynicism and hope. They had talked as the man repaired his small wooden fence, hands skillful and sure, speaking of the sea as a place both treacherous and bountiful. George saw his own path reflected in those modest chores of repair, a task of tradition and insight.

When George reached a particularly knotted section of his walk where roots broke through the earth, he thought of Jacob wrestling the angel. That struggle left Jacob limping but blessed, marked by God yet closer to understanding his own divine struggle. George touched his own side, feeling an old ache—perhaps from running, perhaps from wrestling with unseen angels of his own.

Ahead, the path curved out of sight behind thick oaks, a darkening of the way that promised more wrestling. He had the option, always, to turn back, to find a simpler route, perhaps one without the oversight of a scrutinizing community. But the article, those letters—they were his angels, his adversaries that shaped his journey.

He paused, looking back toward the college buildings that shimmered in the heat haze. They represented his public life, a life now questioned and castigated. Yet, he turned away, choosing instead to walk further into the wooded shadows.

As he walked, he pondered the irony of the well-established Christian institution where he worked, their name professing liberty yet their letters speaking of strict doctrinal boundaries. He considered his own role, not just as an administrator but as a spiritual wanderer among them. Could he be a bridge, however flawed and strained?

By the time George emerged from the other side of the woods, the campus was far behind. He was sweaty, his shirt sticking to his back, his feet sore in his formal shoes. But his eyes were clear, his mind resolute. He had chosen to walk this path, thorny and uncertain as it was, and he would continue, one precarious step at a time.

Perhaps, he thought, the true pilgrimage was this: not the reaching of a sacred destination but the willingness to keep walking, to keep wrestling, even when the divine touched you, marked you, and asked you to walk on, limping but blessed, into the uncertain day.

Christian Themes and Values

Jacob Wrestling with the Angel: George's reflection on the story of Jacob wrestling with the angel (Genesis 32:22-32) is a central motif. This biblical account is often interpreted as a metaphor for grappling with God, with faith, and with one's own identity. Like Jacob, George's experiences a personal transformation through struggle, emerging with a new understanding of his path, albeit with metaphorical wounds.

Pilgrimage and Spiritual Journey: The theme of pilgrimage—walking a path that not only leads through physical landscapes but also deep into the spiritual and moral complexities of one's life—is evident. This reflects the Biblical journey of faith where believers are often depicted as sojourners in the world, navigating the challenges of earthly existence while striving towards spiritual goals, much like the Israelites' journey through the wilderness in Exodus.

Interfaith Understanding and Universal Salvation: George's controversial belief in Christ manifesting in all faiths touches on themes of universalism found in the Bible, particularly in scriptures like 1 Timothy 2:4, which states that God "wants all people to be saved and to come to a knowledge of the truth." This perspective challenges traditional exclusivist views and emphasizes a broader, more inclusive approach to salvation.

Confrontation with Institutional and Community Expectations: The conflict between personal convictions and the expectations of a religious community reflects Biblical themes where prophets and disciples often found themselves at odds with prevailing religious authorities. For instance, Jesus frequently clashed with the Pharisees over interpretations of the law (Matthew 23) and Paul faced opposition from Judaizers who questioned his teachings (Galatians 2:11-14).

Faith Under Fire: The letters of condemnation George receives are reminiscent of the trials faced by Biblical figures who stood firm in their faith despite persecution. This theme is encapsulated in James 1:2-4, which encourages believers to consider trials as opportunities for joy because they test faith and develop perseverance.

Perseverance and Continuation on the Path: George's decision to keep walking, despite the difficulty, aligns with the Biblical exhortation to perseverance and endurance in faith, as seen in Hebrews 12:1-2, which urges believers to "run with perseverance the race marked out for us, fixing our eyes on Jesus."

This story explores the complexities of faith in a modern context, challenging traditional boundaries and highlighting the eternal struggle and beauty of seeking divine truth in a changing world.

Prayer

Holy Transcendent God, we come before You with hearts open to Your transformative power, just as Jacob wrestled with the angel until he received Your blessing. Like Jacob, we wrestle with our doubts, fears, and struggles, seeking Your guidance and blessing in the midst of our trials. Lord, we thank You for Your faithfulness to meet us in our wrestling. You do not turn away from our questions or our struggles, but You meet us where we are and lead us to a deeper understanding of Your will and Your ways. Grant us, Lord, the courage to confront the things in our lives that keep us from fully surrendering to You. Help us to wrestle with our doubts and fears, trusting that You will bring us to a place of greater faith and trust in Your promises. Lord, like Jacob, may we persevere in seeking Your blessing, even when it seems elusive. May we cling to You with all our strength, knowing that Your blessings are worth the struggle and that You are faithful to fulfill Your promises. Help us, Lord, to surrender our own plans and desires to Your perfect will. May we submit to Your authority in our lives, trusting that Your ways are higher than our ways and Your thoughts higher than our thoughts. Thank You, Lord, for Your patience and grace as we wrestle with You. May we emerge from our struggles with a deeper understanding of Your love and a renewed commitment to follow You wholeheartedly. In Jesus' name we pray, Amen.

104

Journey Toward
Spiritual Awakening

Monica sat on the cold wooden bench by the marina, her eyes tracing the horizon where the gray sea melted into a starker gray sky. She had a habit of watching the boats as they bobbed with a sort of idle resignation against their moorings, each one captive but appearing ready to challenge the vast open waters. Monica felt much like those boats: tethered, defined by visible strings, yet inherently free if she dared to cut loose.

She was a nurse by profession, a mother to two boys, recently divorced—a set of circumstances and labels that the world used to define her. Each role came with its own script, expectations written long before she had any say in them. The hospital where she worked demanded a compassionate but composed caregiver, her sons needed a figure of unwavering strength and nurturing warmth, and the end of her marriage cast her, unwillingly, as a survivor. She played each part, but as the evening wore on and the boats creaked, she wondered about the authenticity of the roles she performed.

That day, her youngest had asked her, "Mom, are you happy?" A simple question, delivered with the unfiltered curiosity of a child, yet it struck her deeply. Was she happy? Or was she merely enacting happiness?

Monica remembered her own mother, a vibrant woman who taught her that life was a canvas, albeit one she herself had filled with cautious, muted tones. "We are beings of light," her mother would say in her less guarded moments, her eyes distant, as if recalling a forgotten dream. Monica used to dismiss such notions as whimsy—not the sort of belief that could guide a real, tangible life.

Now, the boats in front of her, each constrained yet inherently buoyant, became a metaphor she couldn't ignore. Was she to stay moored by roles and expectations, or could she embody the light her mother spoke of? It was alluring yet terrifying, the idea of redefining herself beyond societal scripts. To be a being of pure energy and light seemed a myth incompatible with the physical demands of her daily existence.

She stood up, feeling the sting of the cold wind against her face, invigorating her resolve. Each step she took away from the bench and back toward her home was weighted with intention. She would start small, she decided. Tonight, she would write, something she hadn't done since she was a girl. Not an email or a list, but a letter to herself. In it, she would attempt to describe her own essence, devoid of the labels placed upon her. She would write about the dreams she still harbored, the silent joys and the stifled sorrows.

She would acknowledge her luminosity, her divinity, and perhaps in doing so, she would begin to live a life of authenticity. A life where she wasn't just a passive vessel, swayed by external forces, but a creator of her own journey.

And as the darkness enveloped the sky, turning the sea an even deeper shade of obsidian, Monica felt a stirring—a faint glow within, ready to redefine her horizon.

Christian Themes and Values

Freedom from Bondage: Monica's situation mirrors the biblical theme of liberation from bondage. In the Bible, this is seen in stories like the Exodus, where the Israelites are freed from Egyptian slavery. Monica feels 'tethered' by her roles and the expectations of society, much like the boats at the marina. Her contemplation and eventual decision to redefine herself can be seen as a personal exodus from these constraints, seeking liberation to live a more genuine life.

Transformation and Renewal: The Bible talks about the renewal of the mind (Romans 12:2), where believers are encouraged to not conform to the patterns of this world but be transformed by renewing their mind. Monica's transformation begins with her introspection and the decision to write a letter to herself, which signifies the start of renewing her understanding of who she is beyond societal labels, akin to a spiritual rebirth.

The Inner Light and Divinity: Monica's mother's concept of humans as "beings of light" echoes the biblical notion that humans are created in the image of God (Genesis 1:27) and are therefore imbued with intrinsic worth and potential. The New Testament further expands on this with Jesus's teaching that believers are the light of the world (Matthew 5:14-16), called to shine forth their inherent divine light. Monica's journey towards recognizing and embracing her inner light parallels the call to live out one's divine purpose and reflect God's light in the world.

Authentic Living: Monica's quest for authenticity can be paralleled with the Christian pursuit of living a life that is true to one's divine calling, as taught by Jesus. The idea of casting off the old self and putting on the new self (Ephesians 4:22-24) reflects the transformation Monica seeks by shedding societal expectations and embracing her true self.

Faith and Doubt: Monica's initial skepticism about the concept of being a "being of light" can be likened to the biblical stories of doubt and faith, such as the Apostle Thomas's doubts about Jesus's resurrection (John 20:24-29). Her journey from doubt to a deeper understanding of her own spirituality mirrors the path from skepticism to faith, emphasizing personal revelation and the importance of personal experience in faith.

In summary, Monica's story from the Bible's perspective is about her journey toward spiritual awakening and authentic living, echoing biblical themes of liberation, transformation, renewal, and the pursuit of an authentic, divinely inspired life. It underscores the concept that true freedom and fulfillment come from understanding and living out one's inherent divine nature and purpose.

Prayer

Gracious God, we come before You on our journey toward spiritual awakening, longing to experience Your presence in a deeper and more profound way. You are the source of all wisdom, truth, and light, and we desire to know You more fully and to be transformed by Your Spirit. Lord, open our eyes to see You at work in our lives and in the world around us. Help us to recognize the signs of Your presence – in the beauty of creation, in the kindness of others, and in the whispers of Your Spirit speaking to our hearts. Grant us, Lord, the humility to acknowledge our need for You and the courage to seek You with all our hearts. May we set aside the distractions and concerns of this world and make room for You to work in us and through us. Lord, as we journey toward spiritual awakening, help us to deepen our relationship with You through prayer, study of Your Word, and fellowship with other believers. May we be filled with Your Spirit, empowered to live lives that reflect Your love, grace, and truth. Thank You, Lord, for the journey toward spiritual awakening. May we walk in faith and obedience, confident that You are with us every step of the way, leading us into a deeper and more intimate relationship with You. In Jesus' name we pray, Amen.

105

The Endurance of Faith

Terrance grappled with the ghosts of his past, their whispers echoing through the corridors of his mind. Memories, long buried beneath the weight of time, resurfaced like specters from the shadows, haunting him with their bitter sting.

As a child, Terrance had sought guidance and support in the embrace of his church, seeking refuge from the stormy seas of life within its hallowed halls. But instead of finding sanctuary, he had been met with betrayal and disappointment, the echoes of his pastor's harsh words and actions still ringing in his ears.

Now, in the twilight of his years, Terrance found himself once again confronting the demons of his past, their presence a constant reminder of the wounds that had never fully healed. The words of his doctor, spoken with clinical detachment, triggered a familiar wave of anger and resentment, their impact amplified by the scars of old wounds.

But amidst the turmoil of his emotions, Terrance clung to the faint glimmer of hope that flickered within his soul. Though his faith had been tested and shaken, it remained an enduring beacon of light in the darkness, guiding him through the labyrinth of his doubts and fears.

With each passing day, Terrance found himself drawing closer to that elusive truth, shedding the layers of anger and bitterness that had long obscured his vision. In the quiet moments of reflection, he found solace in the gentle embrace of a loving God, whose presence transcended the confines of church walls and human frailty.

And so, as Terrance journeyed through the final stages of his life, with the help of a friend and chaplain, he found comfort in the knowledge that, despite the trials and tribulations of his past, he was never truly alone. For in the depths of his soul, he carried the indelible imprint of a Divine Love that would never falter or fade.

Christian Themes and Values

Struggle with Faith and Betrayal: Terrance's experience of betrayal within the church echoes the Biblical stories of betrayal, most notably Judas' betrayal of Jesus (Matthew 26:14-16). This theme illustrates the pain and conflict that can arise within spiritual communities, testing the faith and resilience of believers.

Healing from Past Wounds: The narrative of Terrance grappling with the ghosts of his past reflects the Biblical theme of healing, both psychological and spiritual. Scriptures such as Psalm 147:3, "He heals the brokenhearted and binds up their wounds," underscore the belief in God's power to heal and restore those who have been hurt or broken by life's experiences.

The Endurance of Faith: Despite the hardships and the initial betrayal by his church, Terrance's enduring faith mirrors the perseverance encouraged in the Bible. James 1:12 offers comfort and promise to those who endure under trial, stating, "Blessed is the one who perseveres under trial because, having stood the test, that person will receive the crown of life that the Lord has promised to those who love him."

Divine Presence and Comfort: Terrance's realization that he carries the "indelible imprint of a Divine Love" aligns with Biblical assurances of God's omnipresence and unwavering support for His followers, as expressed in Deuteronomy 31:6, which encourages believers to be strong and courageous, not fearful or dismayed, for the Lord is always with them.

Redemption and Forgiveness: The story hints at themes of redemption and forgiveness, reflecting Terrance's journey towards releasing his anger and bitterness. This is a core element of Christian theology, as seen in Ephesians 4:31-32, where believers are urged to let go of all bitterness, rage, and anger, and instead be kind and compassionate to one another, forgiving each other just as in Christ God forgave them.

Solace in Spiritual Reflection and Prayer: Terrance's moments of reflection and his interaction with the chaplain illustrate the comfort that can be found in prayer and spiritual counsel. Philippians 4:6-7 advocates for presenting requests to God through prayer and thanksgiving, which brings peace that transcends understanding.

The Role of Spiritual Guides: The chaplain's role in aiding Terrance's journey highlights the importance of pastoral care and spiritual guidance in navigating faith crises, reflecting the Biblical model of shepherding seen in leaders like Moses and Jesus.

Terrance's journey from hurt through healing to an enduring faith encapsulates the profound Biblical truth that redemption and divine love are accessible even in the depths of despair and disappointment. His story serves as a testament to the power of unwavering faith and the presence of God in overcoming life's greatest challenges.

Prayer

Holy Loving God, we come before You, acknowledging the challenges and trials that test our faith. In the midst of adversity, help us to endure with unwavering faith, knowing that You are faithful and that Your promises are sure. Strengthen our hearts and minds to withstand the storms of life. Grant us the courage to persevere through difficult times, trusting in Your unfailing love and sovereignty over all things. Help us, Lord, to fix our eyes on Jesus, the author and perfecter of our faith. May His example of endurance in the face of suffering inspire us to persevere, knowing that He has gone before us and walks with us in our trials. Grant us the wisdom to discern Your purposes in our struggles, and the faith to believe that You are working all things together for our good. May our endurance in faith bring glory to Your name and testify to Your power and grace. Lord, when we are weak, strengthen us. When we are weary, refresh us. When we are tempted to doubt, remind us of Your faithfulness and the hope we have in Christ. In Jesus' name we pray, Amen.

106

Love and Redemption

The autumn sun had begun its slow descent behind the industrial rooftops, casting a harsh, reddish glow through the grimy windows of Curt's small room in the rundown assisted living facility where he was receiving hospice care. He sat in an aged recliner that, like him, had seen better days, its fabric worn and fraying. Curt's hands, still strong but unsteady, trembled as he lifted his cigarette to his lips, the smoke curling upward before being lost in the stale air.

"You know, Chaplain," Curt began, his voice a gravelly echo of the roar of engines and crowds from his past, "it wasn't just a few years ago that I was driving very fast cars and winning races. NASCAR was my life and so was the open road. When I wasn't in a race, I was climbing up a mountain road or going down a dune in a buggy. It was a wonderful life of speed, hot metal, booze, and cigarettes." His eyes, once sharp and clear like the desert sky, now mirrored the dull gray of the room's flaking walls.

There was a profound sadness about Curt, the way his yellowed fingers clung to the cigarette, his grease-stained shirt clinging to his gaunt frame. "When Shirley took a hike and we separated, she left a big hole inside of me. Probably bigger than the cancer that's eating me up now." He took a long drag, the cigarette's end glowing briefly like the taillights of a 1958 Corvette speeding away into the night.

Curt gulped his beer, the can sweating in the warm room. "If I said that Jesus still loves me, you might laugh, but I know that it's true. He still loves me and will always love me." His declaration, tinged with both defiance and

399

relief, hung in the air between us. I didn't laugh but nodded, acknowledging his truth, his resolution, his peace.

"I'm ready to die when God wants me. Not sure if He needs me, but when He's ready, He can just tap me on the shoulder, and we'll both get into that classic '68 Mustang in heaven." A laugh escaped his lips, a sound rough and sincere, but it faded as quickly as it came, leaving behind a somber silence. He stared at the floor, his eyes searching.

Just then, the door creaked open, and in lumbered Thelma, a Newfoundland Hound as grand and solemn as a bear. She moved with a gentle grace incongruous with her size and settled down next to Curt, her body pressing against his leg. "This is Thelma, my favorite love on this planet. I don't think she can live without me, but I guess she'll have to."

Curt's hands, veined and spotted, buried themselves in Thelma's thick, dark mane. "They let dogs in heaven, don't they, Chaplain? Even big, hairy ones like Thelma?"

I smiled, the simplicity of his faith, his love for this creature beside him, was both touching and profoundly human. "I'm sure God allows dogs of all sizes into heaven, even those noisy little chihuahuas, and even pet rats."

His eyes, suddenly glassy, didn't meet mine. "Please say a prayer for me, Chaplain, and also for Thelma, because I'm not sure who's going to care for her when I'm gone."

"Okay?" he asked, the tremor in his voice belying the toughness of a man who had once lived life at full throttle.

"Sure, Curt," I replied, my voice soft but clear in the quiet room. We bowed our heads, the only sounds, the gentle hum of the assisted living facility and Thelma's deep, even breaths. I prayed for peace for Curt, for comfort in his final days, and for Thelma, that she might find a new home filled with as much love as Curt had given her.

As I finished, Curt lifted his head, his eyes clear for just a moment, as if he could see that finish line, not the end of the race but a new beginning, a promise of peace. "Thank you," he murmured, and settled back, Thelma nuzzling closer as if to anchor him to life for just a moment longer.

In that hospice room, as the light faded and shadows grew long, I witnessed the profound connection between a man and his dog, between human and divine. It was a reminder that even in our darkest moments, the bonds of love, the hope for redemption, they endure, speeding us over speed bumps on our way to whatever lies beyond.

Christian Themes and Values

Redemption and Forgiveness: Curt's acknowledgment of his past life filled with "speed, hot metal, booze, and cigarettes," and his separation from Shirley, highlights a theme of seeking redemption. Despite his past, Curt speaks of Jesus's enduring love, reflecting the Christian belief in unconditional love and forgiveness. This mirrors the parable of the prodigal son (Luke 15:11-32), where forgiveness and redemption are freely given upon the son's return.

Divine Love and Acceptance: Curt's statement, "If I said that Jesus still loves me, you might laugh, but I know that it's true. He still loves me and will always love me," taps into the fundamental Christian doctrine of God's unwavering love for His children, regardless of their past actions. This theme is echoed throughout the New Testament, which emphasizes that salvation and love are available to all who surrender in their faith journey. (John 3:16).

The Hope of Heaven: Curt expresses a hope for heaven, imagining it as a place where he can race cars, reflecting the Christian belief in an afterlife where believers find peace and fulfillment. This hope is in line with Biblical descriptions of heaven as a place where there is no pain or sorrow (Revelation 21:4).

Companionship and Care: The relationship between Curt and Thelma, his dog, highlights the theme of companionship, which is important in the Bible. God's recognition of humanity's need for companionship (Genesis 2:18 - "It is not good for the man to be alone") supports the idea that relationships are crucial for well-being. Curt's concern for Thelma's future reflects the stewardship entrusted to humans over animals, a responsibility mentioned in Genesis 1:26.

Faith and Peace in Facing Death: Curt's readiness to face death, "I'm ready to die when God wants me," demonstrates his faith and acceptance of God's will. This acceptance reflects the peace that comes from trusting in God, similar to Jesus's peace mentioned in John 14:27 - "Peace I leave with you; my peace I give you."

Prayer and Spiritual Support: The chaplain's role in providing spiritual support through prayer reflects the Christian practice of intercessory prayer, which is thought to bring comfort and peace to those who are suffering (James 5:14-15).

Enduring Legacy and Love: Finally, Curt's reflection on his legacy and his enduring love for Thelma highlights the Biblical theme of love as the greatest of virtues (1 Corinthians 13:13). Curt's story is a testimony to the enduring power of love, which remains one of the most potent themes throughout the Bible.

These themes collectively underscore the journey of a man who, despite his flaws and the trials of life, finds solace in his faith and relationships. They remind us of the transformative power of faith, the hope of redemption, and the comfort of divine assurance even in life's final moments.

Prayer

Divine Healing God, we come before You in awe of Your boundless love and the transformation You offer us through Jesus Christ. Help us, Lord, to comprehend the depth of Your love and to respond with hearts full of gratitude and praise. Grant us, Lord, the humility to accept Your love and forgiveness, recognizing our need for You in every moment of our lives. May Your redeeming love transform us from the inside out, freeing us from the chains of sin and enabling us to walk in the fullness of Your grace. Help us, Lord, to extend Your love and forgiveness to others, just as You have done for us. May we be agents of reconciliation and healing in a broken world, sharing the hope of redemption with all who are lost and hurting. Thank You, Lord, for Your unending love and the redemption You offer us through Jesus Christ. May we never take for granted the depth of Your grace, but may it compel us to live lives that reflect Your love to the world. In Jesus' name we pray, Amen.

107

Responsibility and Compassion

Jill and Paul, both Bayside Hospital employees, grabbed a rare moment to dine together in the dreaded hospital cafeteria. They teased each other about the dismal food, joking that it was still better than what the patients received. Jill, a nurses' aide on the medical-surgical floor, and Paul, a physical therapist, had crossed paths months ago. They soon found they cared deeply for each other, bonding over their shared interests in bird watching and finding simple pleasure by the river, sitting on rocks and being with nature.

Paul also had the responsibility of caring for his grandfather, who lived with him in their small downtown apartment. His grandfather had recently been diagnosed with senile degeneration of the brain, a tough blow for Paul as he watched the rapid decline of the man who had raised him.

The strain of caregiving often weighed heavily on Paul, leading to bouts of anger and frequent alcohol binges. But Jill stood by him, offering her calming presence and sage advice, along with her heartfelt prayers.

As months passed, Paul found it increasingly challenging to meet his grandfather's needs. Eventually, he made the painful decision to place him in an assisted living facility with a memory unit to manage his dementia and other age-related disorders. Despite knowing it was the best option for his grandfather's care, Paul couldn't shake the feelings of guilt and failure, believing he had let his grandfather down when he needed him most.

During this difficult transition, Jill remained a steadfast source of support. She accompanied Paul on his visits to the assisted living facility, providing emotional and spiritual care to both him and his grandfather. Paul often thought of Jill as a divine gift, sent to him and his grandfather in their time of need.

Christian Themes and Values

Love and Compassion: Jill and Paul demonstrate love and compassion through their care for each other and Paul's grandfather. This reflects the biblical commandment to love one another (John 13:34) and to care for the elderly (Leviticus 19:32).

Suffering and Redemption: Paul's struggle with caring for his grandfather and his feelings of guilt and failure reflect the biblical theme of suffering and redemption. Through his hardships, Paul learns and grows, finding redemption in his decision to place his grandfather in a facility where he can receive proper care (Romans 5:3-5).

Faith and Prayer: Jill's offering of heartfelt prayers for Paul and his grandfather underscores the theme of faith and prayer. It reflects the biblical teaching to pray for one another (James 5:16) and trust in God's plan (Proverbs 3:5-6).

Responsibility and Duty: Paul's sense of responsibility towards his grandfather and his decision to ensure his well-being by placing him in an assisted living facility align with the biblical theme of responsibility and duty, particularly towards family members (1 Timothy 5:8).

Community and Support: The story emphasizes the importance of community and support during difficult times. Jill's steadfast presence and support for Paul and his grandfather, as well as their shared experiences with other hospital staff, highlight the biblical principle of bearing one another's burdens (Galatians 6:2).

God's Provision: Paul often thinks of Jill as a divine gift sent to him and his grandfather in their time of need, which reflects the biblical theme of God's provision and care for His people (Philippians 4:19).

Overall, the story intertwines themes of love, faith, redemption, and community, reflecting the biblical values of caring for others, trusting in God's plan, and finding strength in times of trial.

Prayer

Heavenly Loving God, we come before You with hearts burdened by the responsibility You have entrusted to us as Your children. You call us to love one another and to care for those in need with compassion and mercy. Grant us, Lord, the strength and wisdom to fulfill this calling faithfully. Lord, help us to recognize the needs of those around us and to respond with compassion and generosity. May we be moved by Your love to take action, showing kindness and empathy to all who are suffering or in need. Grant us, Lord, the courage to take responsibility for our actions and the consequences they may have on others. Help us to live with integrity, seeking justice and righteousness in all our dealings. Lord, teach us to be good stewards of the resources You have given us, using them wisely and generously to help those who are less fortunate. Thank You, Lord, for the privilege of serving You by serving others. May we always remember that it is Your love and grace that empowers us to be responsible and compassionate stewards of Your blessings. In Jesus' name we pray, Amen.

108

Inherent Worth and Dignity

Elmer sat in his new room at the assisted living facility, surrounded by boxes and bags filled with his belongings. As he looked around, he couldn't shake the feeling of displacement. The sterile white walls and generic furniture made him feel like just another number in a system designed to care for the elderly. But Elmer knew he was more than that. He was a person with inherent worth and dignity, and he was determined to make that known.

"I am a person, not just a patient," Elmer said aloud to himself, as if trying to convince himself of his own worth. He had always been fiercely independent, and the thought of being in a place where he was dependent on others for his care was unsettling.

He had moved to the facility reluctantly after his health declined and living alone became too difficult. His children had convinced him it was for the best, but Elmer couldn't help but feel like he was losing a part of himself in the process.

As the days passed, Elmer struggled to adjust to his new surroundings. He found himself feeling isolated and ignored, as if he were invisible to the staff and other residents. Despite his attempts to engage with those around him, he often felt dismissed or overlooked.

"Please respect my space and all of my stuff," Elmer pleaded with the staff one afternoon as they rearranged his room without his consent. He had spent years collecting his belongings, each item holding sentimental value and memories of a life well-lived. He couldn't bear the thought of strangers coming in and rearranging everything without his permission.

But his words seemed to fall on deaf ears, and Elmer couldn't shake the feeling of frustration and helplessness. He longed for a sense of autonomy and control over his own life, but it seemed that even that was being taken away from him in his new living space.

As the weeks went by, Elmer's sense of worth and dignity continued to erode. He felt like he was losing himself in the monotony of life at the facility, becoming just another face in the crowd. But deep down, he knew he was still the same person he had always been, with dreams and desires that deserved to be acknowledged and respected.

"Please don't ignore me," Elmer pleaded silently to anyone who would listen. He longed for meaningful connections and interactions, for someone to see him for who he truly was and not just another elderly resident in need of care.

Despite his struggles, Elmer refused to give up hope. He held onto the belief that he was worthy of love and respect, no matter his age or physical condition. And slowly but surely, his determination began to pay off.

One day, as Elmer sat in the facility's common area, lost in thought, he felt a gentle tap on his shoulder. Startled, he looked up to see a young caregiver smiling down at him.

"Hey, Elmer, would you like to join us for a game of cards?" she asked, gesturing to a group of residents gathered around a table.

Elmer hesitated for a moment, surprised by the unexpected invitation. But then he felt a flicker of excitement deep within him. Maybe, just maybe, this was the connection he had been longing for.

With a grateful smile, Elmer nodded and followed the caregiver to the table. As he joined the game, he felt a sense of belonging wash over him, as if he were finally seen and recognized for who he truly was.

From that day on, Elmer's days at the assisted living facility began to change. He formed friendships with fellow residents, engaged in activities he enjoyed, and regained a sense of purpose and fulfillment. And through it all, he held onto the truth of his inherent worth and dignity, knowing that he was more than just a patient or a resident. He was Elmer, a person deserving of love, respect, and the opportunity to live life to the fullest, no matter his circumstances.

Christian Themes and Values

Human Dignity: Elmer's plea to be seen and respected as a person, not just a patient, reflects the biblical idea that every individual is created in the image of God and therefore possesses inherent worth and value (Genesis 1:27). Elmer's struggle against feeling like just another number in the system echoes the biblical principle that each person is unique and deserving of dignity and respect.

Self-Determination and Personal Agency: Throughout the Bible, individuals are called to take responsibility for their own choices and actions, and to assert their rights in the face of oppression or mistreatment (Galatians 6:5, James 4:17).

Community and Fellowship: Elmer's loneliness and isolation in the facility reflect the human need for companionship and fellowship, which is emphasized throughout the Bible (Ecclesiastes 4:9-10). When Elmer finally finds a sense of belonging and connection with the young caregiver and other residents, it speaks to the biblical value of community and mutual support.

Justice and Compassion: Throughout the Bible, God calls on his people to care for the vulnerable and marginalized, and to treat others with fairness and kindness (Proverbs 31:8-9, Matthew 25:40). Elmer's plea for respect and understanding highlights the importance of compassionate care for the elderly and those in need.

Ultimately, the story reflects the biblical message of hope and redemption. Despite his initial struggles, Elmer finds a sense of purpose and fulfillment through meaningful connections and a renewed sense of self-worth. His journey reminds us that no matter our circumstances, we are all deserving of love, respect, and the opportunity to live life to the fullest.

Prayer

Heavenly Father, we come before You acknowledging the inherent worth and dignity You have bestowed upon every human being, for we are fearfully and wonderfully made in Your image. Help us, Lord, to see ourselves and others through Your eyes, recognizing the value and dignity that You have placed within each one of us. Lord, in a world that often measures worth by external standards such as wealth, status, or achievements, remind us that our true worth is found in being Your beloved children. May we find our identity and value in You alone, rather than in the opinions or judgments of others. Grant us, Lord, the grace to treat every person with respect and honor, recognizing the dignity that You have given them. Help us to see past outward appearances and to love others as You love us, unconditionally and without judgment. Lord, may we be advocates for justice and equality, standing up for the rights and dignity of all people, especially those who are marginalized or oppressed. May we work to build a society where every individual is valued and respected, regardless of race, gender, ethnicity, or socioeconomic status. Thank You, Lord, for the precious gift of life and for the dignity You have given us as Your children. May we honor You by honoring the worth and dignity of every person we meet. In Jesus' name we pray, Amen.

109

Faith, Inner Conflict, and Courage

Francine sat at her desk, the words of D.H. Lawrence echoing in her mind like a haunting melody. The typewriter before her remained silent, the blank page staring back at her, demanding to be filled. She tapped her pencil against the desk, lost in thought.

"Francine, are you alright?" Rose's voice broke through the silence, drawing her attention away from the words swirling in her mind.

Francine looked up, offering a faint smile. "Yeah, just trying to find the right words."

Rose leaned against the doorway; her arms folded across her chest. "You look like you've got a storm brewing in that head of yours."

Francine chuckled softly. "You could say that. Just wrestling with some ideas."

Rose stepped further into the room; her gaze fixed on Francine. "You've always been one to wrestle with ideas, haven't you?"

Francine nodded, her gaze drifting back to the typewriter. "I suppose so. It's like Lawrence said, my soul feels like a dark forest sometimes."

Rose raised an eyebrow. "A dark forest, huh? Sounds like you're in for an adventure."

"More like a battle," Francine replied, her fingers tracing the edge of the desk.

Rose took a seat opposite Francine, leaning in closer. "What's got you so tangled up?"

Francine sighed, her shoulders slumping slightly. "Just this idea that my known self will never be more than a little clearing in the forest. That there are gods, strange gods, lurking in the shadows, waiting to emerge."

Rose listened intently, her eyes reflecting a mixture of curiosity and concern. "And what do you plan to do about it?"

"That's the thing," Francine said, her voice tinged with uncertainty. "I have to have the courage to let them come and go. To recognize and submit to the gods within me and within others."

Rose reached out, placing a reassuring hand on Francine's shoulder. "You're a fighter, Francine. I have no doubt you'll navigate that forest with grace."

Francine managed a weak smile, grateful for Rose's support. "Thanks, Rose. I just hope I can find my way through."

Rose squeezed her shoulder gently. "You will. And I'll be right here to help you every step of the way."

As Francine returned to her typewriter, the words of Lawrence continued to dance in her mind. But now, with Rose by her side, she felt a glimmer of hope amidst the darkness of the forest, ready to face whatever gods may come.

Christian Themes and Values

Wrestling with Ideas and Faith: Francine's struggle with her thoughts and ideas reflects the biblical concept of wrestling with faith and understanding. This idea is present in the story of Jacob wrestling with God (Genesis 32:22-32) and the apostle Paul's intellectual and spiritual struggles (Acts 17:16-34).

The Inner Battle Between Good and Evil: Francine's metaphor of her soul being like a dark forest, with strange gods lurking in the shadows, alludes to the biblical theme of the inner battle between good and evil. This theme is often portrayed in the struggle between the flesh and the spirit (Galatians 5:17, Romans 7:15-25).

Courage and Submission to God: Francine's recognition of the need to have the courage to recognize and submit to the gods within herself and others reflects the biblical concept of surrendering to God's will and trusting in His guidance. This idea is present in verses such as James 4:7, where believers are encouraged to submit to God and resist the devil.

Support and Encouragement from Others: Rose's reassurance and support for Francine reflect the biblical concept of community and fellowship among believers. The Bible emphasizes the importance of supporting and encouraging one another in faith (Hebrews 10:24-25, 1 Thessalonians 5:11).

Hope Amidst Struggle: Despite Francine's inner turmoil, the story ends with a glimmer of hope, symbolizing the biblical theme of hope amidst struggle and darkness. This hope is rooted in the belief that God is present and offers guidance and strength to overcome challenges (Romans 15:13, Psalm 23:4).

Overall, the story explores deep themes of faith, inner conflict, courage, and the importance of community, all of which resonate with biblical concepts and teachings.

Prayer

Divine Creator, we come before You in the midst of our inner conflicts and struggles, seeking Your guidance, strength, and courage. You know the depths of our hearts and the battles we face within ourselves. Help us, Lord, to navigate these challenges with faith and courage, trusting in Your wisdom and grace. Lord, in times of doubt and uncertainty, grant us the faith to believe in Your promises and the courage to stand firm in Your truth. May Your Word be a lamp to our feet and a light to our path, guiding us through the darkness of our doubts and fears. Grant us, Lord, the wisdom to discern Your voice amidst the conflicting voices and desires within us. Help us to align our hearts with Your will, surrendering our own desires and agendas to Your perfect plan for our lives. Help us, Lord, to find peace and rest in Your presence, even in the midst of our inner turmoil. May Your love and grace fill us with confidence and courage, enabling us to walk boldly in the path You have set before us. Thank

Richard Gordon Zyne

You, Lord, for Your faithfulness and steadfast love that never wavers, even when our faith falters. May we find courage and strength in You, knowing that You are always with us, leading us onward in our journey of faith. In Jesus' name we pray, Amen.

110

Grief and Comfort in Loss

Sarah, a chaplain in a small community hospital, stood at the cliff's edge, the salty breeze tousling her hair as she gazed out at the vast expanse of the sea. Max, her faithful companion, lay beside her, the loyal black Labrador panting in the midday sun. Max had been by her side for years, a steadfast companion and presence through Sarah's quiet times walking in the woods by her home and, of course, on the wide beach.

But now, as Sarah watched the waves crash against the rocks below, she knew that their time together was drawing to a close. For weeks, Max had been growing weaker, his once bright eyes dulled with pain. Sarah had done all she could to ease his suffering, but it was clear that the end was near. As she sat by her beloved dog, a wave of grief washed over her, heavy and suffocating.

Max had been more than just a pet; he had been a friend, a confidant, a source of unwavering love and support. They had shared countless moments together, from long walks along the bay to quiet evenings by the fire. Now, as the sun dipped below the horizon, casting hues of pink and gold across the sky, Max took his final breath.

Sarah held him close, tears streaming down her weathered cheeks as she whispered a silent prayer. In that moment, as the stars began to twinkle overhead and the world grew quiet, she felt a sense of peace wash over her. For though Max may have left this world, his spirit would live on in the memories they had shared, and the love that would never fade.

As the days passed, Sarah found peace and hope in the memories of their time together. She would often find herself sitting by the cliffside, lost in thought as she watched the waves roll in, Max's presence still felt keenly in the silence.

But life went on, as it always did. The hospital floors and units continued to bustle with activity, patients coming and going, each with their own struggles and triumphs. And though Max was no longer by her side, she found comfort in the knowledge that she had been able to provide comfort and support to those in need, just as Max had done for her.

In the weeks that followed, Sarah found herself drawn to a new patient—a young girl battling cancer, her spirit as bright as the sun on a summer's day. She would sit by her bedside, offering words of encouragement and prayers for healing, the memory of Max guiding her through each visit.

And as she watched the girl's strength and resilience in the face of adversity, she couldn't help but feel a sense of gratitude for the time she had shared with Max. For though their journey together had come to an end, the love they had shared would remain a guiding light in Sarah's heart, forever illuminating her path.

Christian Themes and Values

Stewardship and Care for Creation: The relationship between Sarah and Max exemplifies the themes of stewardship and compassionate care for all of God's creatures. In Genesis 1:28, humanity is given dominion over animals, which is often interpreted as a call to responsible stewardship and kindness. Sarah's efforts to ease Max's suffering highlight this duty of care and respect for the life and well-being of animals.

Grief and Comfort in Loss: The chaplain's deep sorrow and the act of holding Max as he passes away touch on the biblical reflections on mourning and comfort. Psalm 34:18 offers consolation, stating, "The Lord is close to the brokenhearted and saves those who are crushed in spirit." The chaplain's grief is palpable, yet there is a biblical assurance that God is present in moments of deep sorrow.

Eternal Peace and Hope: As Max dies and Sarah feels a wave of peace, this aligns with the Christian hope of eternal rest and peace for all of God's creatures. Romans 8:21 suggests that "the creation itself will be liberated from its bondage to decay and brought into the freedom and glory of the children of God," which can be comforting when considering the fate of beloved pets after death.

Lasting Legacy and Memory: The idea that Max's spirit will live on in the memories they shared together echoes the themes of a lasting spiritual legacy. Proverbs 10:7 states, "The memory of the righteous is a blessing," and although this typically applies to humans, the cherished memories of Max serve as a blessing and a source of ongoing comfort to Sarah.

This story, rich with biblical resonance, underscores the profound connections between humans and animals, the emotional depth of such relationships, and the spiritual comfort that can be found even in the midst of loss. It highlights the transcendent nature of love and companionship that scripture often celebrates.

Prayer

Holy Creator God, In the midst of our grief and loss, we turn to You, our source of comfort and strength. You are the God who walks with us through the valley of the shadow of death, and we cling to Your promise to never leave us nor forsake us. Grant us, Lord, the comfort of Your presence as we grieve. May Your spirit minister to our hearts, bringing healing, hope, and peace in the midst of our pain. Help us, Lord, to support and comfort one another in our sorrow, bearing one another's burdens as we journey through this time of loss. May our love for one another be a reflection of Your love for us, bringing light into the darkness of our grief. Thank You, Lord, for Your faithfulness and love that never fails. May we find comfort and strength in You, knowing that You are our refuge and our strength in times of trouble. In Jesus' name we pray, Amen.

Printed in the United States
by Baker & Taylor Publisher Services